A Brief History of English Syntax

T0349556

In its 1,500-year history, the English language has seen dramatic grammatical changes. This book offers a comprehensive and reader-friendly account of the major developments, including changes in word order, the noun phrase and verb phrase, changing relations between clausal constituents and the development of new subordinate constructions. The book puts forward possible explanations for change, drawing on the existing and most recent literature and with reference to the major theoretical models. The authors use corpus evidence to investigate language-internal and language-external motivations for change, including the impact of language contact. The book is intended for students who have been introduced to the history of English and want to deepen their understanding of major grammatical changes, and for linguists in general with a historical interest. It will also be of value to literary scholars professionally engaged with older texts.

Professor Emeritus of Germanic Linguistics at the University of Amsterdam, OLGA FISCHER is a contributor to the *Cambridge History of the English Language* (1992), co-author of *The Syntax of Early English* (2000), and author of *Morphosyntactic Change: Functional and Formal Perspectives* (2007). She has been an editor of the Language chapter in the Year's Work in English Studies since 1998, and is co-editor of the book series *Iconicity in Language and Literature*. She has written widely on topics within English historical linguistics, grammaticalization, iconicity and analogy.

HENDRIK DE SMET is a BOF research professor at KU Leuven. He is the author of *Spreading Patterns: Diffusional Change in the English System of Complementation* (2013) and co-editor of *On Multiple Source Constructions in Language Change* (2015). His work is primarily on mechanisms of language change, including reanalysis, analogy and blending. He is also involved in the compilation of several freely available text corpora for historical research, including the *Corpus of Late Modern English Texts* and the *Corpus of English Novels*.

WIM VAN DER WURFF is Senior Lecturer in Linguistics at Newcastle University, UK. He is co-author of *The Syntax of Early English* (2000), *Colloquial Bengali* (2009), and has co-edited volumes on reported speech, modality, imperatives and diachronic syntax. His recent work focuses on the way factors of different types interact in the emergence and decline of syntactic constructions.

A Brief History of English Syntax

Olga Fischer

Universiteit van Amsterdam

Hendrik De Smet

Katholieke Universiteit Leuven, Belgium

Wim van der Wurff

Newcastle University, UK

CAMBRIDGE
UNIVERSITY PRESS

CAMBRIDGE
UNIVERSITY PRESS

University Printing House, Cambridge CB2 8BS, United Kingdom

Cambridge University Press is part of the University of Cambridge.

It furthers the University's mission by disseminating knowledge in the pursuit of education, learning, and research at the highest international levels of excellence.

www.cambridge.org
Information on this title: www.cambridge.org/9780521747974
DOI: 10.1017/9781139049559

© Olga Fischer, Hendrik De Smet and Wim van der Wurff 2017

First published 2017

Printed in the United Kingdom by Clays, LTD.

A catalogue record for this publication is available from the British Library

Library of Congress Cataloging-in-Publication Data
Names: Fischer, Olga, author. | De Smet, Hendrik, author. | Wurff,
Wim van der, author.
Title: A brief history of English syntax / Olga Fischer, Hendrik De Smet,
Wim van der Wurff.
Description: Cambridge : Cambridge University Press, 2017. | Includes bibliographical
references and index.
Identifiers: LCCN 2016047639 | ISBN 9780521768580 (Hardback) |
ISBN 9780521747974 (Paperback)
Subjects: LCSH: English language–Syntax. | English language–Grammar, Historical.
Classification: LCC PE1361 .F57 2017 | DDC 425/.09–dc23 LC record available at
https://lccn.loc.gov/2016047639

ISBN 978-0-521-76858-0 Hardback
ISBN 978-0-521-74797-4 Paperback

Contents

Preface and Acknowledgements

This book has been a long time in the making. The first ideas for it were developed after the publication of the chapter on syntax in Hogg and Denison (2007) by two of the present authors. Since we had a lot more material for which there was no room in that chapter, it looked like a good idea to use this material for a more elaborate book on the history of English syntax. And indeed this book builds further upon the 2007 syntax chapter. To it we have added additional chapters on the handling of data, the theoretical background and the changes syntax underwent due to contact. Some of this material was also based on earlier work, such as Fischer (2007) for Chapter 3 and Fischer (2013) for Chapter 5. We have everywhere updated the information with the latest research done in the area, which constituted a fair amount due to the spate of handbooks that have appeared in the last decade, and to the flourishing of the field of historical linguistics with more and more PhDs and journal articles seeing the light of day (although no doubt the pressure to "publish or perish" also plays a role here). We therefore had to make choices, and we hope we have made the right ones.

The present volume is intended for everyone who has an interest in the way English has changed syntactically over a period of more than 1,000 years. For that reason, we have tried to avoid theoretical jargon as much as possible, so that the book can be used both in and outside of universities. It can be used as a textbook but has not been set up as one. It is not restricted to one particular approach to syntax; rather, it is broad in its scope and takes surface phenomena as a first point of departure. Where possible, we have tried also to explain why the changes occurred, making use of the various models of syntax and change, of both a formal and a functional nature, that are around.

We would like to thank Cambridge University Press and especially our editor, Andrew Winnard, for the encouragement given and patience shown. We also thank the Faculty of Humanities of the University of Amsterdam for granting Olga Fischer a six-month leave of absence in 2011. Finally we are most grateful to Sune Gregersen Rygård for his careful reading of the last version of the text and his useful and pertinent suggestions.

1   Introduction

The purpose of this book is to present an outline of the history of English syntax. The main changes in this component of the English language will be discussed and – where possible – something will be said about the factors that played a role in causing the changes and about the effects of individual changes on other structures. Overall, it could be said that English in its earliest stages was a heavily inflected language with a relatively free word order and a lexical base of mainly Germanic words, rather like modern German today. A host of changes over the centuries has made it into what it is today: a language with a morphology and syntax radically different from that of German. The main causes of these changes are the rapid loss of inflexions brought about both by internal phonological weakening and by intense contact with other languages after the Viking and Norman invasions and perhaps by the continuing presence of a Celtic substratum. Throughout the volume, we will document the ways in which these factors have led to a radical transformation of English syntax.

In doing so, we will be able to draw on the considerable volume of descriptive, explanatory and exploratory work on English historical syntax. However, rather than going for breadth of coverage, we will try to go for representativeness of material in terms of importance and interest, providing a full discussion of the major developments and a selection of additional changes that we think are illuminating and/or intriguing. Inevitably, there are many other changes that we could not include. Our apologies to these changes and the scholars that have identified and written about them. We focus on syntactic change in the common core of English, for reasons of both space and availability of materials (though we have allowed ourselves one or two digressions on non-standard developments). In the discussion of individual changes that we have included, we try to reflect the current state of scholarship so that various kinds of approach to historical syntax are represented. Nevertheless, we have attempted at all points to tell a coherent story rather than present an inventory of what has been said and written. At regular points in this story, we alert the reader to the fact that particular changes have not been adequately explained or even described yet – a sobering but also encouraging message, because on the one hand it forces us to recognize that progress in this field can be tantalizingly slow, while on the other it entails that the field is not cut-and-dried and finished, and that there is still plenty to discover and explain.

As one sobering and encouraging example, we may briefly mention here the general changes in word order that English has undergone over the centuries (for discussion of the details, see Chapter 9). The fact that word order in earlier English showed certain resemblances to that of modern German and Dutch was realized long ago, but it has taken a surprisingly long time for the precise extent of the similarities and dissimilarities to become fully appreciated. This, it must be admitted, is not because the basic data are hard to find – a look at any Old or Middle English (OE/ME) text will suffice to establish that both German/Dutch-like and Present-Day-English (PDE)-like orders occur side by side. What is more difficult is to systematically analyse the word orders found in a large number of texts, from various stages of the language, and to do so in a theoretical framework which enables meaningful comparisons to be made. This is more difficult not only because it requires more time and effort (and the availability of a generally accepted and adequate framework), but also because there is a strong temptation to be resisted: the temptation to move from description to explanation as soon as possible. This urge to explain, while admirable in itself, has resulted in some accounts of the word-order changes that are virtually divorced from any empirical findings and that basically leave intact all the questions and puzzles that there were in this field. The other side of the coin, of course, is that answers to these questions and puzzles are still welcome, and that even relatively modest or small-scale studies, provided they are firmly grounded in what is already available, can make a real contribution.

Our own view is that additional studies are most likely to produce answers if they combine detailed philological work (or full consideration of relevant existing work of this type) with the use of theoretical tools. Although this volume, which deals with syntax in the entire history of the English language, is based on the results of research accumulated over the years rather than on a completely new investigation of the field, such a combined empirical-theoretical approach is a line of recent enquiry that we think will lead to additional interesting findings in the years to come. Thus, in the field of word order again, it is easy to find very broad and general claims in the earlier literature to the effect that English word order was influenced by word order in Old French or Old Norse, or in the indigenous Celtic languages. What one usually looks for in vain are claims about the precise locus and nature of this influence, or indeed empirical backing of these ideas which goes beyond the facts to be explained. However, current work by several scholars explores dialectal differences in word order in early English, working with carefully chosen materials and a well-informed theoretical model that promises to finally enable us to substantiate some of the earlier claims and to discount others.

In the pages that follow, we have adopted as a working principle that changes first need to be described and only then explained. The result is a discussion in which description is preponderant, which we take to be a good thing for a presentation of the topic. Nevertheless, we also show for many changes what kinds of explanations have been advanced and where they are still absent. As will become evident, the best and most detailed explanatory work on English historical syntax so far has been structural in nature, in the sense that the rise and decline of syntactic constructions have been ascribed to specific structural properties of the language at the time concerned. This, however, is no doubt partly a result of the scarcity or relative inaccessibility of other types of empirical information for large periods of the history of English. The reader should therefore keep in mind that we present a picture of the subject that in many places is oversimplified, and not only because we have had to cram more than a thousand years' worth of changes in English speech and writing into a relatively brief historical overview.

The basic method of presentation in the following pages is simple; we first deal with general issues before we tackle various syntactic constructions and their developments in detail. We start with a chapter on the nature of the data and how to use it (Chapter 2), followed by an overview of the theoretical models that are currently used in syntactic change (Chapter 3). Chapter 4 offers a discussion of the extent to which English syntax has been influenced by other languages, concentrating on the OE and ME periods when this influence was most pervasive. Next follow five chapters that deal with the syntactic changes themselves. We start with the composition of the noun phrase (NP) (Chapter 5) and the verbal group (VP) (Chapter 6), and then move on to discuss the way these can be combined to form sentences. This is dealt with in Chapter 7 on clausal constituents; changes in negative and interrogative clauses are also discussed here. Chapter 8 deals with subordinate clauses, both finite and non-finite. Finally, Chapter 9 provides a separate discussion of word order, where we again look at the clausal constituents but concentrate on the position they have in the clause, and especially the changes that took place here, which also affected other areas of syntax, such as, for instance, verbal and complementation patterns discussed in Chapters 7 and 8. Other topics have been included where they fitted in most conveniently; where necessary, cross-references are given to help readers find their way to specific subjects.

Additional help is provided by Table 1.1, which contains a summary of the material dealt with in the book. It is organized as follows: in the first column, a list of the changes discussed in the various chapters is found. They are ordered in the same way as the chapters are – that is, elements within the NP are given first, followed by the four systems (mood, tense, etc.) that play a role in the VP. This is supplemented by changes that have taken place in the negative and interrogative systems. What follows next is the constituents of the clause

Table 1.1 *Overview of syntactic categories and their changes*

Changes in:	Old English	Middle English	Modern English	Chapter
case form and function:				
genitive	various functions	genitive case for subjective/poss.; *of*-phrase elsewhere	same	4.3.4; 5.3.2
dative	various functions/PP sporadic	increase in *to*-phrase; impersonal dative lost		7.3–7.5
accusative	main function: direct object	accusative case lost, direct object mainly marked by position		7.3–7.5
determiners:				
system	articles present in embryo form, system developing	articles used for presentational and referential functions	also in use in predicative and generic contexts	5.3.1
double det.	present	rare	absent	5.3.3
quantifiers:				
position of	relatively free	more restricted	fairly fixed	5.4
adjectives:				
position	both pre- and postnominal	mainly prenominal	prenominal with some lexical exceptions	4.3.4; 5.5.1; 5.5.2
form/function	strong/weak forms, functionally distinct	remnants of strong/weak forms; not functional	one form only	5.5.1
as head	fully operative	reduced; introduction of *one*	restricted to generic reference/ idiomatic	5.2.2
'stacking' of adjectival or relative clause	not possible	possible	possible	5.5.1
	relative: *se, se þe, þe*, zero subject rel.	new: *þæt, wh*-relative (except *who*), zero rel.	*who* relative introduced	4.3.4; 5.5.3
adj. + to-inf.	only active infinitives	active and passive inf.	mainly active inf.	4.3.1; 8.2.1
aspect-system:				
use of perfect	embryonic	more frequent; in competition with 'past'	perfect and 'past' grammaticalized in different functions	6.3.2

4

form of perfect	BE/HAVE (past part. sometimes declined)	BE/HAVE; HAVE becomes more frequent	mainly HAVE	6.3.2
use and form of progressive	BE + *-ende*; function not clear	BE + *-ing*, infrequent, more aspectual	frequent, grammaticalizing	2.5; 4.3.3; 6.5.1
tense-system: *'present'*	used for present tense, progressive, future	used for present tense and progr.; (future tense develops)	becomes restricted to 'timeless' and 'reporting' uses	6.3; 6.3.1
'past'	used for past tense, (plu)perfect, past progr.	still used also for past progr. and perfect; new: modal past	restricted in function by grammaticalization of perfect and progr.	6.3; 6.3.2
mood-system: *expressed by*	subjunctive, modal verbs (+ epistemic advbs)	mainly modal verbs (+ develop. quasi-modals); modal past tense	same + development of new modal expressions	6.2 6.2.1–6.2.3
category of core modals	verbs (with exception features)	verbs (with exception features)	auxiliaries (with verbal features)	6.2.2
voice-system: *passive form*	*beon/weorðan* + (inflected) past part.	BE + uninfl. past part	same; new GET passive	6.4
indirect pass.	absent	developing	(fully) present	7.5
prep. pass.	absent	developing	(fully) present	7.5
pass. infin.	only after modal verbs	after full verbs, with some nouns and adject.	same	4.3.1; 8.2.1
negative system	ne+verb(+ other negator)	(ne)+verb+*not*; rare *not*+verb	Aux+*not*+verb; (verb+*not*)	7.7
interrog.system	inversion: VS	inversion: VS	Aux SV	9.2
DO as operator	absent	infrequent, not grammaticalized	becoming fully grammaticalized	4.3.3; 6.6
subject: *position filled*	some *pro*-drop possible; dummy subjects not compulsory	*pro*-drop rare; dummy subjects become the norm	*pro*-drop highly marked stylistically; dummy subj. obligat.	7.2

6

Table 1.1 (*cont.*)

Changes in:	Old English	Middle English	Modern English	Chapter
clauses	absent	*that*-clauses and infinitival clauses	new: *for* NP *to* V clauses	8.2; 8.3.1; 9.7.1
subjectless/ impersonal constructions	common	subject position becomes obligatorily filled	extinct (some lexicalized express.)	7.4
position with respect to V	both S(..)V and VS	S(...)V; VS becomes re-stricted to yes/no quest.	only S(adv)V; VS > Aux SV	4.3.2; 4.3.4; 6.6; 9.2
object:				
clauses	mainly finite *þæt*-cl., also zero/ *to*-infinitive	stark increase in infinitival cl.	introduction of a.c.i. and *for* NP *to* V cl.	8.2; 8.3; 9.7.1
position with respect to V	VO and OV	VO; OV becomes restricted	VO everywhere	9.3
position IO - DO	both orders; pronominal IO-DO preferred	nominal IO-DO the norm, introduction of DO *for/to* IO	IO-DO with full NPs; pronominal DO-IO predominates	7.3; 9.4
clitic pronouns	syntactic clitics	clitics disappearing	clitics absent	4.3.2; 9.2; 9.3
adverbs:				
position	fairly free	more restricted	further restricted	9.6
clauses	use of correlatives + different word orders	distinct conjunctions; word order mainly SVO	all word order SVO (exc. some conditional clauses)	8.3.2
phrasal verbs	position particle: both pre- and postverbal	great increase; position: postverbal	same	9.5
preposition stranding	only with pronouns (incl. R-pronouns: *þær, etc.*) and relative *þe*	no longer with pronouns, but new with prep. passives, interrog, and other relative clauses	no longer after R-pronouns (*there,* etc.) except in fixed expressions	9.7.2

(subject, object, etc.), and the way in which these positions can be filled (e.g. by zero, by a lexical NP, a clause, etc.). The next three columns in each row show the overall changes that each construction has undergone in the three main periods of the history of English. The last column indicates where the relevant discussion can be found.

We have everywhere tried to give as many examples as space allowed us. Also for space considerations, we have tried to draw these from two main corpora for the OE and ME periods, so as not to overburden the reference system. Thus OE examples have all been taken from the Toronto *Dictionary of Old English Web Corpus* (concentrating on prose rather than poetry), and the ME examples are taken from the *Corpus of Middle English Prose and Verse*.[1] In other cases, references to the primary or secondary source have been provided.

---

[1] See http://tapor.library.utoronto.ca/doecorpus/ and http://quod.lib.umich.edu/c/cme/, respectively.

2 Data and Data Handling

2.1 Introduction

In this chapter, we discuss several general issues in the use of data for the history of English syntax, having to do with data collection and the process of making initial sense of the material collected. We begin by considering the use of handwritten and printed texts (Section 2.2). Until the late 1980s, 'texts on paper' were virtually the only source of data available for historical studies of English syntax, and this means that many of the handbooks and standard treatments of the subject still in use today are based exclusively on such materials. Because paper texts also form the input to more recently developed materials, a proper understanding of their nature and characteristics remains vital for all historical syntactic work. After discussing the practice, problems and benefits of working with paper texts, we turn to the possibilities opened up by the use of more recent resources, in particular digital corpora (Section 2.3). We give a brief overview of the different types that are currently available for diachronic syntactic work, the advantages that their use can bring and also some of the problems associated with the use of corpora as data sources. Next, we consider two general issues that arise in the handling of historical syntactic data. The first is the issue of variation, in terms of dialect, social variety, text-type and – broadly speaking – style (Section 2.4). It is now generally recognized that there can be no change without variation, so this is an obvious focus of interest for all diachronic syntactic study. A second, partly overlapping issue is that of data patterning (Section 2.5). Once paper texts and/or corpora have been mined for relevant data and these have been grouped according to factors like dialect, social provenance and text-type, what are then the patterns that we could or should look for and what are some of the problems that might arise in identifying them?

It will be clear that there are many theoretical decisions that will influence the selection and handling of data in the study of any specific topic in the history of English syntax. Thus, if one's aim is to characterize the internal grammars of speakers of English at different points in time, the lack of spoken records for all but the most recent periods makes it necessary to draw motivated inferences on the basis of necessarily incomplete data, whether these are in paper or digital form. Moreover, unlike in research on present-day syntax, there are – in spite of what Lightfoot (1979: 6) suggests – no native-speaker judgements for earlier English; hence it is impossible to be certain about the grammaticality of many types of sentences. In historical studies with a sociolinguistic focus, such considerations may be less of a problem, but it should not be thought that such work therefore stays 'closer' to the data in any real sense of the word. The attribution of geographical, social or stylistic properties to a text is the result of a complex process of reasoning, involving decisions about the overall system of categorization to be adopted, the establishing and weighing of criteria for assignment to specific categories, and comparison with other texts. If evidence on which to base these decisions is incomplete, as it usually is in historical work, the whole enterprise goes well beyond what is in the data as such. Clearly, the kind of patterns on which one wants to focus should have some connection with the data, but their nature will also inevitably be influenced by the general view of syntax and syntactic change that is adopted.

This chapter aims to make explicit certain methods and concepts on which there is a large degree of consensus and which are indispensable for developing an initial description of any set of diachronic syntactic data. The next chapter gives an overview of how such initial descriptions can be and have been interpreted further, in sometimes widely divergent ways. All of this, we hope, will give the reader a sense of the evidential and theoretical basis underlying the accounts of specific syntactic changes presented in Chapters 4 through 9.

2.2   Data from Handwritten and Printed Texts

Data in English from before the year 1473, when William Caxton – still in the Low Countries at the time – printed the first book in English, are all written by hand. They include some early inscriptions, such as the runes on the Franks Casket and the Ruthwell Cross, but – unlike scholars working on early North Germanic – historical syntacticians of English have not paid much attention to such materials, which are few and tend to be short anyway. This is more than compensated for, however, by the large number of manuscripts surviving from the medieval period, many containing substantial amounts of English text. For purposes of syntactic inquiry, it is actually rather unusual to work with these first-hand sources: the standard method is to use printed editions of the texts in which one is interested.[1] A rich collection of this type is the volumes in the

---

[1] Although there are exceptions, such as Meurman-Solin (2007).

various series published by the Early English Text Society (EETS), set up in 1864 partly to facilitate historical lexical research for what later became the Oxford English Dictionary. But these editions, the total number of which now approaches 500, are obviously also eminently suitable as sources for historical syntactic work. In fact, until the development (around the year 1990) of computer corpora containing historical texts, the EETS volumes, together with editions in other series, such as the Scottish Text Society and the Camden Society, and one-off editions of single texts formed the main source for any serious data work on medieval English syntax. For the post-medieval period, there are very large numbers of printed texts, in which additional data can be found. Of course, handwritten texts did not stop being produced after the fifteenth century, and indeed many early Modern English (eModE) and late Modern English (lModE) diaries, personal notebooks and collections of letters have been published in printed versions suitable for historical syntactic work.

Diligent and intelligent perusal of enormous amounts of material of these various kinds has led to the large-scale descriptions of the history of English syntax found in works like Jespersen (1909–49), Mustanoja (1960), Mitchell (1985) and Visser (1963–73), as well as a host of smaller-scale investigations of particular syntactic phenomena (many of them conveniently reviewed in Denison, 1993). The wealth of detailed descriptive studies of this type has meant that the history of English syntax has become a favourite testing ground for ideas and hypotheses concerning syntactic change in general. Several of the theoretical models discussed in the following chapter were originally developed with reference to changes in English, with data often being drawn from reference works like those mentioned here.

One of the issues that all historical linguistic studies have to grapple with is that of the dating of texts. For example, there has been an (implicit) tendency in the study of OE syntax to regard the period as being rather homogeneous. However, given that the OE materials suitable for syntactic study span more than three centuries, this cannot be right. Hence, it is necessary in collecting and reporting data to make at least initially a distinction between early OE (as attested mainly in the works associated with King Alfred, of the late ninth century) and late OE (as attested in a more diffuse body of work, a prime representative being Ælfric, who wrote around 1000 AD). It has also been demonstrated, in particular by Allen (1992), that many manuscripts containing OE works are actually late copies, produced in the early ME period, thus making them potentially unreliable witnesses to properties of OE grammar. In dealing with texts from the Modern period, more subtle questions about dating issues can sometimes be addressed, such as whether texts should be seen as representing the state of the language during their year of composition or during the formative years of their authors. Thus, Arnaud (1983, 1998) presents data on the progressive in the nineteenth century which suggest that some authors appear to show stable usage through time, while others exhibit what Sankoff (2005) calls 'lifespan change'.

Although work based on paper texts has yielded impressive results, in the form of detailed descriptions of many changes in English syntax through the centuries, there are obvious problems that it faces due to the nature of its data sources. The main problem is that reading texts for the purpose of finding examples of specific syntactic phenomena can be enormously time-consuming. In earlier work, this led to the inclusion of statements about the frequency of constructions that were quite imprecise and/or impressionistic (Visser, 1963–73, is particularly notorious in this respect). Moreover, it is often impossible to achieve full accountability, in the sense of considering all potential variants that express a certain meaning or share a common formal property. For example, in a study based on a large number of paper texts, Foster and van der Wurff (1995) consider changes in the frequency of clauses with object-verb order in late Middle English but are unable to provide full comparable data for clauses with verb-object order, instead relying on smallish samples of such cases. Yet another problem is that data work of this type can often not realistically be replicated. This is particularly problematic when, after data collection, it is realized that some crucial variant or alternative has been mistakenly omitted from the search. Reliance on data from paper texts can thus be an obstacle in implementing the 'virtuous' cycle where increased insight triggers the collection of additional data, which in turn increases insight, and so on and so forth.

Nevertheless, there are also advantages to the use of paper texts in searching for data. For one thing, the careful reading that it necessitates ensures that the researcher gets a sense of the complete syntactic system of the language of the text, rather than limiting this attention solely to the one phenomenon under consideration. If one believes the structuralist tenet that language is a system where everything coheres (*un système ou tout se tient*), this is obviously important. From a practical point of view, it can be helpful in identifying phenomena which have similar functions or forms. For example, while doing an exploratory search in some eModE texts for the NP *the same* used as an anaphoric marker, as in (1) (with antecedent given in italics), Leung and van der Wurff (2011) noted the frequent occurrence in the same texts of NPs of the type *the said* N with rather similar function, as in (2).

(1) The Cooks they wrought both day and night in many curious devises, where was no lacke of gold, silver, or any other costly thing: the Yeomen and Grooms of his Wardrobe were busied in hanging *the Chambers* with costly Hangings, and furnishing *the same* with beds of silke and other furniture for *the same* in every degree (1641, Cavendish, *Th.Woolsey*, 74).

(2) ere we came to *Standingfield*, the Cardinall of Lorraine a goodly young Gentleman gave my Lord a meeting, and received him with much joy and reverence, and so passed

forth with my Lord in communication untill wee came neere *the said Standingfield,* which is a religious place standing betweene the English, French, and Imperiall Dominions (1641, Cavendish, *Th.Woolsey,* 42).

Accordingly, it was decided that developments affecting these two expressions should be compared, as part of a study of anaphoric devices that were frequent in eModE but that have since become rather minor variants – not an earth-shattering idea in itself, but it might not have arisen at all if attention during data searching had been limited to sentences of type (1) only. In working with material from older periods, there is a certain danger that expectations based on present-day English will create blind spots or colour the perception of earlier data. Reading longer stretches of text is no guarantee that this will not happen, but it may help avoid at least some of its negative effects.

2.3   Digital Data

Over the past two decades, there has been great activity in the creation of digital corpora of texts suitable for English historical linguistic work. As with corpora for PDE, various types of historical corpora can be distinguished, according to how they have been planned: balanced (i.e. containing specific proportions of material of different kinds) versus opportunistic (i.e. containing material within the period of interest chosen simply because it is easily available); general (covering a wide range of materials) versus specialized (focusing on texts that meet some very specific criteria); bare (not enriched with linguistic coding) versus tagged (enriched with part-of-speech labels) versus parsed (fully syntactically analysed). Such classifications, though, should not be taken as more than somewhat imprecise labels which can be convenient for identifying corpora of certain kinds but which may not be helpful in discussing other kinds (see e.g. Lüdeling and Kytö, 2008–09, Bennett *et al.,* 2013, for full discussion of these and many other aspects of corpus use, planning, creation and classification).

The mother of all diachronic English corpora is the Helsinki corpus, a 1.6-million-word, largely balanced, general and initially bare collection of texts approximately spanning the years 730–1710, compiled at the University of Helsinki in the late 1980s and described fully in Kytö (1996). Data from this corpus have been used in a tremendous number of historical syntactic studies – some early examples can be seen in the papers in Rissanen *et al.* (1993, 1997). Several additional corpora have been created collaboratively by the University of Pennsylvania and the University of York. These are partly based on the Helsinki corpus materials but add full syntactic annotation to the texts. They cover the OE period (the York-Toronto-Helsinki Corpus of Old English Prose, which contains all major OE prose texts, and the York-Helsinki Corpus of Old

English Poetry, containing all surviving OE verse), the ME, eModE and lModE periods contained in the three Penn-Helsinki Parsed Corpora of these periods. All of these are general and balanced. They use the same system of syntactic annotation and the same query language (named CorpusSearch), which takes some learning effort but allows users to easily search for syntactic patterns through the entire history of English.

In addition, there are now dozens of specialized historical corpora, covering many specific text-types and/or subperiods. Several of these also have been compiled at Helsinki, such as the Corpus of Older Scots (with nearly 1 million words of Middle Scots) and the Corpus of Early English Correspondence, in its first version containing the text of c.6,000 letters written in the period 1410–1680 (Raumolin-Brunberg and Nevalainen, 2007). There is a corpus containing the proceedings of the Old Bailey in the eighteenth and nineteenth centuries (Huber 2007). The Corpus of Late Modern English Texts (currently at version 3.1) contains 34 million words of British English prose from the years 1710–1920 (De Smet *et al.*, 2015). A collection of early newspaper writing (1660–1800) can be found in the 1.6 million-word Zurich English Newspaper Corpus (Lehmann *et al.*, 2006). Of particular note are also the corpora developed by Mark Davis at Brigham Young University, which include the Time Magazine Corpus (containing the full text of this magazine since its inception in 1923) and the Corpus of Historical American English (spanning the period 1810 until 2006 and comprising 400 million words), both with part-of-speech tagging and searchable with the same intuitive search engine. In addition, many more corpora exist and others are currently being compiled or planned (for fuller descriptions of some corpora, see e.g. Beal *et al.*, 2007; for more recent corpora see Section 2.4).[2]

Some of these corpora have no linguistic tagging, but this need not be an obstacle to their exploitation for diachronic syntactic work. As long as the researcher is examining a pattern which has one or more specific lexical items uniquely (or nearly uniquely) associated with it, data for many syntactic phenomena can be collected. This can also be done in online text collections primarily created for the purpose of literary or historical rather than linguistic investigation, such as 'Early English Books Online' (containing all English books published before 1700) and the historical archives of *The Times of London* and *The Guardian*, which can all be treated as large digital sources of data.

---

[2] The Research Unit for Variation, Contacts and Change in English at the University of Helsinki acts as an informal repository for basic information about English-language corpora, see www.helsinki.fi/varieng/CoRD/corpora/index.html. Another useful repository is http://tiny.cc/corpora.

The advantages of working with digital corpora will be obvious: because it is many times faster than the method of reading through paper texts, it is possible to inspect much larger amounts of text and, in some cases, to aim for full accountability to the data; it is also replicable. In addition, when one has access to the complete digital files of a corpus, there is the possibility of enriching it with additional linguistically relevant information. In terms of hypothesis generation and testing, if one has a hunch about an explanation or a pattern based on initial corpus data, it is usually fairly easy to do a quick search in the same corpus to see if the hunch might be worth exploring in further detail. Corpus work therefore accommodates itself well to the virtuous cycle of data triggering new ideas, to be checked against additional data.

But working with corpora also has some potential disadvantages. In the interviews with fourteen corpus linguists collected in Viana *et al.* (2011), one of the questions addressed was the possible weaknesses of corpus analysis. Although none of the interviewees specifically focused on the use of corpora for historical syntactic study, they identified the following areas of concern which are also relevant to our discussion:

(i) there can be tension between what is easily retrieved through corpus searches and what is thought to be linguistically most significant; a historical syntactic case in point involves patterns of co-reference of noun phrases, as in (1) and (2); these have been largely neglected because they involve information status, which is currently not part of any standard annotation scheme (but see Komen, 2009, for ideas on how to incorporate it);

(ii) when a data search yields large numbers of hits, there may be a temptation to interpret corpus results merely as numbers, which is a severely reductive approach; in cases of grammaticalization, for example, changes in frequency may act as tell-tale signs (see Hopper and Traugott, 2003: 126ff), but an exclusive quantitative focus will mean that one is ignoring the changes in meaning and context that form the core of the process;

(iii) the substantial amounts of data that can be collected from a corpus can also blind researchers to the dangers of making generalizations about the language as a whole on the basis of a partial view of it; this is a particularly relevant problem for diachronic research, because we only have very incomplete evidence for the state of the language in any historical period (see Section 2.6 for further discussion);

(iv) trying to achieve greater representativeness by collecting and comparing data from various corpora can also be tricky: principles guiding text inclusion vary widely, there is little standardization in user interfaces, and they can require a significant time investment to learn to operate.

2.4   Data and Variation

From whatever source one's historical syntactic data are collected, a vital part of processing the findings for further interpretation is categorization in terms of a number of parameters of variation. The first of these – not surprisingly – is temporal, as expressed by date of writing of the texts and/ or date of birth of the authors. Because syntactic change tends to be somewhat slow, there is usually little point in comparing data separated by a time span of only a few years. Hence, in many studies, the periods investigated cover from 50 up to 150 years. In the study of medieval English, the nature of the data sources sometimes makes it impossible to set very precise boundaries, but it would generally be felt that treating a period longer than two or three hundred years as one single data point (e.g. by taking the average frequency value of some phenomenon in this period) will result in too much loss of information. At the lower end of the scale, a period of about thirty years can already yield interesting syntactic change, as demonstrated by several studies of recent change in written English (e.g. Mair and Leech, 2006, Leech *et al.*, 2009), using the so-called Brown family of corpora, currently consisting of the Brown corpus and the London-Oslo-Bergen (LOB)-corpus (each containing 1 million words of English from the 1960s, from the United States and the UK, respectively), the Frown corpus and the FLOB corpus (with comparable materials from the 1990s) and the BLOB-1931 corpus (a BLOB-1901 corpus is in the making). The existence of such relatively fast change has also been reported in specialized studies of historical texts (e.g. Arnaud, 1983, 1998; Raumolin-Brunberg, 2009).

Another obvious dimension of variation lies in the dialectal or regional nature of the material examined. On the whole, historical syntactic research has tended to adopt the dialect divisions developed in phonological and lexical studies and tried to establish whether there are also syntactic differences reflecting these divisions. A major problem in this is the strong dominance in much writing of standardized kinds of English. Even in OE, the West-Saxon variety was in use in Anglian areas as well, making it somewhat difficult to spot dialectal variation, certainly at the syntactic level. But there is some. One well-established case concerns incorporation of the negative marker *ne* into verbs (forms like *nis* 'not is' and *ne-wat>nat* 'not knows', a feature most typical of West-Saxon OE; see Hogg, 2004). In ME, there is much more dialectal diversity in the texts (Milroy, 1992), and although the syntactic side of this has been somewhat neglected until recently, it is now clear that there are, for example, North-South differences in the position of the finite verb in main clauses (Kroch *et al.*, 2001), in subject-verb agreement patterns (de Haas, 2011) and in the use of relative markers (Suárez-Gómez, 2009). One possible avenue for further work might be to examine closely the prose texts in manuscripts localized by means of the 'fit' technique in work for the *Linguistic Atlas of Late Middle English* (McIntosh *et al.*, 1985) and try to determine whether the phonological and spelling variation exploited in that project is matched by syntactic differences.

For the eModE period, syntactic investigation has until recently largely concentrated on printed works, which right from the start show rather uniform use of syntactic constructions. In fact, Görlach (1999b: 492) states that 'evidence of Early Modern English dialect syntax is almost nil'. But progress in this area is now being made by careful exploration of hand-written texts, for example in the Corpus of Early English Correspondence. Nevertheless, the amount of dialectal grammatical variability detected so far is not very great and tends to be more morphological than syntactic in nature (for examples, see Nevalainen, 2011). For lModE, there is a certain amount of printed dialect writing available and there are some contemporary comments on dialectal features (see Ihalainen, 1994), but the work done so far on dialect syntax is limited and few results have been reported within British English (see Kortmann and Wagner, 2010, for an overview). The best prospects in this area seem to lie in first identifying differences in syntax between present-day regional varieties as is done in Trousdale and Adger (2007; a good example of this can also be found in Anderwald, 2005) on the use of double negation in the North versus the South of England), and then to examine earlier materials for their possible presence.

This method has been used to good effect in tracing the development of several syntactic differences between British and American English during the nineteenth and twentieth centuries. Present-day differences are reasonably well documented (in works like Tottie, 2002 and Algeo, 2006), and there are now several corpora that can be used to study their historical origins. Rohdenburg (2009), for example, argues that corpus data show American English increasingly favouring less explicit grammatical marking, as shown by the fact that it has led the way in changes like the loss of reflexive marking with verbs such as *to straighten* (*oneself*) and the loss of *to be* in passive complements of 'order' verbs, as in *He ordered it* (*to be*) *done*.[3] Additional studies making such historical trans-Atlantic comparisons can be found in Rohdenburg and Schlüter (2009).

Syntactic variation conditioned by social factors is probably not recoverable for the OE and early ME periods, owing to the sparsity of texts for comparison

---

[3] Seidlhofer and Widdowson (2007: 366–68) suggest that American English favours greater semantic simplicity, as indicated by the use of general-purpose vocabulary in several proverbs (e.g. AmEng *the early bird gets the worm*, BrEng *the early bird catches the worm*). They argue this could be a consequence of English having to some extent the status of a *lingua franca* in multilingual communities in the United States from the nineteenth century onwards. This would shed a different light also on American-British syntactic differences.

and the total absence of information about many of the authors of this time. For late ME and eModE, however, some good results have been achieved. Bergs (2005) studies the effect of social networks in the language of the Paston Letters and, again, the Corpus of Early English Correspondence has been an important source of useful data of this type (see Nevalainen and Raumolin-Brunberg, 1996, 2003, where a range of morpho-syntactic features are examined). For the eighteenth century too there has been some work, with letters again being a favourite data source (see Tieken-Boon van Ostade, 1987, on social class and gender as factors influencing use of auxiliary *do*, Sairio, 2009, on the use of preposition stranding and of the progressive within one specific social network, and Laitinen, 2009, on gender variation in the use of *you were* and *you was*). For the nineteenth century, there are many incidental observations on socially conditioned grammatical variation (e.g. Phillips, 1984) and a few more systematic studies of certain topics (Pratt and Denison, 2000, on the diffusion of the passive progressive, Kytö and Romaine, 2006, on gender differences in adjectival comparison), but there is clearly scope for further work.

Yet another source of variation is differences in text-type or register. This is a factor that is taken into account in the creation of virtually all historical corpora, and it is usually not difficult to pinpoint the more obvious text-typical features of the material one is working with. The general finding in work that has considered the role of this factor is that it can cause very big differences in syntax between texts. An obvious case in point is the differences between poetry and prose. These have been studied in particular for the medieval period, for which much of the surviving textual evidence consists of verse. With regard to word order, for example, Foster and van der Wurff (1995) show that, in the fourteenth and fifteenth centuries, poetry and prose increasingly diverge in their use of pre-verbal objects, with prose showing a clear decline but poetry maintaining stable levels, a clear sign that this order is becoming a marked option for language users. Attempts have also been made to exploit the rhythmic organization of verse to draw inferences about the relation between word order and intonation characteristics of the language, something which is otherwise very difficult or impossible to do in historical material. Thus Pintzuk and Kroch (1989) argue on the basis of data from the poem *Beowulf*, which they take to represent a very early type of OE, that post-verbal position of objects in English was originally restricted to NPs separated from the verb by an intonation boundary. Comparing *Beowulf* with the rhythmical prose of Ælfric, Taylor (2005) argues that this restriction was gradually loosened in the course of the OE period, suggesting that post-verbal objects were becoming a more freely available option.

In spite of these and other ways in which data from verse can provide insight into processes of syntactic change, poetic usage must be treated with care because part of it may be the result of hard-to-pin-down literary conventions and the even more intangible effects of a poet's attempt to create local meaning. Most studies of historical syntax therefore focus on prose. Within this category, there are also big differences in the use of syntactic options so that, normally, finer distinctions are made, often depending on what kind of material is available for different text-types in the period of interest. The Helsinki Corpus, for example, contains texts in the following, partly overlapping general categories: statutory (legal and official documents), secular instruction (handbooks, texts on astronomy, medicine, philosophy and education), religious instruction (treatises, homilies, sermons), expository (texts on astronomy, medicine and education), non-imaginative narration (history, biography, religious treatises, travelogues, diaries) and imaginative narration (fiction, romance, travelogues). Grouped in one way or another, these are naturally also the categories distinguished in the numerous studies based on data from the Helsinki corpus. The overview of historical corpora in Section 2.3 reveals some of the other text-types that have been singled out for special attention, such as letters, newspapers and court-room language.

Although the majority of studies focus on the development of a single syntactic phenomenon or a small set of related phenomena in one or more text-types, there have also been studies examining the textual distribution of clusters of features. For example, inspired by Douglas Biber's (1988) work on text-types in PDE, Biber and Finegan (1989) show that, since eModE, the text-types of fiction, essays and letters have become steadily more oral, in the sense of having higher frequencies of features associated with a more involved, less elaborated and less abstract style. Concretely, this means they have come to use, for example, more present tense verbs, more second person pronouns, more *that*-deletion, more time adverbials, fewer passives and fewer adverbial clauses. The same method has since been used to trace the development of other text-types, such as scientific writing (Atkinson, 1999) and newspaper editorials (Westin and Geisler, 2002).

For some researchers, the holy grail of historical syntactic study is the identification of properties of everyday spontaneous speech in historical periods. We have only glimpses of what this text-type was like, but – on the basis of work on PDE – certain other text-types can reasonably be taken to provide approximations to naturalistic speech, in particular personal letters, court-records and (certain kinds of) drama.[4] Work exploring such registers is now abundant (see Claridge and Walker, 2001, and Laitinen, 2008, for some examples, in addition to several mentioned earlier in this section). Where such texts converge in their use of syntactic constructions while diverging from

---

[4] For the medieval period, such texts are largely absent, but it has been observed that, in ME, some poetry contains features that may reflect spontaneous informal speech.

other text-types, it does seem reasonable to say that they to some extent provide a window onto properties of earlier speech, including its role in the origin and propagation of innovations.

A method for investigating change in spoken data more directly is now also available: a Diachronic Corpus of Present-Day Spoken English has been developed at UCL. This contains transcribed versions of different categories of spoken British English dating from the 1950s till the 1990s. Study of such data is interesting also from the perspective of the idea that the grammar of speech is fundamentally different from that of written text, as claimed by researchers like Brazil (1995) and Miller and Weinert (1998). If they are correct, the question arises whether the relevant properties can be subject to diachronic change and how such change would take place. Obviously, only direct comparison of diachronic spoken data can lead to answers. But even if one believes that speech and writing do have shared fundamentals, there is much to be gained from studying changes in speech. Modern corpus work on everyday speech has firmly established that it is characterized by great amounts of repetition and very high proportions of fixed and semi-fixed phrases or lexical bundles (see Greaves and Warren, 2010, for an overview). It is natural to suppose that such pervasive features of speech have an effect on its development over time. Unfortunately, these features are underrepresented even in the historical registers mentioned earlier that come closest to speech. Yet if certain general pathways for syntactic change in speech driven by these features can be deduced from examination of contemporary material, it may be possible to project these back in time and make use of them in accounting for historical change. For some work along these lines, see Bybee and Cacoullos (2009).

A rather special text-type which is abundantly attested during all stages of the English language is translations, in particular from Latin (during all periods) and French (in ME and eModE). The interpretation of data from such texts requires extra care, because specific features may partly reflect the syntactic system not of English but of the language of the original. One safeguard against faulty interpretations due to this is comparison with texts that have not been directly or indirectly influenced by a process of translation; comparison with the text in the source language is of course also essential. Using such methods, it has been established, for example, that some syntactic phenomena found in OE texts, such as raising-to-object were not native to OE and occurred only as a result of literal translation from Latin (see Chapter 4). Note that such comparisons give the researcher something resembling negative evidence (i.e. information about syntactic constructions that were not licensed by the underlying grammar of the language at that point in time).

The foreign feature can also manifest itself in differences in relative frequency. An example is the use of object-verb word order in late ME: in most prose texts this is not frequent but there are a few translations from French with very high numbers of preverbal pronominal objects, closely reflecting usage in Old French (Foster and van der Wurff, 1995). Yet another way in which features of the source language can affect the language of the translation is through suppression of certain variants. Thus, Taylor (2008) notes that OE prepositional phrases are normally head-initial, but can have complement-P order if the complement is a pronoun, as in (3).

(3) *Þa   cwæþ se Hælend **him to**, Aris hal   of   ðam bedde*
    then said   the Saviour him to arise whole from the   bed (*ÆHom*.2,38)
    'Then the Saviour said to him, 'Arise whole from the bed''

Examination of non-translated and translated texts reveals that the word order in (3) is less frequent in texts translated from Latin.[5] The reason appears to be that this order does not occur in Latin (except with the single preposition *cum* 'with'); adoption of the Latin word order therefore has the effect that the translation has far fewer instances of what seems to have been an otherwise productive option in OE.

Of course, the (non-)use of certain syntactic constructions in translated texts due to influence of the source language can in the longer run lead to change, where such uses spread to other texts and may eventually become a general feature of English. Raising-to-object, for instance, eventually became part of the grammar of English. The topic of contact-induced syntactic change of this and other types is addressed in Chapter 4.

A final source of syntactic variation in historical texts that we should mention is style. This factor is difficult to operationalize for historical material, but one way it has been done is through levels of formality. Some of this is captured through the concept of register, as when a comparison is made between, say, everyday talk between friends (informal), a conversation with a stranger (moderately formal) and an address to a larger unknown audience (formal). But variation is certainly possible within these and other registers, and style may be a good term to refer to such variability. It could then include cases of jocularity, semi-serious use of old-fashioned or archaic grammar (as perhaps in (8) later in this chapter), and other special uses of language. Identifying such cases can be difficult and requires reading of paper texts – this is another area in which exclusive use of corpora is likely to lead to incomplete descriptions of the data. In spite of these difficulties, the effects achieved by speakers' and writers' stylistic choices are important. Recent work on syntactic change suggests that it is often very local in nature; hence, it is important to be aware of all factors that have an effect on the local selection of syntactic options.

---

[5] Though, as Taylor (2008: 349–53) shows, the effect can only be clearly seen once various other factors influencing the order of preposition and pronominal complement are taken into account.

2.5   Data Patterning

Although studies of different topics will naturally focus on different types of configurations in the data, there are some general patterns that many historical syntactic studies will try to identify. One such pattern is related to the conditioning of syntactic choices. In essence, this boils down to the question when certain options are used and when they are not. The conditions can of course relate to the dimensions of variation discussed in the previous section, but they can also be entirely linguistic in nature. A good example of the latter possibility is the word-order phenomenon in OE and ME known as verb-second, illustrated for OE in (4), where the initial element *eall ðis* 'all this' is immediately followed by the finite verb *aredað* 'arranges'.

(4) *eall ðis   aredað   se   recere suiðe ryhte*
    all this arranges the ruler   very rightly (*CP*.169.3)
    'all this the ruler arranges very rightly'

In the early 1980s, it was known that use of this word order is an option characteristic of main rather than subordinate clauses and that it is categorical in interrogatives, except when these are introduced by the word *hwæðer* 'whether' functioning as a kind of question particle (cf. Allen, 1980). Later, it was realized that verb-second tends not to occur in OE if the subject of the clause is a personal pronoun, except after a small set of specific clause-initial elements (Van Kemenade, 1987). Later still, the (non-)occurrence of verb-second with subjects that are not pronouns was shown not to be random but to depend on the nature of the clause-initial element (Pintzuk, 1991, Koopman, 1998). Furthermore, it was demonstrated that verb-second does sometimes occur in subordinate clauses but only when the verb is passive or unaccusative (Van Kemenade, 1997).

This example is in no way exceptional: usually more is going on in the data than one might initially be inclined to think. Failure to recognize the more fine-grained aspects of the conditioning of a syntactic option results in descriptions that are lacking in precision, and this in turn means that questions about the how and why of syntactic change become difficult or impossible to address successfully. It is true that progress in understanding is a cumulative and protracted process, but when reading historical syntactic work carried out a few or more decades ago, it can sometimes be difficult to avoid the feeling that the writers could have achieved more if they had inspected more carefully the way the data are patterned. The best precaution to ensure that one's work will not provoke such a response at some point in the near future is to look at the data long and hard before drawing any conclusions from it. One can never be sure in advance what the relevant conditions are but it is always worthwhile to spend time on one's data to determine the linguistic contexts which may cause variation in the use of a particular syntactic phenomenon (more on this in Chapter 3).

Another aspect of the patterning of historical data that is obviously important is the following: when is the phenomenon under investigation attested for the first or last time? In theory, these should be straightforward questions to answer, but in practice there can be various difficulties. An instructive example here is the search for the earliest cases of the progressive BE+*being* followed by an adjective or past participle. The latter sequence forms the passive progressive, a relatively recent innovation in the history of English. Nehls (1974: 158) gives (5) and (6) as the earliest cases.

(5) Sir Guy Carlton was four hours being examined
    (1779, J. Harris, *Letters, ibid.*: 158)

(6) like a fellow whose uppermost upper grinder is being torn out by the roots by a
    mutton-fisted barber
    (1795, Southey, *Life & Correspondence, ibid.*: 158)

However, Denison (1993: 431–32, 444) argues that (5) is not a secure example since *being examined* may be 'a participial or gerundial phrase ... used absolutely' (*ibid.*: 431), leaving (6) as the earliest case. Denison (1998: 152), after having looked at more texts, is able to give an even earlier instance, from the year 1772. But this too has been antedated: Van Bergen (2013), searching in several lModE corpora that have become available since the late 1990s, has identified several instances that are even earlier, including examples from several London-based newspapers in 1761.

For cases of progressive BE+*being* followed by an adjective, Visser (1963–73: §§1834–35) gives examples like (7)–(9).

(7) With tendre youth was he hote being
    'He was hot (was being hot) with tender youth'
    (a1500, *Partenay*)

(8) but this is being wicked, for wickedness sake
    (1761, Johnston, *Chrysal*)

(9) You will be glad to hear [...] how diligent I have been, and am being
    (1819 Keats, *Letters*)

While data like this suggest that the construction has been in use since the start of the eModE period, Denison (1993: 396) points out that (8) and similar examples from the eighteenth century are actually not instances of progressive BE. The meaning of (8) is 'this amounts to being wicked', where *being wicked* is a gerund clause functioning as subject complement and *is* is the simple present tense of the copula. The result is that there are a few instances of this construction attested around the year 1500, then a long silence, followed by additional examples from the early nineteenth century onwards.

These examples with BE+*being* illustrate several of the problems that can make the search for earliest attestations difficult:

(i) there may be doubt (sometimes resolvable, sometimes not) over whether a concrete instance is actually an example of what one is looking for; because new constructions often seem to be based on ambiguous instances of constructions already in existence, this is a recurrent problem;

(ii) findings are inevitably affected by the (lack of) availability of texts, which in turn reflects the amount of scholarly work on text edition and corpus creation for the relevant period as well as the vagaries that determine the loss and survival of historical texts;

(iii) if one has to search for data in unparsed texts (as Visser, Denison and van Bergen did in trying to find passive progressives), the work can be very time-consuming;

(iv) even if one has all the texts and all the time that could exist in any possible world, there will probably be cases in which an early example of an innovative construction is found, followed by a period without any examples and then what looks like a restart, sometimes with several cases attested closely together.

Similar problems can arise when trying to determine the date when a construction passes out of use. In particular, problem (iv) – in this case taking the form of unexpectedly late instances of a construction – can be troublesome. The reason for such late survivals may be that a particular usage is not completely extinct but continues as a stylistically or lexically restricted option, for example as a marker of old-fashioned language or as a feature of certain more-or-less frozen expressions. An example is the use of negatives without *do* in PDE, as in (10).

(10) I kid you not.

Tieken-Boon van Ostade (1987) has traced the decline in frequency of *do*-less negatives in the eighteenth century and Varga (2005) shows they become very infrequent in the course of the nineteenth century (with verbs of cognition surviving longest and strongest). Yet the continued use of cases like (10) makes it impossible to assign a definite date of disappearance to this option. Instead, we have to recognize that the construction is undergoing obsolescence very gradually.

Part of every change, including the process of obsolescence, is quantitative and that is the final aspect of data patterning that we discuss here. Study of the frequency of diachronic data always involves comparison: of frequencies at different time periods and/or in different text-types, produced in different regions and/or by different types of authors (in terms of gender, social class or other characteristics). Moreover, it is often necessary to consider not just one syntactic phenomenon but to make a comparison between two phenomena, regarded as subtypes of a larger category. It is not always the case that there is patterning involving each of these factors, but if a phenomenon has undergone change over a longer period of time, all of them may well have played some role at some point. For example, in research on the history of possessive marking in English, Mustanoja (1960: 75) reports that there was a steep increase in the use of the *of*-phrase as compared with the genitive in the course of the ME period. If this shift was partly due to French influence (see Chapter 4), the social factor of prestige may have played a role in it. After 1400, the shift was to some extent reversed, with the genitive regaining some ground (Rosenbach *et al.*, 2000). In terms of text-type, it has been shown that in the seventeenth century the genitive was frequent in poetry but also in texts reflecting language use at a personal and informal level (Altenberg, 1982). Work on more recent periods, such as Rosenbach (2003) and Mair and Leech (2006), has demonstrated that the genitive is still increasing in frequency as compared with the *of*-phrase, in particular in text-types belonging to more informational genres.

Quite complicated patterns can emerge once linguistic conditioning factors are also taken into account (e.g. the preference for genitives when the possessor NP is short has human reference and encodes given information). The recognition that quantitative patterns in data can result from the interaction of many different factors has led to the use of increasingly sophisticated statistical methods of analysis. For example, Hinrichs and Szmrecsanyi (2007) examine possessive marking in the Brown family of corpora using multivariate analysis to establish the relative weight and interaction of no less than sixteen factors, including genre, dialect (UK or U.S. English), time, the nature of the final segment of the possessor NP (sibilant or not), length of possessor NP and possessum NP, etcetera. Like earlier work, they find an increase over the past few decades in the frequency of the genitive in press texts; their detailed findings on the factor weighting allow them to attribute this to a process of economization, where – all else being equal – shorter expression is favoured, rather than to a process of colloquialization, as had been suggested before.

2.6   Conclusions

In this chapter, we have covered some of the issues that arise in the collection and description of data for historical syntax. We have discussed the material basis of these data in handwriting or print (often coming to the researcher only after a certain amount of scholarly pre-processing, as in editions of earlier texts), the care that is needed in interpreting such materials with respect to date of creation and origins, the problems that arise when trying to extract precise and accountable information from them and the benefits that can come from reading entire texts on paper. We contrasted this with the use of digital corpora, available in increasing numbers and types and searchable with much greater speed and accuracy.[6] Yet, it is important when using the latter to strike a balance between number-crunching and interpretation of the data in light of the (textual) world outside the specific pattern under examination. Aspects of this world that are likely to be relevant include the different dimensions of variation that have also been found to be relevant in non-historical work: dialectal or regional variation, social variation and variation in text-type. Usually, it will be found that syntactic data pattern along one or more of these dimensions, which may also play a role in the causation of change. In addition, there is nearly always language-internal patterning, in the form of linguistic conditioning of syntactic options, making for a total configuration that is potentially quite complex and may require the use of statistical analysis. At a simpler level, an obvious aim of practical data work on syntactic change is often to determine when a construction first appears or is lost – but this too can be more difficult than it sounds, particularly given the fact that constructions tend to fade away very slowly rather than disappear abruptly.

In studying data and all the types of patterns in which they can be involved, it is necessary to firmly keep in mind the limitations of the evidence that we have for most of the history of the language. Instead of a rich spectrum of vernacular regional dialects, what we have for OE are documents in mostly standardized versions of the dialect of South-Western England (with the early and later texts representing different localities in this area), with uncertain amounts of influence from Latin, from which many texts are translated, and with Celtic possibly still present as a substrate language (see Chapter 4). For ME, the evidential database is much richer, but there are huge gaps for early ME when writing in French occupied much of the space that writing in English might have done. Throughout ME there is also a dearth of materials that reflect more spontaneous types of language, and when these come in towards the end of the period (as in plays and personal correspondence) there is simultaneously an increasing effect of standardization. For eModE and lModE, existing materials are much richer but – certainly when it comes to texts that are easily available – they are heavily slanted towards the formal usage of middle-class males. And they are all written. While it is entirely possible for a change to find its origin in writing (see Biber and Gray, 2011, for an example), it is probably

---

[6] Although there are by now many studies of the English used in digital communication (e.g. Baron, 2008), too little time has elapsed since their first use for them to undergo any noticeable syntactic change. But no doubt this will become an area for future study.

much more usual for innovations to start in speech. This means that historical material gives us only an imperfect data-set to work with. Because of the gaps in the written record and the complete absence of speech, including its patterns of intonation and its heavy use of fixed phrases and interactional routines, we cannot claim to have a good idea of what many regard as the normal locus of syntactic change. Some of the fluctuation and variability that is typically found in historical data may therefore well be noise, masking the regularities of an underlying system that we can access only very indirectly and incompletely.

3 Theoretical Models and Morpho-Syntactic Change

3.1 Introduction

As in any science, we need to abstract away from the purely physical data (in our case, texts or recorded spoken language) in order to find recurring underlying patterns. These should help us to streamline the data, to describe and categorize them in a coherent fashion, and thus give us an understanding, via the formulation of principles, laws, rules or schemas, as to why the data are the way they are. With the help of such 'induced' abstract patterns, we build theoretical models that, ideally, should enable us to understand how language is structured, how language is learned and hence how it may change; and they may even help us to predict possible new developments.[1] At the same time, it is important to remember that any rules or categories or schemas that we may set up are indeed 'tools': they do not necessarily represent anything that speakers actually make use of when they learn or process their native language.

The data we have to work with are highly complex, incomplete and vary enormously per language and even within language. They do not constitute purely natural phenomena (in contrast to data in the physical sciences), nor purely artifactual ones (as is the case for instance in logic and mathematics) because they are the product of *both* natural processes *and* human interference. For this reason, understanding how language works and changes cannot be reached by 'simple' induction and deduction; in many cases language learners and language users abduce the 'wrong' pattern, 'wrong' in the sense that they do not follow what has become conventional in the speech community

---

[1] Cf. Lass (1980), Keller (1994), McMahon (2000), who all discuss the nature of the linguistic data and the three logical processes used to organize the data into a system. The latter are the well-known methods of induction (the establishment of a law/pattern/principle on the basis of available data), deduction (to predict or create new data on the basis of an established law) and abduction (inferring the most plausible law on the basis of the then available data). Notice that what linguists do is not necessarily different from what speakers do. Abduction, although unreliable, is extremely important because it is the only inferential process that creates *new* forms; it, therefore, plays a crucial role not only in linguistic theory formation, but also in actual linguistic change.

(cf. Note 1 in this chapter). This is one of the reasons that language is forever in flux; another reason is the changing world around us and its impact on how language is used. This situation puts limits on how far we can go in formalizing language or on how precisely we could ever predict language change. In practice, the most that we may hope to achieve is an explanation for a change *after* the fact, and the ability to say something about the likelihood of a particular change under certain conditions. Even that is hard, however, because of the way the human mind functions (it works by leaps and bounds rather than purely logically (cf. Hofstadter, 1995 and Kahneman 2011) and because the external (socio-cultural) circumstances in which language functions, keep changing too.

Still, in spite of these hurdles, it makes sense to set up theoretical models because it is the only way to advance our understanding of language and language change. Thus, linguists of various persuasions set up hypotheses, test them and adapt or replace them when falsified. The two best-known models used to understand morpho-syntactic change are the formal Principles and Parameters [P&P henceforth] model and the functional model of Grammaticalization Theory [GT]. More recently, they have been joined by a diachronic approach to Construction Grammar [CxG] which resembles GT in some ways but has a wider application and more of an eye for form (for the differences, see Noël, 2007).[2] We discuss these models in some detail, explicating how, where and why they differ in terms of matters such as attention paid to the language output or the underlying system, the role played by both form and function, differences in the types of rules, schemas or principles (cognitive or otherwise) proposed, and so on.

First, however, we need to say a few words about the relation between synchronic and diachronic linguistics.

3.2   The Position of Historical Linguistics *vis-à-vis* Linguistics

The structuralist movement that started at the beginning of the last century with Bloomfield and Saussure and was continued by the generative-transformational school of Noam Chomsky and his followers in the late 1950s and 1960s and beyond has led to a different way of describing and investigating grammar, which has also affected historical linguistics. It has had a great influence on our understanding of how grammar works and has led to a deepened interest in the theory of language acquisition, and mental models of grammar. Looking for the system behind language has proven fruitful and successful and has laid bare connections between aspects of grammar that had not been seen before. It has uncovered important principles

---

[2] Recent publications in this framework are Traugott and Trousdale (2010, 2013), Hilpert (2013), Barðdal *et al.* (2015).

and universals, such as the role played by word-order patterns and the behaviour of anaphors and clitics.

However, this interest in the system underlying language (variously termed *langue*, 'competence' or more recently 'I-language') has also led to a loss of interest in the study of 'performance' – that is, the study of language utterances as they are processed by speakers and hearers against a historical, socio-cultural background. Not surprisingly, the attention paid to speakers' competence rather than their performance resulted in a lowering of the status of historical or diachronic linguistics, which by its very nature must rely on (written) utterances rather than living speakers whose competence can be studied by introspection. The philological approach to language (where the language output itself was the object of investigation) was then put on the backburner, so to speak, because the dominant mode of thinking held that change could only be detected *indirectly* via a comparison of *synchronic* linguistic states or systems, which had now become the primary object of investigation. This only changed with the rise of sociolinguistics in the 1960s (especially through the work of William Labov and his followers), which investigates synchronic *variation*. Variation is the seed of change. Variant forms became neglected in the search for competence because they were generally considered to be part of performance. The emphasis on the system *behind* language also meant that pride of place was given to *internal,* more purely linguistic, mechanisms. This in turn also affected the study of linguistic change, in that here too socio-historical factors and the context in which the utterances occurred became less important than the internal grammatical mechanisms that were seen to steer a change. For generative historical linguists, 'grammar change' rather than 'language change' became the proper object of investigation as is clear from the following quotation:

our focus here is grammars, not the properties of a particular language, or even general properties of many or all languages. A language on the view sketched here is an epiphenomenon, a derivative concept, the output of certain people's grammars. ... So when we think about change over the course of time, diachronic change, we shall now think not in terms of sound change or language change, but in terms of changes in these grammars, which are represented in the mind/brains of individuals. (Lightfoot, 1999: 74)

Our line of reasoning here is that we indeed need grammatical models in order to describe and understand morpho-syntactic change, but apart from investigations into the language system, we also inevitably rely on the way utterances are used in their context (in the widest possible sense), involving (historical) sociolinguistics, pragmatics and discourse, and on investigations of a comparative nature (i.e. typological studies) in order to both deduce what the grammar of a language at a particular period may have been like and to understand the circumstances that lead to changes occurring between periods.

In other words, for a fuller understanding of a linguistic innovation or of change in general we need a model, we need knowledge of internal mechanisms (including cognitive principles) and we need an awareness of the external circumstances affecting the historical data themselves; in addition, we need to take note of the frequency of linguistic phenomena, as well as the registers and text genres in which they occur. When a change is described in terms of the grammar only, we in fact describe merely the endpoint of a change. In order to understand why something started changing, we must look at the variations over time as they begin to occur on the performance level. Linguistic structures or patterns may change, for instance, because speakers 'see' an analogy (in form and/or function) with other structures; they may change via pragmatic inferencing when they are frequently used in certain contexts; they may change because the language community is 'invaded' by speakers with a different linguistic background, and so on. These performance variants, to be found in the output of adults, are central to language change. For example, they may serve as 'primary linguistic data' (henceforth PLD) to children in the next generation and may ultimately cause these children to set up grammars that are slightly different from those of the adults. Therefore, to understand change, we need to investigate the innovation stage as well as the later grammar change. For a full understanding of the system of grammar within which language users innovate, we should look at how they innovate. In sum, what we cannot ignore is that, both as historical linguists and as language users, our knowledge of the grammar system is indirect, it depends fully on our interpretation of the (physical) data.

As already mentioned in this chapter, most changes involve a combination of internal systemic and external socio-cultural factors (cf. Gerritsen and Stein, 1992; Labov, 1994, 2001, 2010); this is what makes change indeed so unpredictable. It is often hard – if not impossible – to distinguish between internal and external factors and to measure what the weight of each factor has been in any particular change. McMahon (2000: 120–21) and Pintzuk *et al.* (2000: 9) both refer to the fact that Lightfoot (1999: 105–06) provides six diagnostic properties which should help us decide whether we are dealing with an internal (systemic) or an external (language) change, simultaneously noting, however, severe problems surrounding these diagnostics. According to Lightfoot, each new grammatical property (which in his model is a result of parametric, i.e. internal, change) is manifested by (i) a cluster of new phenomena, (ii) the frequent setting off of a chain reaction, (iii) rapid change in the form of an S-curve, (iv) obsolescence of other structures as a structural domino effect, (v) significant changes in meaning in the construction concerned, and, more generally, it involves (vi) a response to shifts in simple, unembedded data.

Finding such diagnostic features may indeed tell us something about internal factors once the change is underway, but even in these cases it is more than probable that external causes led up to the change, and may therefore be said to provide a 'deeper' understanding of why the change took place. Lightfoot himself in the course of time moved away from overall explanatory principles such as his 'Transparency Principle' (1979), via specific principles of the theory of grammar (cf. Lightfoot, 1981), and his notion of cue-based learning (1999), towards a closer inspection of the PLD, and to the role the PLD plays. McMahon (2000: 124) indeed observes that 'Lightfoot's ideas on the *explanatory* scope of his theory seem to have modified over the years . . ., [which] might suggest that explanation lies ultimately in the changes in the triggering experience (i.e. the PLD), which Lightfoot accepts he cannot deal with at all' (emphasis added). This would, McMahon (*ibid.*) concludes, 'reduce the potential for explanation [away] from internal aspects of the formal theory'. The current trend in theory formation is for this multifactorial view of causality to be formulated more and more explicitly. This is true both of models that accommodate multiple language-internal causes, typically with roots in the grammaticalization literature (Fischer, 2007; Traugott and Trousdale, 2013), and of models that seek to combine language-internal and language-external explanations of change (e.g. Labov, 1994, 2000, 2010; Croft, 2000; Schmid, 2015).

3.3   Models Relevant to Diachronic Linguistics

In this section, we review the various mechanisms, principles, parameters, constraints, and, ultimately, explanations that have been put forward for morpho-syntactic change within GT, CxG and P&P. When comparing the three approaches, we refer to all the factors that somehow condition changes – whether as mechanisms, causes, principles or constraints – with the neutral term 'factors', so as not to prejudge the issue. The reason for this circumspection is that, what may be seen as an explanation within a particular theoretical model, in the end depends on the principles or constraints that are part of that model, which need not have been accepted as such by other models. Theory-internal explanations indeed risk being circular because what the model sees as a cause or explanation in terms of its principles, may in the end be no more than a description. 'True' (or at least more long-lasting) explanations can only be found outside the theory, and outside the subcomponent of linguistics in which one is working (cf. McMahon, 2000: 133). Faarlund (1990: 181) concurs with this when he writes: 'model-internal principles' only serve as an 'explanatory device' when they 'can be shown to reflect cognitive processes'.

One of the problems in the present discussion is that there is indeed a wide divide between the generative P&P model on the one hand, and the cognitively oriented CxG and GT approaches on the other, which has to do with the question as to what constitutes the primary object of research, the language output (as in CxG and GT) or the underlying grammar system (as in P&P). The dichotomies that have often been noted with respect to the two schools of thought – the most important of which are given in (1) – are to a large extent bound up with this performance versus competence difference.

(1)   EMPHASIS ON   EMPHASIS ON
       PERFORMANCE /   COMPETENCE /
       LANGUAGE OUTPUT   LANGUAGE SYSTEM
       (a)   product-oriented   process-oriented
       (b)   emphasis on function (in CxG   emphasis on form
              also form)
       (c)   locus of change: language use   locus of change: language
                                               acquisition
       (d)   equality of levels   centrality (autonomy) of syntax
       (e)   gradual change   radical change
       (f)   heuristic tendencies   fixed principles
       (g)   fuzzy categories/schemas   discrete categories/rules
       (h)   contiguity with cognition   innateness of grammar

In what follows, we describe these two main approaches in broad outline, whereby we refer to the dichotomies enumerated in (1). Inevitably, this survey provides a rather general picture of some of the central points involved and therefore will not always do justice to all the variants that exist between linguists and their treatments. We focus first on how the general architecture of the various models leads their practitioners towards specific objects of study, certain kinds of explanations and specific types of evidence. Next, we home in on what change looks like when viewed through the lens of the different approaches.

3.3.1   Objects of Study, Explanations and Evidence

In the more narrow GT approach, the primary focus has been on how (lexical) forms adopt new (grammatical) functions because of how they are used. Given this focus on function and use, linguistic forms or facts tend to be considered as if they float freely through time and space, as if the patterning of the overall synchronic system in which these elements function at each point in time is not relevant. Because of the emphasis on the stages of grammaticalization – that is, the way in which a (referential) lexical element or cluster of elements loses its autonomy and acquires a more and more grammatical function – research in this area involves mostly an investigation of the diachronic pathway of the specific structures being considered: how they gradually (in unidirectional clines) change their function in context, and how this function change is manifested later in changes in form. In other words, the semantic-pragmatic function of a form is considered more important than its formal manifestation. Not surprisingly, grammaticalization is seen by most of its practitioners as basically a type of semantic change, which is the result of pragmatic inferencing and subjectification (cf. Diewald, 2011; Nicolle, 2011). In addition, the changing structure is scrutinized mostly in isolation: not much attention is paid to 'neighbouring' structures (i.e. structures with similar meanings and/or similar forms). In this way, neither the systemic pressure that the underlying grammar may exert on the change is considered, nor is the possibility that analogous structures could also play a role.

Many of these problems are solved within the CxG framework in that here more attention is paid to formal matters and, most importantly, to other constructions which may have influenced the construction that is changing. In other words, similarity (analogy) in form and function and the overall synchronic system in which the construction functions has come to play a much more crucial role.

In the P&P approach, the synchronic forms are also viewed in isolation but in a different way compared to GT. Here, possible semantic-pragmatic motivations or indeed phonetic or phonological ones (cf. Schlüter, 2005), are neglected because the syntactic system is deemed to be autonomous; the form's meaning and/or function in communication is thus downgraded. Variant forms, which provide the staple diet in CxG and GT, are also given much less attention.[3] Generally, the P&P model can be described as a modular and computational system of grammar, geared towards an optimal design, which is closely linked to the LAD (Language Acquisition Device). Central in this model is the syntactic component, which generates the phrase structures that will be expanded further with information from another component, the lexicon. Lexicon and syntax together provide the base which feeds the interpretive modules of PF (Phonological Form) and LF (Logical Form; in the later Minimalist program this is replaced by 'Spell-out', which constitutes a single point of interaction between syntax and the interfaces). The syntactic component consists of categorial (phrase structure) rules and transformational rules, the latter having been reduced to just one type (i.e. Move-α [in the Minimalist program reduced to the two basic operations of Merge and Move]). The whole system is constrained by principles which may work on one or more of the subcomponents, such as the principles of X-bar theory, Government (dropped in the Minimalist program), Binding, Bounding, Case and θ-theory and Control. The principles always obtain, but

---

[3] One way of dealing with variant forms is by hypothesizing that there exist simultaneous competing grammars (cf. Pintzuk, 1991, on the so-called Double-Base Hypothesis). The problem, however, with this solution is, where does multiplication stop? Do we postulate a separate grammar for each variant structure? For a more fine-tuned view on this, see Pintzuk and Taylor (2012).

there is some room for parametric variation. Parameters will be set on the basis of UG and the PLD that the child is faced with during the period of language acquisition. The setting of the parameters forms the basic mechanism for change (see e.g. Roberts, 2007).

There are significant differences between P&P and GT in how the principles and terms of the model are established. The principles in GT are 'tendencies': they are not fixed, they are of a general nature and formed heuristically, and their formulation has remained more or less the same in the theory over time. An important principle is that of *unidirectionality*, which is made visible in a number of semantic-pragmatic and formal *clines*, an example of which is shown in (2).[4] The idea of these clines is that changes follow the given stages and that, generally, they do not go in the opposite direction. Accepting the universality of these clines brings with it the danger of missing any evidence that runs against a cline, and of oversimplifying the change in question (for some discussion see Fischer, 2007)

(2) a *Cline of modality (formal):*
       lexical verb > vector verb > auxiliary > clitic > affix > zero
    b *Cline of modality (semantic):*
       fully lexical verbs > root modals: dynamic/deontic > epistemic
       modals/future > subordinate marker/subjunctive)
    c *Cline of modality (discourse-pragmatic):*
       propositional/non-subjective > (textual/subjective)[5] > expressive/attitudinal/
       intersubjective

Unidirectionality does not play a role in the CxG model. In principle any construction can influence another as long as there are some 'islands of regularity' (Hilpert, 2013: 203) between the variant forms that may influence one another. At the same time, this constitutes one of the problems of diachronic CxG, because it is not immediately clear of what these 'islands' may or at a minimum must consist. This is related to the fact that similarity or the workings of analogy is difficult to capture. Spotting analogies, as Hofstadter (1995) so convincingly shows, depends on what is available in one's language, one's culture and one's experience, and on the frequency of constructions and on all the links that may have been formed between them.

Tendencies, probabilistic generalizations and/or explanations based on similarities in GT and CxG are typical of an inductive approach to building linguistic theory (cf. Labov, 1994: 13). In contrast, the principles of a generative grammar such as the P&P model are typical of a deductive approach; they

---

[4] More information on this can be found in the Grammaticalization Handbook (Narrog and Heine, 2011).
[5] Traugott (1989) suggests that there need not be a strict linear order (i.e. the interpersonal stage may also be derived directly from the propositional one).

are precise, discrete and fixed (as in fully man-made systems like logic or mathematics). They may be altered or replaced whenever new facts arise or whenever a more elegant principle (comprising more facts) can be established. The principles are meant to be falsifiable, with the search for falsification causing modifications in the model. It is to be expected therefore that the model changes over time, ideally becoming more adequate and explanatory, the ultimate aim being the establishment of 'laws' (i.e. a completely fixed model).

Much more so than the P&P model, then, GT has change built into its very terms and principles. Similarly, CxG has built change into the constructions themselves, relying mainly on similarity between constructions, and type and token frequencies to establish change. By contrast, in P&P the terms and principles themselves are fixed. The 'genotype' or 'biological grammar' provides the blueprint, on the basis of which the child, during the process of language acquisition, fixes the parameters of its 'phenotype' (i.e. a speaker's mature grammar).

Because our models represent abstractions, they necessarily practise a certain amount of 'cleaning'. The cleaning process in the generative and functional-cognitive approaches, however, is fundamentally different. It is common in the P&P model to purify the facts to be explained, by reducing them to what is considered to form the competence. Often, this has resulted in reducing them to the standard, *written forms* of language, ignoring spoken and variant forms as well as the circumstances under which language forms are used (which shed light on the referential and social aspects of the forms).[6] In addition, generative grammar looks at language as a product of the *competence* of speakers; this competence is itself a mental system, and hence does not represent observable facts but native-speaker intuitions. GT and CxG, on the other hand, are concerned with linguistic utterances as they occur in a social, communicative context (which automatically incorporates a *time factor*, which in the generative approach is fully controlled and thus missing); they are concerned with the observable facts, their *forms* as connected to their *functions*. The problem here is that function is not directly observable from the language forms but has to be inferred from the circumstances in the situational context as they are interpreted by the human mind.

We may conclude that both theories have weaknesses (in order to make them strong!), which lie in those areas that escape direct observation (i.e. 'competence' and 'function'). In both cases, this may result in circularity of

---

[6] Of course there are exceptions here, especially with synchronic linguists working with non-standard, non-written languages and linguists interested in diachronic and/or dialect variation (see e.g. Pintzuk *et al.*, 2000). On the whole, however, these linguists are less concerned with context and the communicative situation.

argumentation. Still, it can be said that both theories provide satisfactory explanations for some of the facts, if not all (see further discussion later in the chapter).

3.3.2   What Does Change Look Like?

When language change is seen through the lens of different theoretical models, it looks very different. This is most apparent in the perceived gradualness or abruptness of change. From the idea within GT that change follows clines ensues that categories are fuzzy rather than discrete (1g) and that change must be gradual rather than radical (1e). Fuzziness and gradualness are likewise incorporated in CxG. In the P&P model, which in contrast has fixed categories, it is just as inevitable that changes must be considered radical or even catastrophic. The problem, however, with the latter view is that when we look at change superficially, it doesn't look exactly radical. The P&P model addresses this problem, which of course their practitioners also recognize, as follows: the model makes a distinction between 'triggers' and 'changes' (see Table 3.1).

Triggers are part of the experience that a child has; this 'varies from person to person and consists of an unorganized, fairly haphazard set of utterances; ... [t]he universal theory of grammar and the variable trigger together form the basis for attaining a grammar' (Lightfoot, 1999: 66). These triggers therefore constitute 'minor changes in the relevant childhood experience', which are said to have an effect on the emerging grammar only when they 'cross a threshold' (Lightfoot, 1999: 79) – that is, when they become too frequent to ignore. On the other hand, there are also *grammar* changes ($\neq$ triggers). Some of these are 'small-scale' and may progress 'in piece-meal fashion', word by word. Others

Table 3.1. *Types of changes according to Lightfoot (1991,1999), taken from Fischer 2007: 108)*

Type of change	1 Triggers (on the PLD level)	2 Minor grammar changes	3 Major grammar changes
Characteristics	involves variables (small changes) on the output level	involves changes in grammar	involves changes in grammar
	progresses gradually until threshold is reached	change is piece-meal, may diffuse lexically	change is abrupt
	is haphazard, but may lead to change in grammar	involves recategorization (morphological and categorial)	involves parameter shifts, and clusters of simultaneous changes

are catastrophic. The minor grammar changes must, like the major abrupt ones, 'take place in direct or indirect response to changes [=triggers] in the PLD' (Lightfoot, 1999: 88).

This division into three types seems clear enough. Under type 1, 'triggers', no formal grammar distinction can be made between one pattern (variant) and another. In type 2, 'minor grammar changes', there is a morphological or categorial distinction: they may involve a loss or emergence of a morphological feature (e.g. inflection) or a change in category. Type 3, the 'major grammar changes', involves the loss or emergence of an abstract syntactic rule or pattern. Because there is little difference between 'gradual progress' and 'piece-meal change', the important distinction between types 1 and 2 is that in type 1 there is no pattern yet visible. If a patterned distribution can be discerned on semantic-pragmatic grounds, it may still not exist within the model, because the model is based on *formal* divisions. Type 2 includes piece-meal progress by lexical diffusion, which is probably as much based on semantic-pragmatic considerations and lexical features as on purely formal ones.

An example of recategorization (type 2) could be the case of the English modals. The present-day modal verbs used to behave more or less as full lexical verbs in the OE period, and developed into a new category (i.e. that of Auxiliary) in the modern period losing the ability, among other things, to appear in infinitival and participial forms and to take a direct object and so on (for details and more discussion, see Chapter 6). Because this change affected the modals one by one and over a lengthy period of time, its description fits type 2. This is how it is seen in Lightfoot (1991, 1999). However, in his earlier work (1979, 1982), this very case was considered a prime example of a catastrophic change, obeying the diagnostic properties described in Section 3.2 – that is, it is considered an example of type 3 (a similar explanation involving a parameter shift can be found in Roberts, 2007: 127–29, 353ff.). Lightfoot could categorize this as type 3, because he did not take into account the behaviour of the individual verbs and their semantic-pragmatic characteristics (for a full discussion, see Fischer, 2007: 161ff.).

Similar problems of categorization as to type arise with other changes. A word-order change from Object Verb (OV) to Verb Oject (VO) as happened in English (see Chapter 9) looks *prima facie* like a parameter shift in the P&P model (type 3 in Table 3.1). If it starts as a type 1 change, with gradual, haphazard changes leading to a threshold, then one would not expect to find patterned variation at that stage. After the parameter has finally shifted, one would expect VO to be the rule for all speakers with a shifted parameter. It is interesting to observe, however, that these same VO speakers still use OV structures at quite a late stage, which *were* also found to be patterned (because certain types of direct objects retained the earlier word order, cf. van der Wurff,

1999; Moerenhout and van der Wurff, 2000, 2005). Such patterning is difficult to account for within the three-type model described in Table 3.1. We would conclude that the historical record must be examined very closely before a change can be established as being of type 1, 2 or 3. It is quite possible that there was a pattern present in the change all the way through (cf. also Pintzuk and Taylor, 2006).

Another obstacle in connection with the type 3 change is the nature of an abrupt change. Firstly, a change can only be abrupt if it involves a para-meter shift. Therefore, and to some extent, the presence of a type 3 change depends on what are seen as parameters in the model. The problem we run up against is that the nature of the parameters (and also the rules and principles) of UG are not (yet) fixed. Newmeyer (2003: 59–60) notes that '[t]he properties of UG are ... anything but clear. There are more than a dozen different and competing theories, each of which presents a different explanandum for the language ... researcher'. Additionally, a type 3 change also depends on the presence of a cluster of changes (i.e. simultaneous surface changes and subsequent chain reactions, cf. Lightfoot, 1991: 167). Hence, timing of all these changes becomes crucial. Again the OV > VO change may serve as an example. Lightfoot (1991: 42ff) describes this as a gradual type 1 process in main clauses, but as an abrupt type 3 change for embedded clauses. To accept this, we have to accept his hypothesis of degree-∅ learnability. According to this hypothesis, the trigger can only consist of unembedded material, more precisely 'it is restricted to data occurring in an unembedded binding Domain' (*ibid.*: 32) – that is, it includes embedded COMPs and Subjects of non-finite clauses. The fact that this case is used to prove degree-∅ learnability as well as that degree-∅ learnability is needed to prove this case, makes it difficult to avoid a suspicion of circularity. Secondly, it is not clear what the role of coordinate clauses is in this order. They also show a sudden shift to VO, like the subordinate clauses; yet, as far as we can tell they do not fall under degree-∅ learnability, as some of them must be main clauses.[7] A final problem is that the loss of OV order in subordinate clauses may not have been as abrupt as Lightfoot takes it to be. OV is definitely still quite common after the twelfth century, the putative date of the abrupt parameter shift (cf. again the studies by Moerenhout and Van der Wurff mentioned earlier), and both orders still show up within the grammars of one and the same author. (Of course, one can avoid this dilemma by accepting the Double-Base Hypothesis, but see Note 3 in this chapter.)

---

[7] Coordinate clauses can be both main and subordinate, depending on whether the first clause of the coordinated set is itself main or subordinate. This distinction is often not made; an example is Mitchell (1985).

The question, then, whether abrupt change exists, is still open. As Nagle (1989: 45) aptly remarks, 'the gradual versus abrupt issue in surface change is largely one of theoretical orientation', adding that 'the broad picture of at least surface change is gradual' (*ibid.*: 46). What we need to do as historical linguists is to examine more carefully the reputed simultaneity of the changes in a cluster, and the simultaneity of the chain reactions. We also need to look at the (in)divisibility of each change in question, because possibly some of these radical changes form themselves a chain of smaller changes.

As we already intimated here, the idea of gradualness is closely connected with the presence of semantic-pragmatic factors involved in a change, an area ignored in P&P but crucial in the cognitively oriented models. For most grammaticalization theorists, the semantic changes come first, only later followed by structural changes (as we already noted), and hence gradualness is the principal player in their model. In CxG, form is given much more space, and also quantitative considerations in the form of type and token frequencies. Explanation in both depends on what happens on the surface, while in P&P true explanations can only be found in changes in competence (i.e. in *grammar* changes, which are typically non-gradual). The emphasis on unidirectionality and gradualness in GT has in turn (in contrast to CxG) led to the idea that the process of grammaticalization is mechanistic, and that it is itself a mechanism or cause of change. Bybee *et al.* (1994: 298), for instance, write: 'Thus our view of grammaticization is much more mechanistic than functional: the relation between grammar and function is indirect and mediated by diachronic process. The processes that lead to grammaticization occur in language use *for their own sakes*' (emphasis added). They even suggest (*ibid.*: 17–18) that we can reconstruct the path of grammaticalization with the help of the 'hypothesis that semantic change is predictable' (cf. also Heine *et al.*, 1991: 9–11).

Let us therefore take a closer look at the factors (or diagnostics) distinguished for grammaticalization in GT. The clearest discussion of this is to be found in Lehmann (1985), whose 'parameters' can be used to represent stages in the development. Lehmann (1985: 306) presents the following table (slightly adapted in order to indicate the *processes* taking place), where the parameters illustrate the degree to which a particular linguistic item has grammaticalized:

Table 3.2. *Diachronic stages in the process of grammaticalization*

Parameters	Paradigmatic processes	Syntagmatic processes
Weight	(loss of) integrity	(reduction of) scope
Cohesion	(increase in) paradigmaticity	(increase in) bondedness
Variability	(loss of) paradigmatic variability: increase in obligatoriness	(decrease in) syntagmatic variability

The 'weight' or substance of a lexical element — or group of elements — (row 1) involved in a grammaticalization process is reduced (in contrast to similar, but non-grammaticalized items within the same field or paradigm) through both semantic and phonetic erosion (also called semantic bleaching and phonetic reduction). This also means that the element may become syntactically less dominant in the clause, as in the case where a full lexical verb such as *go* in the expression BE + *going to* V, first dominates a purposive adjunct (as in *I am going (to the market) to get her some fish*), and next develops into a semi-auxiliary, becoming part of the VP headed by the infinitive (as in *She's going to/gonna marry that boy someday*).

Concerning 'cohesion' (row 2), the more grammaticalized a linguistic element is, the less choice there is formally (i.e. within the paradigm of forms that have a similar function). Thus, in the expression of a thematic role, an inflection for case is more paradigmaticized than a preposition (to express the same function) because usually only one choice exists within the paradigm of case-forms, whereas often more than one preposition can be used to express the function in question. Syntagmatically, cohesion is increased in that the grammaticalized item may fuse with other linguistic elements; for example, *going* + *to* has developed into the reduced *gonna*.

Paradigmatic 'variability' (row 3) refers to the degree to which a particular linguistic element is obligatory within the clause. Thus, the verbal past tense marker in English is a highly grammaticalized element because it occurs obligatorily within the clause, whereas adverbial markers of past time such as *yesterday, last year, recently*, and so on can occur much more freely, their presence being determined not by the grammar but by discourse. Syntagmatically, a grammaticalized element becomes less variable because it takes up a fixed position in the clause. For example, the tense-marker must follow the matrix verb, while the adverbial marker of time can occur in quite a number of positions within the clause.

It is important to note that grammaticalization theorists have observed that not all of these parameters hold true in each case of grammaticalization. The discourse-pragmatic type of grammaticalization (see Traugott, 1989; Sweetser, 1990; and many later studies), in which a lexical item moves from the more concrete propositional domain into the textual domain, and from there into the expressive or epistemic domain (see (2c) earlier in this chapter), diverges from these parameters on almost all levels. The item in question undergoes pragmatic enrichment rather than bleaching, increases in scope rather than decreases, there is no 'increase in bondedness', and so on. This strange behaviour forms a problem for the theory and needs to be explained or further investigated. It is clear that GT cannot account for this type adequately if its principles do not apply.

Next we should consider the kind of factors that have been recognized in grammaticalization on the level of the speaker. These are again functional, centered as they are around pragmatic inferencing: they relate to the communicative situation and/or to the workings of the mind. We have a clear contrast here with the P&P model, where the factors are strictly formal (parameter shifts). There is a difference in another respect, too: the emphasis in grammaticalization is on innovations made by adults in actual communication (here CxG concurs), while parameter shifts take place during the process of language acquisition in childhood (cf. (1c) earlier in this chapter). For most linguists writing on grammaticalization, the main factors involved at this level are metaphorical and metonymic in nature (cf. Hopper and Traugott, 2003: 84–98).

Metaphorical change is a pragmatic/semantic phenomenon and can be related to the cognitive process of analogy. It is a type of paradigmatic change whereby a word used for a concrete object such as the word 'back' (referring to the part of the body that is opposite to the belly) can be reinterpreted more generally to refer to anything that has a front as well as a back part (e.g. the 'back' of a book, the 'back' of a house and others) because of some element that these concepts have in common. Next, it may come to be used on a more abstract level as an indication of location (at the 'back' of the shed) or even of time ('back' in those days). It is important to note that many metaphorical extensions, especially of a natural (i.e. non-poetic) type are often simultaneously metonymic in character, too. Rubba (1994) shows in detail how the extension of the sign for a body-part like the 'back' to a locative noun has as much to do with the relational orientation of the body as with a similarity between the back part of the body and the back of some other object. It is thus a type of metonymic inferencing that arises out of the link between ourselves, our own bodies in space, and the way we conceptualize and order the world around us. Both metaphoric and metonymic thinking are related to 'inferencing', but unlike metaphor (which is analogical and paradigmatic), metonymy functions strictly on the syntagmatic (associative) plain and has to do with cause and effect, with contiguity and associations between objects rather than similarities.

3.4   Evaluation and Further Use of the Models in This Volume

A theoretical model in which both form and meaning play equal and independent roles, would be a great advance, providing more in the way of explanation. McMahon (2000: 115) notes in this connection: 'The more general question arising from these analyses is whether linguistic change can be modelled, and explained, in formal theories at all'. She believes that explanation can be improved by taking formal and functional factors into account: 'Progress in terms of external explanation can only be achieved if functional considerations are incorporated into the [formal] model, or if it is accepted that such considerations are relevant and remove explanation of at least some change types from the scope of the formal theory involved' (*ibid.*: 125). Even more helpful in terms of explanation would be to make use of the investigations of linguistic facts in other domains, such as first and second language acquisition (which relate to immature speakers, and hence present different language facts), language evolution, language pathology, neuro-linguistics, and also to look at data coming from other cognitive domains (such as vision, motor development, and others). Similarly, results obtained via psycholinguistic experiments and computer simulations should also advance our understanding. Tomasello (2003: 94), for instance, emphasizes that investigating the systems of communication that are simple and not 'full-blown' is important if we wish to make progress. This includes the language of children and our nearest primates, but also the language of pidgin speakers, aphasics, and others. Hurford (2003: 53ff.) notes that using computer simulation is important to probe the evolution of language, which presents another system that is not 'full-blown'. There is not enough space to go into all this here (a convenient summary can be found in Fischer, 2007: Ch.3). What is clear, however, is that explanation will always be 'work in progress'; any explanation is inevitably temporary and inadequate. Here, we will therefore concentrate on the models we have discussed paying attention to both form and function, to context, and a consideration of both internal and external factors.

Briefly reconsidering the current diachronic models, we would like to note that there is something very neat and pleasing about the strict scenario for change prevalent in the P&P model; the decisive advantage is that it gives direction to our enquiries. It enables us to develop clear hypotheses that can be tested and, if it so happens, falsified; it encourages (historical) linguists to look for a bundle of changes occurring on the output level, which appear unrelated. Their simultaneity could then indicate the presence of a more fundamental shift in the grammar. Because it may indicate on the grammar level that the superficial phenomena *are* related to some deeper principle, it may also vindicate the existence of the principle itself. This approach is valuable and worthwhile if it is combined with detailed corpus research. It may then have two positive results. It could provide evidence for already posited parameters (and thus strengthen the case for them), and it could unearth new parameters (and perhaps disqualify some posited ones). Secondly, it could inspire historical linguists to look for evidence of additional surface-like connections between the 'unconnected' changes that have simultaneously arisen. It is easier, after all, to find connections when a link has already been established.

When this strict scenario for change is combined with extensive corpus study, its idea of simultaneous or radical change may be corroborated, but it is also possible that researchers discover that the new phenomena were linked on a less abstract or non-formal level (e.g. there may have been functional connections). This would be the case, for instance, when the researchers discover that there were other more gradual (less radical) small shifts on the output level that preceded the postulated grammar change. If these small shifts cannot be directly connected to any principle of grammar, a generative linguist would classify them as mere PLD 'triggers', which serve to build up towards a catastrophic or radical grammar change. On the other hand, if these small shifts *are* recognized as independent changes within the grammar (and this of course also depends on the model used), then it would mean that there is no build-up towards a radical grammar change. And if that is so, it would not provide evidence for a parameter shift, nor for the validity of that parameter within the theory.[8]

Trying to find evidence for simultaneity is thus in itself useful in that it may support or falsify the existence of parameters, and it is useful as a heuristic device in that it stimulates historical linguists to dig deeper into the historical data. In a similar way, some of the principles of the grammar posited in the P&P model have been used as heuristic devices in neuro-linguistic work, and have been found to comply with neural networks. For instance, the X-bar principle and the principle of Subjacency can both be fitted into a simple neuronal network of sequential learning (Kirby and Christiansen, 2003: 275ff.).[9] This would mean that these principles are not necessarily language-specific but are the result of the properties of neuronal sets dealing with language in sequence. Quite a few scholars, often from outside linguistics proper, indeed argue that the universals of UG cannot be confined to formal linguistic ones. Tomasello (2003: 101) writes in this respect:

'I do not mean to imply that there are no linguistic universals, of course there are. But these do not consist of specific linguistic categories or constructions; they consist of general communicative functions such as reference and predication, or cognitive abilities such as the tendency to conceptualize objects and events categorically, or information processing skills such as those involved in dealing with rapid vocal sequences'.

These extra-domain findings may thus vindicate the principles of UG and show at the same time that these are not necessarily inherently linguistic.

When we come to summarize the functional-cognitive and formal models in terms of the factors that are considered relevant or motivating in

---

[8] An interesting case opposing 'parameter shift' and 'small change/trigger' in the explanation of new passives in English can be found in Lightfoot (1999: 127–29) versus Allen (2001).

[9] Stated informally, the X-bar principle holds that all syntactic categories have similar projections and that within one language they tend to branch out in the same direction. The Subjacency principle limits the distance to which an element can be moved. It is believed to be related to the strength of reverberation of neuronal sets, and to the limits of the 'active memory'.

morpho-syntactic change (some of which may serve as *internal* explanatory factors), we can list the following:

(3) *Main explanatory factors involved in the cognitively oriented and formal models:*

GT   (i) problem-solving and pragmatic inferencing: by means of (semantic-pragmatic) (a) metaphorical and (b) metonymic thinking
(ii) the process of grammaticalization itself steered by (a) frequency and (b) economy/erosion, with the latter leading to unidirectional clines

CxG   stronger emphasis on the role played by form, on type and token frequencies and analogy

P&P   (i) changes in the (external) triggering environment, the PLD (N.B. these need not lead to change)
(ii) steering by the (formal) principles and constraints of UG
(iii) (formal) reanalysis through (a) parameter resetting during the period of language acquisition, involving (b) a frequency factor (i.e. the so-called threshold)

It is clear that in two cases there are theory-internal factors (UG and the process of grammaticalization proper are both seen as 'causes'), adjacent to more general ones, which predominate within CxG. Among the latter we find the factor of frequency (to which economy/erosion may be considered related), and metaphorical and metonymic thinking, which are related to analogy and reanalysis, respectively. We now consider these general factors in somewhat more detail, whereby we pay special attention to the role played by analogy, which is especially prevalent in CxG.

3.5   Analogy, Reanalysis and the Role Played by Frequency

As we mentioned earlier in Section 3.3.1, in GT, metaphor and metonymy (as part of pragmatic inferencing) are discussed strictly from a functional point of view. According to Hopper and Traugott (2003: 39) they are 'semantically motivated mechanisms', while analogy and reanalysis are characterized as 'general mechanisms by which grammaticalization takes place' (*ibid.*). Additionally, they write (p. 71): 'Although it is possible to describe change in terms of successive strategies of reanalysis (rule change) and analogy (rule generalization), the important question remains *why these strategies come about* – in other words, *what enables the mechanisms we have outlined*' (emphasis added). Quite clearly then metaphor and metonymy provide the motivation, while analogy and reanalysis only show the possible pathways through which the new interpretation emerges. In addition, Hopper and Traugott consider reanalysis to be the 'most important mechanism for grammaticalization, ... because it is a prerequisite for the implementation through analogy' (*ibid.*). In Traugott's later work (e.g.

2011), influenced as it is by CxG, analogy has begun to play a much more dominant role.

Within the P&P model, reanalysis is also much more crucial than analogy, but here it is seen as a mechanism involving a parameter shift in the way elements are structured or placed in the derivation. The reanalysis, in fact, stands for the abduction which takes place during the process of language acquisition, and in that sense forms part of the explanation (together with UG). Analogy, on the other hand, is almost completely neglected in the P&P model as it is not possible to formalize it in terms of a fixed principle or constraint. On the whole, generative linguists consider analogy to be a superficial process only, which merely affects the influence concrete forms may have on other concrete forms. In this respect, it is interesting to note the definition in the generatively inclined *Lexicon of Linguistics* by Kerstens *et al.* (1996–2001): '**Analogy:** MORPHOLOGY: a diachronic process which changes words after the model of other forms', after which follows an extensive example explaining how in Gothic the noun meaning 'foot' shifted from one noun-class to another due to the fact that the accusative form became indistinguishable from the accusative form of another class. Thus, analogy seems to be reduced to just one level, that of morphology, it is restricted to proportional analogy, and applies only to changes in concrete forms, not to more abstract structures.

When we look at the two factors, analogy and reanalysis, from a wider perspective however, it seems quite obvious that analogy must be the more substantial of the two because it is linked to the general cognitive ability to spot similarities between items, whether concrete or more abstract (cf. Holyoak and Thagard, 1995; Hofstadter, 1995). This is also the direction that diachronic CxG has taken. We likewise argue here that analogy is a motivating factor and not merely a mechanism or pathway. Analogical thinking or behaviour is an ability present in all mammals and also in lower forms of life. Also, it is evolutionarily very old (cf. Deacon, 1997). Analogy may take place when some creature perceives a similarity in form, or in function, or indeed both. Itkonen (2005: xii) therefore proposes to treat analogy as a 'psychologically real phenomenon which has *causal* efficacy both in language and in culture' (emphasis added), and not just as a 'merely descriptive device'. Moreover, it is not necessarily the case that function takes priority over form, as seems to be the GT way of thinking. We can see analogy clearly at work in folk etymology where form as well as function can be initiators of a change. Thus, language users or learners may associate two forms because they are formally similar, and hence they may make them similar in meaning, as can be seen to have happened in the pair 'flout/flaunt'. Or the form of a word may be changed towards another existing but functionally unrelated form to make it meaningful, as happened in the word 'hangnail'. OE *angnægl* became modified when the morpheme **ang* 'narrow, tight, painful' was no longer understood as most

OE words that contained it had disappeared. Another form *hang* was found, close to *ang* in form, and one that could be made to be meaningful with respect to the object concerned. Or two forms may be similar in meaning, leading to a similarity in form, as happened for instance with the Dutch reflexive verb *zich ergeren* 'to be annoyed', which caused the non-reflexive verb *irriteren* with a similar meaning of 'annoyance' to develop a reflexive form too: *zich irriteren.* What helped here, too, is a formal similarity as regards structure: both *ergeren* and *irriteren* were used causatively without a reflexive pronoun in the sense of 'causing annoyance'.

Metonymic thinking, too, is closely linked to analogical thinking. For Anttila (2003: 426), linguistic signs (words, structures of words) are 'double-edged': they are not only 'combinations of form and meaning', but in addition 'meaning and form are combined in [a] symbolic colligation': the paradigmatic (similarity) and syntagmatic (contiguity) axes are part of what he calls the 'analogical grid' or the 'warp and woof of cognition'. We can see the close link between metaphor and metonymy at work in, for instance, the grammaticalization of the GOING TO construction from main verb to auxiliary, to which we already alluded. An utterance of *I am going to the corner shop to buy some cookies* must have occurred frequently without the indication of place: *I am going to buy some cookies* so that an interpretation from 'actual going to a place' to 'future reference' could take place (because the emphasis is now on the *purpose* of 'going' – that is, the activity expressed in the infinitive, which lies in the future). This is a typical metaphorical change from concrete location to abstract time, which we saw earlier in the development of the word 'back'. At the same time, the change involves a metonymic shift in the sense that *to* with its sense of purpose becomes associated with *going* rather than the infinitive (later the two forms even become one: *gonna*) turning the phrase BE + *going* into an indicator of future time; this shift takes place on the syntagmatic axis through contiguity.

Next, the development must have spread further, again via analogy. Formally, this spread happened via the *category* of infinitives: through other infinitives that could be collocated with the concrete movement expressed by *going* (such as 'to buy' in our example), it could spread to infinitives indicating mental activities (as in *You are going to love this*), and then also to subjects that were inanimate or empty rather than animate and agentive (as they necessarily were in the earliest constructions when *go* was still a verb of movement), as in *It's going to rain*. All this became possible through higher, more abstract analogical thinking, through grammatical similarities between (different types of) infinitives and (different types of) subjects. What may have helped the analogical shift is the fact that other grammatical patterns with a similar *function* (i.e. the future pattern *I will go*) also allow both animate and inanimate subjects, and also allow both concrete and mental infinitival verbs. This in turn could have led to the formal melting into *gonna* because of the fact that the auxiliary in *I will go* is also followed by a bare infinitive, the infinitive most common after auxiliaries.

Deacon (1997: 74–75, 99), in his study of language evolution, also links metonymy (which he calls 'indexical thinking') with analogy (which he calls 'iconic thinking') and he shows their importance in the evolution of language towards 'symbolic thinking'. Most of the forms used in human language are arbitrary (symbolic), that is purely conventional, even though they may have been motivated to begin with. Deacon further suggests that symbolic reference is still connected to iconic and indexical reference in a hierarchy. This makes clear that symbolic reference *can* only take place on the basis of the two other forms of reference, the indexical and the iconic, whereby iconic reference is evolutionary earlier and forms the basis for *all* interpretation.

There is another reason why analogy may be considered more crucial than reanalysis in change.[10] Most cases of reanalysis takes place *after* an *analogical process* – that is, reanalysis tends to be confined to and shaped by the formal structures that already exist. The reanalysis of a structure, as a rule, does not result in a totally new structure, but in one that is already in use elsewhere (cf. also Itkonen, 2005: 110–13). It is the superficial similarity (analogy) that a language user perceives between two structures and between two communicative uses of them that causes a reanalysis in one of them, so as to bring it in line with the other. Hence, the *perception of similarity* must be logically primary to the reanalysis. In fact, it may not be so much the perception of a similarity between one form and another that causes the speaker to make one structure/form analogous to another. Rather, it may be the fact that the speaker does *not* see a difference between the two forms/structures (because they are so much alike), and therefore by *misperception* as it were, unconsciously, makes the one form look like the other. This would explain why such analogies (or reanalyses) occur so easily in language (change) (cf. Deacon, 1997: 74; De Smet, 2009, 2013b). Hofstadter (1995: 201 and *passim*) uses the term 'conceptual slippage' for these misanalyses, which, as he makes clear by his examples, involve both similarity and proximity. Thus, to use again the development in *I am going to buy* ... from [*I am going* [to *buy* ...]] to [*I am going to* [*buy*...]], this may indeed have been caused by metonymic and metaphorical inferencing, but it may have been caused as much by the fact that the language user already had [Aux V]-type structures in his language system. It is quite likely that the development towards *gonna* would not have

---

[10] More detailed discussions on the relation between analogy and reanalysis can be found in De Smet (2013b) and Traugott (2011). Traugott (2011) makes a distinction between analogy as motivation (which she terms 'analogical thinking') and analogy as mechanism (which she terms 'analogization'). The latter is the case when the analogy is 'exemplar-based' or form-based. Because we believe that analogy or analogical thinking involves either form or function or both at the same time, we do not see how such a distinction can be made.

taken place if the language system had not already contained an auxiliary category and bare infinitives.

Another general factor mentioned at the end of Section 3.4 was frequency. The frequency of an item or construction may, on the one hand, be directly tied up with external circumstances in the sense that the more frequently an item is used in the external world of utterances, the more likely it is to undergo erosion through 'ease of effort'. This is especially true for grammatical or function words. Frequency on this concrete surface level may also be influential with respect to analogy – that is, it almost goes without saying that the more frequent forms are more likely to function as a pattern for other forms than infrequent forms (cf. Paul, 1909: 84, 109; Hilpert, 2013). On the other hand, frequency may also concern the frequency of patterns in the underlying system. The more frequent or basic a particular formal structure is, the more likely it is that other structures may conform to it by analogy. We see this often in word-order patterning. Thus in English, the SVO word order, which already in OE was more frequent than other possible orders like SOV and VSO, became more or less the only available word order in Modern English. Similarly the order Noun Adjective, slowly gave way to the much more frequent Adjective Noun pattern in English (for details of both, see Chapters 5 and 9).

3.6   Concluding Remarks

It looks as if the factors found to be relevant for learning, in both language evolution and acquisition, are the *iconic* and *indexical* reference systems, in combination with *repetition* (frequency). Repetition is necessary to entrench the iconic and indexical links in one's experience and to enable a higher form of thinking (i.e. abstract or symbolic thinking). Given that the same primitives play a role in the two areas of language evolution and language acquisition, it is likely that they should also play an important part in language change. An advantage of this approach is that these primitives are part of the biological endowment inherited from our non-human forebears, and are significant in other, non-linguistic cognitive domains as well. If in the future, we can also link these primitive features to features of a neuronal theory of grammar, it would further strengthen our proposal to consider them crucial.

The attention we have given to the importance of analogy, to an analogical approach to language, and hence to the importance of both form and function, implies that we see language use and language learning as a continuous dynamic process rather than a reliance on a fixed rule system like UG. We see the use of language as process-driven, invoking procedures and local schemas rather than overall rules. This is the approach also taken in diachronic CxG (cf. Note 2). The advantage of postulating a rule system is of course that it minimizes the number of procedures (rules) and simplifies contextual specification. The disadvantage of a rule system, however, is that it is not clear where the rules come from in the first place (unless one assumes they are innate), and that next to the rule system, one needs a separate lexical system to account for all the exceptions to the rules. In an analogically based system, there is only one system. The disadvantage of an analogical system is that one needs more fine-grained lexical categories (based on semantic and formal criteria) and more 'construction-types' or schemas.

Taking an analogical approach to language would mean, in other words, that we assume that in language learning humans rely more on particular and small (er) scale constructions and on concrete surface forms, than on deep, abstract rules and principles. In this sense, the analogical CxG approach is less elegant than the generative one. The question is: is this a problem? It depends on what one wishes to do with a grammatical model or theory, or what kind of status one wishes to give to it. If one wishes to give clear direction to one's search for the language system and the way language changes, the P&P model with its clear hypotheses may well be preferable. If one wishes the model to resemble or come closer to the way we actually learn or process language, the analogical model may be preferable. Does the lack of elegance matter? According to the Chomskyan notion of grammar, a language is only learnable when the underlying system is economic and elegant, and when this system is innate. According to generative thinking, this is necessary in order to explain why children learn their native language so fast in spite of the 'messy' data they are confronted with (this is the so-called 'poverty of the stimulus' argument). According to linguists working with a usage-based grammar, the large number of schemas to be learned is not an obstacle because the learning takes place in a concrete setting and ties in with other forms of learning and general cognitive principles. One could, therefore, also maintain that the analogical approach is more elegant because it has no need of an innate grammar. In this respect, it is interesting to observe that in neurological terms, a less elegant model that makes use of more surface-like (lexical) structures and schemas and which functions via associative learning is quite possible: recent studies on the workings of the mind/brain emphasize that retrieval from memory is the preferred strategy, and that people's brains (containing an immense amount of neurons that are connected to each other by innumerable synapses) are able to store vast numbers of prefabricated units (cf. Dąbrowska, 2004: 27). An inelegant system may in fact be more efficient.

Only the CxG model can be easily aligned with this analogical approach, as it fully combines form and function. We would like to note, however, that some of the principles of GT and P&P could well be accommodated within our analogical approach here, such as the structure-preserving sequence of constituents defined by the X-bar principle, or the hierarchies of construction-types defined by government and c-command (cf. Chomsky, 1981: 162 ff.). Similarly, the clines and hierarchies distinguished within GT would also conform to constructions or schemas linked in order of abstraction. As heuristic devices, therefore, these 'factors' are all very useful. And, indeed, they may be easier to work with for a researcher, because they supply 'handy terms' to the different levels and hierarchies that have to be distinguished; they provide the researcher with tools with which to confront the data. However, the use of such terms at the same time may obscure how the grammatical system really works, because they may begin to lead independent lives (i.e. there is the danger of reification).

An additional advantage of an analogical learning system is that it is more parsimonious from an evolutionary point of view, and it better fits the neurological findings briefly alluded to earlier in this chapter. There is a similar advantage as far as language change is concerned: the same mechanisms are now available for morpho-syntactic and lexical change.

To conclude, we think that it is essential to make use of theoretical models when we investigate morpho-syntactic change, but it is also good, when we wish to offer some degree of explanation for the changes involved, to be eclectic in our use of these models. In the chapters that follow, therefore, we take note of both formal and functional facts and factors, we stress the importance of corpus evidence wherever available and we pay attention to both internal and external factors, to the conventional grammar system as well as the context in which utterances take place and to comparative and typological evidence which may also serve to give us ideas about how and why something changed.

4   The Role of Contact in Syntactic Change in English

4.1   Introduction

In this chapter, we look at the role contact has played in the way the grammatical system of English developed. We concentrate on the medieval period since foreign influence on standard British English after that period was mainly restricted to lexical loans. We first introduce (Section 4.2) the theoretical framework that is used in this chapter, including the terminology current in discussions of contact change. An important distinction to be made is one between 'borrowing' and 'substratum influence', because of their different effects on the receiving language. In Section 4.3, the influence of four contact languages – Latin, Scandinavian, Celtic and French – are considered, as they affected English in the OE and ME periods and in some cases beyond. We first give a description of the socio-historical circumstances under which this contact took place, after which the influence of the four languages will be discussed in more detail.

4.2   Syntactic Change and Contact: General Background

English has undergone an enormous amount of change in the course of its development, more so than other Germanic languages, with the possible exception of continental Scandinavian.[1] It is plausible that this is to a large extent due to invasion and conquest, which had an impact on all linguistic levels but most notably, and recognizably, on the lexical level.

Whereas lexical change and lexical loans are fairly easy to spot, syntactic change and syntactic loans are much harder to observe because this usually involves abstract patterns rather than concrete lexical items. Thomason (2003: 709) notes in this connection that 'the easy cases are those in which both form and function have been adopted from another language', but such cases are

---

[1] Word order in mainland Scandinavian is pretty much fixed, both main and subordinate clauses generally have SVO order; it also clearly has fewer inflexions than the other Germanic languages. Still it retains some vestiges of the V2 rule (cf. e.g. McWhorter, 2002, and additional discussion in this chapter).

rare: 'the hard cases are those in which the interference features consist of structure alone' (*ibid.*). Another factor that makes syntactic interference harder to spot is that syntax, as 'the most central component of language', is 'most open to interaction with other components ... syntax is too much the opposite of a closed system for the effects external forces can have on it to be easily predictable' (Gerritsen and Stein, 1992: 12). It may be the case, for instance, that the syntax is affected by contact only indirectly – that is, via changes on the morphological or lexical level (see the discussion later in the chapter).

Effects of contact on syntax vary in nature and intensity, depending on the kind of contact situation – that is, how (the speakers of) the source and target languages relate to each other. One important distinction is between 'shift-induced interference' or 'imposition' (cf. Thomason, 2003: 709) and 'contact-induced changes' (often termed 'borrowing' in a more narrow sense). Contact-induced changes are especially prevalent when there is full bilingualism, and where code-switching is also common, while shift-induced interference is usually the result of imperfect learning (i.e. in cases where a first language interferes in the learning of a later adopted language). To distinguish between contact-induced change and shift-induced interference, Van Coetsem (1988: 7ff.) uses the terms 'recipient-language agentivity' versus 'source-language agentivity', respectively, and in doing so links them to aspects of 'dominance'. Concerning dominance, he refers to (i) the relative freedom speakers have in using items from the source language in their own (recipient) language (here the *recipient* language is dominant), and (ii) the almost inevitable or passive use that we see with imperfect learners, when they adopt patterns of their own (source) language into the new, recipient language, which makes the *source* language dominant. In (i), the primary mechanism is 'imitation', which only superficially affects speakers' utterances and does not involve their native code, while in (ii), the primary mechanism is 'adaptation', where the changes in utterances are a result of speakers' (= imperfect learners) native code. Not surprisingly, Van Coetsem (*ibid.*: 12) describes recipient-language agentivity as 'more deliberate', and source-language agentivity as something of which speakers are not necessarily conscious. In source-language agentivity, the more stable or structured domains of language are involved (phonology and syntax), while in recipient-language agentivity, it is mostly the lexicon that is involved, where obligatoriness decreases and 'creative action' increases (*ibid.*: 26).

It is clear that 'language contact is always the historical product of social forces' (Sankoff, 2002: 640). Therefore, in order to understand the linguistic consequences of any contact for the speech-community and ultimately for the language itself, we need to know what the contact involved/ involves, and whether it is the result of immigration or conquest, or mere social contact between communities. It is also possible that contact takes place via written or indirect oral sources (books, the internet, radio/television, etc.) without any speakers directly communicating, in which case the effect of the contact is usually less strong (cf. Britain, 2002: 609). In cases of immigration, we need to know how large the number of newcomers is compared to the native population, and what their social (economic, political) status is in the newly mixed community. More generally, we need to know the prestige status of the source language that provides the loans. In the case of language shift via substratum or imperfect learning, we also need to know how much access there is to the target language, whether schooling or a standard language is involved, whether the rate of language shift is rapid or slow, and what the amount of bilingualism is among the speakers. It is to be expected, for instance, that more structural borrowing will take place if the newcomers are not fluent speakers of the target language because, in that case, they will fall back on the structures of their own (source) language (cf. Thomason, 2003: 691). Finally, we need to know the ins and outs of the grammatical systems internalized in speakers of both the source and the target languages during the period of contact, and in addition we need to compare in a quantitative manner the constructions used in the target language before and after this period in order to throw more light on the effects the interaction may have had. Furthermore, the nature and intensity of syntactic borrowing will also be affected by the structural relations between source and recipient language. A special situation is that in which languages in contact are of more or less equal status, and mutually intelligible (in which case they are more likely to be 'dialects' rather than separate languages). In such circumstances, a *koine* may arise. Transfer of structures or lexical items from one language to another may take place here too, but other aspects of a more indirect, internal kind, come more to the fore. Thus, Kerswill (2002) remarks that, apart from a more thorough mixing, reduction is a frequent phenomenon in such situations, in the form of levelling and simplification. Levelling can be observed in the removal of marked forms and in an increase in morphological and syntactic regularity (cf. also McWhorter, 2002).

Apart from these practical considerations, the likelihood of syntactic change through 'borrowing' tends to be perceived differently depending on the theoretical framework used. Some generative historical linguists – because of their interest in the autonomy of syntax and the parameters and universal principles of 'innate grammar' – tend to ignore external factors, paying much more attention to internal ones. Approaching the issue from the other direction, there are the more functionally oriented linguists, who take languages in general rather than individual competence as a basis and seek explanations in typological universals. Other historical linguists with a more sociolinguistic background believe that, given enough intensity and/or length of contact, anything can happen (cf. Thomason and Kaufmann, 1988: 14; Harris and Campbell, 1995: 149). Yet another group, which includes many philologically trained linguists, believes that the idea that virtually anything can ultimately be borrowed, puts far too much emphasis on the mere force of social pressures and neglects *quantitative* research, which could throw light on the interaction with internal developments. In this connection Sankoff (2002: 640–41) remarks:

> in rejecting the contribution of internal linguistic structure T[homason] and K[aufman] have thrown out the baby with the bathwater. The cumulative weight of sociolinguistic research on language contact suggests that although it may be true that 'anything can happen' given enough social pressure, T and K are very far from the truth in their blanket rejection of internal constraints.

It appears that an open mind, not weighed down by the pre-eminence of a particular approach or model, is the best way to explore the possible occurrence of syntactic borrowing or interference. Methodologically, it is most sound to give heed to and study quite a number of aspects of both an external and an internal kind, having to do with the type of contact, the socio-cultural make-up of the speech-community, and the state of the conventional internalized code that individuals in the community have developed during the period of language acquisition and beyond.

4.3   The External Circumstances Affecting the Linguistic Consequences of Contact with Latin, Scandinavian, Celtic and Medieval French

Before turning to the linguistic details, we summarize, on the basis of available studies, the circumstances of the contact situations themselves.[2] Table 4.1 takes into account the various parameters discussed in Section 4.2.

Some first conclusions can be drawn from this. The situations of Latin and French contact are fairly similar, they share the parameters given in (1), (4)–(6) and (12), and are closer to each other with respect to (2)–(3), (7)–(9) and (11) in comparison with the position of Scandinavian. Scandinavian shares no parameters with Latin and French, and takes the more extreme or opposite position on (2)–(3), (7)–(9) and (12). The position of Celtic is rather different in most respects; this is also because much less is known about what happened to the native British population after the Germanic invasion in 476 (see additional discussion in Section 4.3.3).

---

[2] General information on the socio-cultural and linguistic circumstances of the contacts can be found in many text- and handbooks on the history of English, and more particularly in Hadley and Richards (2000), Filppula *et al.* (2002), Hickey, (2010), Kastovsky and Mettinger, (2003), Schendl and Wright, (2011) Miller, (2012), Schreier and Hundt, (2013).

Table 4.1. *Socio-cultural and external-linguistic parameters involved in contact with Latin, Scandinavian, Celtic, and French.*

Parameters (social and linguistic)	Latin Contact – OE/ME period and Renaissance	Scandinavian Contact – OE (/ME) period	Celtic Contact – OE/ME period and beyond (in Celtic varieties of English)	French Contact – mainly ME period
(1) Type of language agentivity (primary mechanism)	Recipient (imitation)	Source (adaptation)	Source (adaptation)	Recipient (imitation)
(2) Type of communication	Indirect	Direct	Direct	(In) direct
(3) Length and intensity of communication	Low	High	Average (?)	Average
(4) Percentage of population speaking the contact language	Small	Relatively large	Relatively large	Small
(5) Socio-economic status	High	Equal	Low	High
(6) Language prestige	High	Equal	Low	High
(7) Bilingual speakers (among the English speakers)	Yes (but less direct)	No	No	Some
(8) Schooling (providing access to target language)	Yes	No	No (only in later periods)	Some
(9) Existence of standard in source/target language	Yes/Yes	No/No	No/No (only in later periods)	Yes/No
(10) Influence on the lexicon of the target language (types of loanword)	Small (formal)	Large in the Danelaw area (informal)	Small (except in Celtic varieties of English) (informal)	Very large (mostly formal)
(11) Influence on the phonology of the target language	No	Yes	Yes? (clearly in Celtic varieties of English)	Some
(12) Linguistic similarity with target language	No	Yes	No	No

As far as (10) is concerned, it is noteworthy that Latin and French are each other's true opposites only here: the number of Latin loanwords in OE and ME is still fairly small,[3] especially when compared to the enormous amount of French loanwords that poured in during the ME period. This has a twofold explanation. On the external side, it can be related to the fact that communication in terms of Latin was far more indirect (mostly via translators of texts), and restricted to the more formal registers. Therefore, contact was never long and intensive for the population as a whole. Additionally, speakers of Latin were always bilingual and in politico-economic terms not particularly dominant. French speakers, on the other hand, as conquerors and subsequent rulers of the country, were highly dominant but not generally bilingual. On the internal side, a lot had happened to the language during the Scandinavian occupation, which explains to some extent the heavy use of French words in the ME period. The language had lost native patterns of word-formation due to the phonological erosion of bound morphemes, and hence it was a 'shorter path' to borrow words rather than to make up one's own, as was still the rule in the OE period concerning the adoption of Latin words (cf. Godden, 1992: 524, 528). Because French had prestige and was prevalent in both formal and literary writing until the thirteenth century, it is not surprising that English speakers started to use French words in their own language when English regained its position in the later Middle Ages.

Judging from the information collected in this table, we may therefore expect syntactic influence, direct or indirect, to be especially strong in the Scandinavian situation and possibly also with Celtic, and to be much weaker in the case of Latin and French because source-language agentivity was strongly present only in the former. In the following subsections, we will look in more detail at the syntactic consequences linguists of various persuasions have noted for each contact in question. By linking what happened linguistic-ally (both in qualitative and quantitative terms) to what happened historically, we hope to present a clearer view both of the general and the specific: a contribution to our knowledge of what we may expect in any contact situation as well as a better understanding of the degree and the amount in which Latin, Scandinavian, Celtic and French shaped English syntactically.

4.3.1   The Case of Latin

We are fortunate in having quite a few investigations on the influence of Latin on English syntax. Most of these concentrate on the absolute construction (*ablativus absolutus*), the passive infinitive, and the *nominativus-* and

---

[3] Loanwords from Latin into English increase in the late ME period (they abound of course in code-switching), but they only become a regular flood in the fifteenth century and the Renaissance. For an overview of loanwords entering English chronologically see Finkenstaedt *et al.* (1970).

accusativus-cum-infinitivo constructions (*nci* and *aci*, respectively).[4] The conclusions concerning the putative influence are mixed. Most linguists agree that the absolute construction and the *nci* are mostly encountered in translations closely based on Latin and therefore did not truly affect English syntax (cf. Kohnen, 2003; Nagucka, 2003; Timofeeva, 2010). Concerning the *aci* and the passive infinitive, opinions are more divided.

Timofeeva's (2010: 186–87) findings on the *nci* are as follows. In a corpus based on glosses and direct translations from Latin, thirty-nine instances were found in the Latin originals, of which only one is rendered by an *nci* (1a):

(1) ... *cogebantur   noua   meditari*
    ... they-were-compelled new [things] to-consider (*G*Dii.3.142.20)
    (a) ... *hi ... wæron geneadode niwe þing to smeagenne*
        ...they   were   compelled new things to consider' (*GD*(ms H)104.20)
    (b) ... *hi   wæron genydede ..., þæt hi   scoldon niwe wisan hycgan and smeagan*
        ...they were   compelled ... that they should new ways think   and consider
        (*GD*(ms C)104.20)

The most usual technique is to use a *þæt*-clause (twenty-six instances) as was indeed done in another manuscript version of *Gregory's Dialogues*, see (1b). In other cases the construction was either omitted or partly omitted (six instances), the main verb made active (four instances), or a participle was used (two instances).

Timofeeva does not present quantitative evidence for the use of the *nci* from her corpus of *native* OE texts but simply gives one example from the *Peterborough Chronicle* to show that the *nci* was used in late OE with the verb *seon* 'see'. Checking all occurrences where *seon* is part of a passive predicate in the complete *Dictionary of OE Corpus*, we found only one more example in original OE from the same chronicle:

(2) *and þa   uppon Eastron ... **wæs gesewen** forneah ofer eall þis land ... swiðe*
    and then at   Easter... was seen   nearly   over all this land... very
    *mænifealdlice steorran of heofenan **feollan***
    manifold   stars   from heaven fall (*ChronE*,1496(1095.12))

What is interesting is that three other examples with passive *seon* do occur but with a present participle rather than an infinitive, a construction also found twice as a replacement in Timofeeva's corpus of Latinate texts:

---

[4] An *aci* is a construction in which the object of the main verb (*him*) also functions as subject of the infinitive, as in *I expect **him** to be late*. The *nci* is the passive counterpart of the *aci*, as in *He was expected to be late*.

(3) ... *and fyrenne dracan **wæron gesewene** on þam lifte **fleogende***
     ... and fiery   dragons were   seen   in the   air   flying
     (*ChronD*,0183(793.1))[5]

These participle constructions can fairly comfortably be interpreted as native because the participle need not be directly dependent on the main verb but can be interpreted as dependent on the NP *dracan* (i.e. 'flying dragons') in spite of the intervening PP. Furthermore, since OE allowed a bare infinitive as well as a present participle after active predicates of *seon*, a construction with a present participle here is also easily formed on analogy with the active construction. Further analogizing could then lead to the use of a bare infinitive even though the *nci* with a bare infinitive does not really fit the native grammar system, as the avoidance of *nci*'s in Timofeeva's Latinate corpus makes abundantly clear. Even the construction used in (1a) is understandable from the point of view of 'least salience' or analogy because the *to*-infinitive used can be seen as conveying purpose, and was in native use next to *þæt*-clauses after verbs of 'persuading and urging', to which *neodian* belongs (cf. Los, 2005: 51ff). Thus, in all cases where a Latin *nci* can be shown or surmised to have influenced the text, the translator prefers to use a construction that is either native to OE, or one that is analogous to a native construction, making it as non-salient as possible.

Concerning the ablative absolute, Nagucka (2003: 259) observes that 'typically, absolute constructions are substituted by native structures' (e.g. *ab urbe condita* [lit. 'from (the) city built'] is translated in *Orosius* [78/1] as *æfter þæm þe Romeburg getimbred wæs* ['after [the time] that Rome-city built was']). Similarly, Timofeeva (2010: 33ff.) found that of the 622 cases of ablative absolutes in her Latinate corpus, it is only the glosses that tend to use a literal rendering (96.94 per cent of the 98 cases are translated with a dative absolute construction), while in the direct translations (524 instances) this occurs only 21.76 per cent of the time. The following patterns were used instead (more details in *ibid.*: 36ff).

  (i)   a prepositional phrase without a verb (*facto mane* 'morning reached' >
        on mergen 'in the morning')
 (ii)   the use of a nominalized phrase instead of a participle (*imperante Constantino ... anno nono* 'Constantine reigning [in the] ninth year' >
        þy nigoðan gere Constantines rice 'the ninth year of-Constantine's reign')
(iii)   the use of a coordinate clause (*Et ascendente eo in navicula secuti sunt eum discipuli eius* 'And, him ascending on ship, his disciples followed

---

[5] The other two instances are in *ChronE*(Irvine)1110.14 and 1114.6. There is also one example with a past participle in *ÆCHom*.I,21,347.76: *wæron gesewene englas mid hwitum gyrelum geglengde* 'were seen angels with white clothes adorned'. Here the adjectival status of the participle is even clearer.

him' > *And he astah on scyp and his leorningcnihtas hym fyligdon* 'and
he went on [board] ship and his apostles followed him')

(iv) the use of a subordinate clause (see the example from Nagucka earlier in
this chapter)

 (v) omission of the *nci* where possible and replacing it by an adverb when it
contained old information (*qua accepta* 'this accepted' > *þa* 'then')

In her corpus of native texts, Timofeeva (2010: 73) found twenty-six instances
of dative absolutes, sixteen of which are found in the writings of Ælfric, which
are often indirectly based on Latin. What is interesting is that most of these
examples are modelled on *concrete* Latin phrases (e.g. *defuncto* X >
X *forðgefarenum* 'X having died' (*ibid.*: 61)). This shows that these are, as
it were, 'loan idioms', which should be considered lexical rather than syntactic
borrowings.

Van de Pol (2016) has also investigated the absolute construction, making
use of a bigger corpus. She first notes that the absolute construction could be
seen as inherited from Indo-European because it occurs in other Indo-
European languages. She argues that it was probably moribund in early OE
(where it is rare in her corpus) and that it revived under the influence of
scholars familiar with Latin in the late OE period. She admits that 'loan
idioms' are a possibility as 83.69 per cent of the ablative absolutes based
directly on Latin are indeed idiomatic, but at the same time she notes that non-
translated texts, such as Ælfric's *Homilies* also contain ablative absolutes.
What is remarkable is that the native examples from Ælfric given in Van de
Pol all seem to admit an instrumental or 'simultaneity' interpretation, thus
coming very close to the instrumental meaning that the dative case could still
carry in OE, and where modern Germanic languages can still use a construction with *with* (see also Chapter 8). They are of the type illustrated in (4a), and
not of the type shown in (4b), which is directly based on Latin and indicates a
temporal sequence:

(4) a *geendedum dagum þære freolstide/bescornum feaxe*
With-ended days   of-the festival/   with-shorn hair
(*ÆCHom.*I,37:501.130/I,32:457.184)[6]
'with the days of the festival over/with his hair shorn'

  b *and ymne acwædene*   *eodon ut   on oelebearwes dune*
and hymn said[DAT] [they] went   out   on of-olive-grove hill (MtGl(Ru)26.30)
'and a hymn having been sung, they went out onto the Mount of Olives'

---

[6] And see also *ÆCHom.*I,27:406.181 and 29:428.287, where *þus cwedendum drihtne/þisum
gewordenum* can be translated as 'with the lord speaking thus/in the words of the lord' and
'with this having happened/with this result'.

Van de Pol and Petré (2015) show an interesting increase in absolute constructions from eModE onwards, one that is not shared by other Germanic languages such as Dutch and German. They argue that this is due to the fact that the absolute construction shows formal and functional overlap with constructions with a gerund (as in *Life was fraught enough . . . without her adding to the problems, ibid.*: 215), and constructions with prepositional postmodification (as in *He is downstage, with his back to her, ibid.*: 216), which both become more frequent in that period. Such long term developments, taking place in this case in the absolute construction, show again that foreign-type constructions are more easily adopted whenever the native language can accommodate them in a natural way. The development of the verbal gerund in later English (see Chapter 8) clearly helped to make the absolute construction become fully acceptable.

Something similar happened in the case of passive infinitives and *aci* constructions. These, too, became part and parcel of the grammatical system of English in the course of time, but by a different route. As for passive infinitives, Fischer's (1991) investigation based on an OE and a ME corpus shows that they were only fully grammatical in OE after modal verbs (as in *Hwæt **mæg beon** mare bliss to gehyrenne* 'What may be a greater joy to hear', *ÆCHom.*II, 25 211.159). They did not occur as a complement after the verb *be* (as in PDE *What is to be done*), as an adjunct to an NP (*A case to be considered is . . .*) or adjective (with only one exception, see Fischer, 1991: 154–55) (*What is best to be done*), nor as a subject (*To be advanced in our company is our chief design*). They were found occasionally in *aci* constructions and after impersonal verbs but mainly in direct translations from Latin. All these types (apart from passive infinitives after modals) only began to emerge in the course of the ME period. Timofeeva (2010: 166ff.) notes that passive infinitives in *aci*'s are 'extremely rare' in her Latinate corpus: she found only five examples out of a total of eighty-eight passive infinitives in the Latin originals. Mostly the translator resorted to finite *that*-clauses or active infinitives.

Concerning the *aci*, quantitative evidence of its occurrence in OE and ME, and comparative evidence from German and Dutch, shows to what extent the introduction of the *aci* was due to contact with Latin, and to what extent other factors were involved. The *aci* is a construction where an NP, which functions as the subject of the infinitive, is not syntactically governed by the infinitive but by the main predicate even though this predicate does not assign a semantic role to the NP in question (cf. Note 4 in this chapter). In OE (and this is still the case in modern Dutch and German) such a construction was only possible (and indeed part of the native code) with a bare infinitive after verbs of direct perception and causatives, where there was a semantic as well as a syntactic link between main verb and accusative NP, as in *I saw/let him go* (where indeed one can actually *see him* in the action of *going,* or directly *allow him* something) – that is, where the situation was concrete and directly observable or the causation direct. In Latin-type *aci*'s, later also found in English with *to*-infinitives, such as *The County Council would clearly think this to be unreasonable* (BNC)[7] or *He expects it* [the CTsystem] *to find a ready market amongst arable farmers and growers* (BNC), these two aspects are not present: the activity expressed by the infinitive is neither observable nor direct or simultaneous in a temporal sense (cf. Fischer *et al.*, 2000). The use of empty *it* in the second example also makes clear that there is no semantic relation between *it* and the main predicate.[8]

Many explanations have been offered for the rise of the *aci* in English. Quite a few linguists working within a traditional model of grammar believe it was native to English. Because the native and the Latin types of *aci* are formally not easily distinguishable on the surface, they see them as belonging to one and the same category (cf. Krickau, 1877; Visser, 1973). In such a model, constructional changes, naturally, do not readily become visible. Others, such as Zeitlin (1908), argue that the *aci* construction spread naturally by means of analogy (in tandem with lexical diffusion) from verbs of physical perception to verbs of mental perception, and then to other cognition verbs and verbs of utterance. Yet other researchers believe it may be an extension of small clauses such as *I found her far too pretty* (BNC) > *I found her to be far too beautiful* (Google; see https://letterboxd.com/settingsun/film/dial-m-for-murder/, more details in Los 2005: Ch.9).

Lightfoot (1981), working in a generative model, ascribes the rise of the *aci* to the influence of Latin. This is surprising because he is otherwise reluctant to invoke foreign influence when parallel forms exist in two languages (cf. Lightfoot, 1979: 383). He argues that a rule of S-bar deletion (current in the P&P model, allowing infinitival subjects to be governed in order to receive a semantic role), which was new to ME, is likely to be 'a result of translating Latin accusative + infinitive constructions', which 'then became part of the linguistic environment' (1981: 113). In a later study (1991: 89ff.), he considers the rise an internal development, arguing that the *aci* is due to a parameter shift in the status of *to*: *to* coalesced with the governing verb enabling this verb to transmit its head government and case properties. Both proposals are highly theory-internal and technical, and both only work as long as the model in which the constructions function is upheld. This is in itself a problem, but more serious is the fact that the philological details to support the explanation are not correct.

---

[7] The BNC stands for the British National Corpus, a corpus we will use to illustrate modern usage.

[8] Bolinger (1967: 48) shows that, even though, strictly, there is no semantic (argument) link between the oblique NP and the main predicate (the *aci* as a whole functions as the complement of the main verb), there *is* a 'surface' link between verb and NP in that 'the string [predicate]+NP when taken as a constituent in its own right has a meaning compatible with that of the sentence as a whole'. This explains why *I believe the report to be true* is well-formed (because the speaker 'believes *what is in the report*'), whereas *I believe the rain to be falling* is not, or at least odd.

There is no space to go into any of these theoretical considerations in detail (we refer the interested reader to a discussion of this in Fischer *et al.*, 2000: 211ff.); instead, in order to understand why it happened, we would like to highlight the comparative aspect and the synchronic state of the grammar system of English at the time of the change. First, it is remarkable that the Latin-type *aci* construction did not spread in Dutch and German, even though the same contact situation as regards Latin applied here too in the same period (cf. Krickau, 1877; Fischer, 1994b). If the socio-cultural circumstances in all three cases can be considered more or less equal, an explanation for the rise must be found elsewhere. Secondly, the Latin-type *aci* spread into native English texts only *after* the OE period.[9] This raises the question of what was different about ME in comparison to both OE, and German and Dutch. The quantitative evidence given for OE in Timofeeva (2010), and for ME in Warner (1982) and Fischer (1992a) speaks for itself. Timofeeva (2010: 161;163) found only two translated *aci*'s in her Latinate corpus after verbs of cognition, out of a total of thirty-seven Latin ones, and only one after verbs of utterance out of forty-eight possible ones.[10] Fischer (1992a) finds a large number of passive infinitive constructions functioning as *aci*'s in a corpus of original ME texts (for the significance of the use of the passive, see below), namely 146 instances after perception verbs and causatives, and nineteen after persuade-type verbs; this is followed in the course of time by more truly Latin-type *aci*'s after cognition verbs and verbs of utterance (30 instances, 17 of which are ambiguous, 6 have a passive infinitive).

Quite a number of studies have pointed to the role played by word order in the rise of new infinitival constructions (involving next to the *aci*, also the so-called *for* NP *to* V constructions, as in *It was necessary for it to happen*, cf. Fischer *et al.*, 2000; Los, 2005; De Smet, 2010, 2013a: 73ff.). In the older Germanic languages the word order was still variable because the languages lacked a written standard; they were still in Givón's (1979: 223) 'Pragmatic Mode', rather than in his 'Syntactic Mode'. Basically, the older Germanic languages could be described as SOV, with Verb-second (V2) regularly operating in main clauses, and with the possibility for pronouns to occur in clitic position before the finite verb, at least in OE. However, none of these patterns was fully grammaticalized. Grammaticalization occurred in all three languages, probably as a consequence of the development of a

---

[9] This time gap also creates a problem for the 'analogy' explanation put forward by Zeitlin (discussed earlier). Analogy may still have played a role but it clearly needed further constructions to support it.

[10] This in contrast to *aci*'s after direct-perception verbs and causatives, where *aci*'s are common in her corpus (*ibid*: 150–60).

written tradition and subsequent standardization, whereby Dutch and German remained strongly SOV, with a highly regular V2 rule, while English became more and more a strict SVO language. We go more deeply into these word-order developments in Chapter 9, the only point we want to stress here is that the move towards a fixed SVO word order in English created an environment in which the Latin *aci* fitted more easily than before because of the availability of an analogous pattern. This can best be illustrated by means of some examples.

In OE, when infinitival constructions were used (bare infinitives after perception verbs and causatives, and *to*-infinitives, expressing purpose, after verbs of 'commanding and permitting' and 'persuading and urging'), the object of the infinitive, when transitive, regularly appeared before the infinitive, as can be seen from the position of *boc* in (5a), thus following basic SOV order. The NP that provided the agent(subject)-role for the infinitive and which functioned at the same time as the syntactic object of the main finite verb, would normally be placed after the predicate and before the infinitival object, as can be seen in (5a): *þone arcebisceop Wulfstan*. It was also quite common for the subject of this infinitive to be left out when it could be understood from the context, as in (5b). When the infinitive was intransitive, the agent-role of the infinitive (again, the syntactic object of the finite verb) was also usually found in this pre-infinitival position: *heora feonda wærod* in (5c).

(5) a *Se cyng   het   þone arcebisceop Wulfstan **þærto boc   settan***
      The king commanded/let the   archbishop   Wulfstan for-this [a] book prepare
      (*Ch.*1460(Rob 83)0002(8))
      'The king had archbishop Wulfstan prepare a book for this'

    b *þa   **het**   **he hine lædan** to beheafdunga*
      then commanded/let   he him lead   to beheading
      (*Mart.*5(Kotzor)1015(Se.14,A.4))
      'then he had him taken away to be beheaded'

    c *a   hi   **leton**   **heora feonda** wærod wexan*
      ever they let/allowed their enemies' army [to]grow (*ChronE*(Irvine)0757(999.7))

In ME, due to the ever-increasing SVO order in all types of clauses, the orders found in (5a) and (5b) are attested less and less. What we see instead is that the infinitival object of (5a) *boc* comes to be placed after the infinitive, as indeed happened with *land* in (6a), a ME instance. The object of the predicate, *heom*, keeps its post-predicate position:

(6) a *and let heom tilien þat lond*
      and let them till   the land (*Laȝ.Brut*(Cal.)8414)

(5b) proved to be an awkward construction in an SVO language. Either an infinitival agent has to be added so that it looks like (6a), or the infinitival object is reanalysed as subject by making the infinitive passive as in (6b), or, if possible, intransitive as in (6c).[11] Construction (5c) is unproblematic because it already has the subject before the infinitive.

(6) b *Þa lette he his cnihtes … æuere beon iwepned*
         then let he his knights … ever be   weaponed (*Laʒ.Brut*(Cal)8156–7)
     c *sir Dynadan herd a grete horne blowe*
         Sir Dynadan heard a great horn blow (*MorteDarthur*,529)

It seems therefore highly likely that the rise of Latin-type *aci* constructions was helped along by the surge of new *passive aci*'s that preceded them.[12] The passive infinitive (which, as we have seen, was formally already available in OE after modal verbs) could be resorted so as to solve the word-order problem noted earlier; simultaneously, however, it made the connection between the predicate and the oblique NP looser. In (5a), there is clearly a semantic (argument) relation between *het* and *þone arcebisceop Wulfstan*. When a passive construction is used, as in *The king commanded a book to be prepared*, this relation is gone, turning *a book to be prepared* as a whole into a theme or complement. The development shows that the Latin-type *aci* construction crept in at a 'weak' spot, where it was least salient, and then spread from there. Warner (1982), Fischer (1992a, 1994b) and Dreschler (2015: 176–77) have found a few more weak spots that helped the construction along, such as the fact that the *aci* first occurred with reflexive oblique NPs, in *wh*-movement constructions, and in passives where the past participle functions like an adjective, again in places where the *aci* was least salient. Similar supportive constructions helped the new *for* NP *to*-infinitive construction on its way (cf. De Smet, 2009, 2013a).

The conclusion must be, as before with the absolute construction, that Latin influence on English syntax was only possible where the synchronic grammar system allowed it. Interesting in this connection is the case of the so-called parasitic gap constructions looked at by Van der Wurff (1990). He found that clauses such as,

(7) a book which you can't understand *t* unless you read *e* well

which are highly marginal in PDE (normally the gap *e* is filled by an anaphoric pronoun, *it*) were quite common in Latinate writings from the Renaissance onwards, but they never really made it into regular standard English because there was 'no grammatical derivation' for them possible within the

---

[11] *Blawan* could be both transitive and intransitive in Old English but there is evidence that quite a few verbs came to be interpreted as intransitive due to these 'awkward' constructions, see Fischer (1992a: 35–36).

[12] De Smet (2013a: 78) also notes with reference to the new *for* NP *to*-infinitives that the earliest ones to appear are 'predominantly passive', as in *the Bysshop of Norwych makyth but delayes in my reasonable desire for an eende to be had* in the xxv. Marc of Hykelyng (1400–1449, quoted on p.77).

grammatical system of English at the time (*ibid.*: 196). And, we could add, there was no need for them because there was already a perfectly adequate construction making use of an (extra) pronoun.

4.3.2   The Case of Scandinavian

There is a lot of controversy about the influence Old Norse [ON][13] may have had on the English dialects spoken in Northern England and later — through migration of Northern and Midlands speakers into the London area — also on the developing Standard. The main problem is that it is not possible to link the archaeological (burial, sculptural and coinage) evidence and the evidence from place-names directly to the number of settlers (cf. Hadley, 1997; Hadley and Richardson, 2000). Sawyer (1971), followed by Thomason and Kaufman (1988: 299, *passim*), had claimed on the basis of this evidence and the lack of continuity in a separate ethnicity of the Vikings, that the number of settlers was relatively small. Hadley (1997: 70), however, notes:

The consensus reached by the end of the 1970s was that although the Viking armies were perhaps not as sizeable as was once thought, they were, nonetheless, not as small as Peter Sawyer had claimed.

Most scholars agree that there must have been a high degree of intermarriage and social mixing and that this 'makes it probable that it would soon have been difficult to distinguish people of exclusively English or Danish descent' (Hadley, 1997: 86; and cf. Allen, 1997: 67). Thomason and Kaufman (1988: 281) concur when they write that the language contact situation must have been 'intense' and that the 'Norse influence on English was pervasive'. They add, however, that this was only 'in the sense that results are found in all parts of the language, but it was not deep, except on the lexicon' (*ibid.*: 302). They believe that '[i]n spite of the relatively large number of grammatical elements of Norse origin in Norsified ME [as shown in detail on pp. 278–79], their effect on English structure was almost trivial' (*ibid.*: 298), and they do not believe that the contact with ON caused simplification 'because the simplifications we see in ME when compared to OE probably were taking place in OE before Norse influence became relevant' (*ibid.*: 303).[14] This seems to contradict their earlier statement on *ibid.*: 277, on which they state: 'Northern

---

[13] The Viking tribes that occupied Northern England from the eighth century onwards, and later from 1016 to 1042, all of England, consisted of Danes, Norwegians and Swedes. Their language is usually referred to as Old Norse.

[14] Their view is the complete opposite of the ideas found in Emonds and Faarlund (2014), who argue that English is basically a Scandinavian language. However, their arguments rest on rather shaky grounds in the sense that many of the changes they ascribe to Scandinavian have

dialects ... show a good deal of morphological simplification when compared to the OE stage or even to old Norse'.

Thomason and Kaufman, followed by Allen (1997), uphold that the simplifications that occurred should be seen as a natural development rather than one caused by contact. They defend this position by arguing that 'most simplifications of Northern ME' already took place in Old Northumbrian, and, secondly, that they are 'not unusual when compared with Modern Dutch, Low German, Danish, or Swedish' (1988: 280–81). Allen (1997: 86) shows that reduction of forms and case syncretism is rife in the early Northern *Lindisfarne Gospels* glosses, and that the 'details of syncretism differed considerably' with those taking place in the South, but she too attributes this to natural processes such as phonological weakening and analogy.

However, this does not answer the question of why the developments in Northern English were, first, so much faster than in the Germanic sister languages, and, second, also much faster compared to the Southern English dialects, where there was no Viking settlement. Simplification (loss of variation) due to imperfect learning of the Vikings would have similar results (with analogy playing a major role) and, in addition, would explain the earlier occurrence in the north. True, the 'processes involved' in this development would not have 'differed fundamentally in the north from those ... in the south' (Allen, 1997: 86), but the timing clearly did. The developments taking place later in the South would also have been speeded up (compared to what happened in the other Germanic languages) by immigration from the North and Midlands as described in Samuels (1969: 411–13), or by the development of an East Midland *koine* or interlanguage as described in Poussa (1982).

Concerning the sister languages, loss of inflexions in Dutch only occurred some 500 years later, and this loss was not nearly as pervasive as the loss in Northern England (i.e. Modern Dutch still has two genders, remnants of strong and weak adjectives, and weak as well as strong plural nouns). A comparison with modern German dialects is even more striking, because they remained highly inflexional. Equally important is the fact that Dutch still has the variation in word order that was present in OE, even though each variant is more grammaticalized; thus it still has Subject Verb inversion after a topicalized element, SOV in subordinate clauses, and the verbal 'brace'-construction (with finite verb and infinitive/participle (em)bracing the object, which is placed in between) in main clauses. Word order in the more 'progressive' Scandinavian languages also is not totally fixed;[15] they still have

---

also taken place in other Germanic languages or were already embryonically present in OE. For some comments see http://languagelog.ldc.upenn.edu/nll/?p=4351.

[15] As is well-known, Icelandic is more conservative and still more highly inflexional than the other four Scandinavian languages: Danish, Faroese, Norwegian and Swedish.

remnants of the V2 rule (cf. Note 1 earlier in this chapter), word-order differences with respect to adverbs between main and subordinate clauses, and they are more highly inflexional, preserving gender, some agreement features, and some distinctions between weak and strong adjectives (cf. Bandle et al., 2005).

Our position here, following McWhorter (2002), is that it is most unlikely that the contact situation between the Vikings and the Northern Englishmen, which was intense, as even Thomason and Kaufman admit, did not lead to a simplification of the language. Thomason and Kaufman base their conclusion on Sawyer's argument that the number of settlers was quite small, and on their idea that they represented a 'small elite', who therefore 'could have influenced the vocabulary of English-speaking peasants merely through a prestigious status' (1988: 304). We would argue for the opposite position – namely that simplification must have taken place through shift or interference due to imperfect learning – on the basis of the following: (i) the archaeological evidence (the lack of continuity in ethnicity, see earlier discussion) suggesting that the Vikings soon fitted in with their new environment; it is likely that this also resulted soon in a common new variety; (ii) intermarriage leading to a new mixed language in which the next generation, having to choose between alternative elements and structures, will tend to opt for the maximally simple via the process of analogy; (iii) the unlikelihood of prestige being involved because the Vikings and English were both farmers; additionally, prestige leads to lexical borrowing (cf. the Norman situation later) but not to a dramatic loss of inflexions and the borrowing of function words; (iv) the mutual intelligibility of ON and OE making it likely that koineization occurred as a result of intensive contact (cf. Kerswill, 2002: 669).

With respect to koineization, Kerswill notes a number of characteristics. He writes that it typically takes only two or three generations to complete, and is even achievable in one (2002: 670). It is composed of three processes: mixing, levelling and simplification (p. 672). Additionally, *koine*-formation typically involves continuity of both dialects, which makes it very different from pidgin and creole genesis (p. 696). Finally, there is no dominant language and prestige is not involved.

Mixing is indeed attested on various levels, phonological, morphological and lexical. We see it in the paradigm of the personal pronoun, which contains Norse (*they, their, them*) as well as English elements, and of the verb *to* BE, which has ON *are, art* and *ware(n)* next to OE *be, beoþ, ben* and so on; we see it in the mixing of phonetic form and meaning, as in the word *dream*, a word that acquired its sound shape from English but its meaning from ON *draumr* (similarly with *dwell* and *bread,* which acquired their meanings from ON *dvelja* and *brauð*); we see it in hybrid compounds such as *liðsmann* 'sailor'

(ON had *liðsmaðr*) from ON *lið* 'fleet' and OE *mann*;[16] sometimes a phoneme might change under the influence of ON as in OE *fæder*, *modor* which became *father*, *mother* under the influence of ON *faðir*, *moðir*. We see it in the mixed core-vocabulary: words such as *die, take, both, though, till, leg* and so on, and the forms *give, get* and others, rather than Southern *yive, yet*, derive from ON. Miller (2012: 134ff.) and Emonds and Faarlund (2014) point to quite a number of syntactic instances (e.g. the omission of the complementizer *that*, the development of preposition stranding) where Scandinavian and English share innovations, which could also be seen as a result of syntactic mixing.

Levelling is clear from the evidence given in Thomason and Kaufman (1988: 279); it affected the nominal case and number system, and most strongly the demonstrative pronoun *se/seo/þæt*, which in the early ME *Peterborough Chronicle* (Peterborough was part of the Danelaw) was reduced to *þe* in all cases where there was no deictic force.

Simplification is evident in the loss of distinction between strong and weak adjectives, loss of gender, loss of distinction between weak class 1 and 2 verbs, loss of the Ablaut distinction between the singular and the plural past of strong verbs, loss of the distinction between indicative and subjunctive and so on.[17]

On the basis of these examples, it is not at all unlikely that Norsification also affected the syntax in terms of simplification. Thomason and Kaufman are extremely hesitant to admit influence here because they see a lack of sufficient evidence and problems with theoretical models making it hard to define 'simplicity' (cf. Note 16 in this chapter). However, if it can be shown that it is the *variation* in syntactic patterns that is reduced, then we need not be concerned about whether one construction is more marked than another because the simplification is one of quantity not of quality.[18]

We are fortunate in having a quantitative study of syntactic patterns found in early ME Northern- compared to Southern-Midland texts in Kroch and Taylor (1997). They note an important syntactic difference between these texts, which they relate to a difference between two types of V2-movement involving two

---

[16] Hybrid compounds and indeed hybrid derivations are a more common form of mixing; they also occur later, in ME, in the contact with French.

[17] OE had two types of *weak* verbs (i.e. verbs that formed their past tense and past participle with a dental suffix [a Germanic innovation]). *Ablaut* is the change of vowel that occurs in strong verbs. In OE, there was a vowel distinction between past tense singular and plural (as there still is in German and Dutch) as in *rad – ridon*, in PDE both have become 'rode'.

[18] Kerswill (2002: 671) indeed notes that simplification involves 'a decrease in irregularity in morphology and an increase in invariable word forms'; this is what we see in Northern texts in both morphology and syntax.

In a similar way, McWhorter (2002: 219–20), defines complexity versus simplicity in syntax as the operation of respectively more or fewer rules in any given area of grammar. He notes overall a much stronger decrease in what he calls 'overspecification' in the history of English as compared to the other Germanic languages, which he ascribes to contact with the Scandinavians.

different positions to which the verb may move: either to CP or to a lower IP position. They see these as representing a 'typological distinction' (p. 297), involving a parameter shift. The technical details of their theoretical model need not concern us here; what is important is that they have found clear surface differences between Northern- and Southern-Midland texts. Southern-Midland texts show the same constraints on V2 as OE texts – that is, we see regular Subject-Verb inversion after all preposed complements and PP adjuncts, but only with full NP subjects not with pronominal ones (for the behaviour of these so-called pronoun 'clitics', see Chapter 9). We also see that the inversion works differently with light adverbs such as 'then' and 'now', which already in OE allowed inversion even with clitic pronoun subjects. In contrast, a considerable simplification has taken place in the North in that, in the application of the V2-rule, subject pronouns are now treated in exactly the same way as full subject NPs, and the variation after 'then' has disappeared – that is, they have lost their clitic status (cf. also Miller, 2012: 144).

Kroch and Taylor themselves, however, do not accept this 'simple' explanation because they have other evidence showing that the OE clitic status of pronouns has been preserved even in the Northern texts. The evidence for this is not very convincing, however. The examples they quote (pp. 314–15) of clitic pronouns still preceding the finite verb are all awkward in one way or another, and clearly different from the normal anaphoric pronouns collected in their Table 3 (for details see Fischer, 2013). Moreover, only a few exceptional constructions of this kind are attested (fourteen in all), in comparison with the much greater amount of regular constructions where the pronoun need not be interpreted as a clitic (226 instances in their Table 3). If one uses another theoretical framework (i.e. a usage-based model), which makes use of ana-logical learning rather than innate principles and parameters, then the handful of exceptions is less problematic. On the contrary, the picture that emerges is that there has been an overall simplification tending towards one simple inversion or V2-rule covering all cases: pronouns as well as nouns, comple-ments as well as adjuncts and light adverbs. Our suggestion, therefore, is that this simplification has been caused by imperfect learning due to language contact with Scandinavian, whereby the most frequent pattern, by analogy, replaces less frequent ones. There is no need to invoke a parameter change from an IP-V2- to a CP-V2-language, as Kroch and Taylor do. A remarkably similar development is described for the V2 rule in immigrant Dutch in Fischer (2007: 290ff.). Here imperfect learners have simplified the rather complex rule in Dutch, where initial manner adverb normally take V2, while sentence adverbs do not. Because the same lexical item can often be used in both functions, the new learners have simply turned all instances into V2 structures.

In summary, the influence of ON on English syntax seems to have been more profound than that of Latin influence, but it was not of a direct kind (if we leave the borrowing of some function words out of account).[19] The suggestion here is that a *koine* arose in the Danelaw which led to the simplification of OE morphology and word order via shift-induced interference.

4.3.3   The Case of Celtic

The influence of the original British language (a branch of Celtic usually referred to as Brythonic) used in England before the invasion of the Germanic tribes in the fifth century may in some ways be comparable to the Scandinavian case (because it is likely that it also involved source-language activity rather than target-language activity), but there are also important differences. Firstly, far fewer loanwords from Brythonic have survived than is the case with Scandinavian (Tristram, 2002: 116, ascribes this to a higher prestige of the source language in the case of Scandinavian). Secondly, the languages involved were very different, precluding a similar kind of *koine* development.[20] Additionally, some of the British may have been Latin speakers, which would create another layer in between the languages involved (cf. Tristram, 2002: 113; Schrijver, 2002). Thirdly, the British were not in a dominant position in most areas where the Germanic tribes settled (especially in the fertile southern parts), so that it is unlikely that their language had any prestige. On the other hand, they must have been larger in number than the incoming Germanic tribes (cf. evidence quoted in Tristram, 2002: 113–16); such numbers would provide fertile ground for substratum influence or language shift.

The main problem in assessing British impact on what becomes the English language is that the evidence here is even scantier than in the ON situation. This has led to a lot of speculation. The dominant nineteenth-century view was that the native population either fled or was enslaved, having no influence whatsoever on the future development of Anglo-Saxon. From recent archaeological (cf. Klemola, 2013) and place-name evidence (cf. Coates, 2002),

---

[19] There have been many suggestions of direct influence. Kirch (1959) deals with four of these suggested by Jespersen (ellipsis of the relative pronoun, and of the complementizer *that*, the genitive before nouns, and the use of *shall* and *will*) and shows there is no evidence for any except perhaps the use of *shall*. Trips (2002: 332) concludes in her book on ON influence on ME: 'All the empirical findings [with respect to] the Scandinavian characteristics like V2 order, object shift and stylistic fronting in the *Ormulum* and other early ME texts, as well as the comparison with these findings and the situation in Old Norse and other early stages of Scandinavian strongly support the hypothesis that Scandinavian influence was so strong then that not only syntactic operations like stylistic fronting were borrowed but also that the change from OV to VO word order was triggered by contact with Scandinavians'. But here again, the evidence is minimal as Cloutier (2005) has convincingly shown.

[20] The genetic grouping of the Celtic languages is still unclear. Wiik (2002) suggests that the Celtic languages belong to an Italo-Celtic branch rather than a Celtic-Germanic branch.

however, it appears that the areas of British settlement may have been some-what wider than often assumed (i.e. not only in the western parts of the British Isles), and evidence brought forward by Higham (2002: 43) suggests that the 'demise of specifically British group identity [i.e. a separate ethnicity] in the lowlands [this in contrast to the 'western uplands', where the British popula-tion remained as the elite group (*ibid.*: 42)] and the spread of 'Englishness' to non-immigrant individuals and communities were arguably both processes characterized more by negotiation and acculturation than either immigration or extermination'. What exacerbates the situation even more is the fact, as Higham and others note, that there is, and has been for a long time, an ideological divide between an Anglo-Saxonist vision and a British one, with the latter one gaining strength only since the 1980s.

We do not intend to choose sides in this discussion, but simply point out that substratum influence is quite possible, but that any proof for this is indirect as there are no records of the state of the language in this early period, neither of the various Anglo-Saxon dialects, nor of Brythonic and the possible British-Latin factor.[21] Scholars supporting the British view have repeatedly pointed out areas of English grammar which both significantly differ from the gram-mars of the other Germanic languages and which can be shown to be charac-teristic of the later Celtic (specifically Welsh and Irish) languages. In this connection a number of suggestions have been made, which we simply enumerate as far as they comprise morpho-syntactic areas (some of these structures will be discussed in more detail in the following chapters):[22]

- attrition of inflexions, loss of case and gender; Tristram (2002) and White (2002) argue that the early loss of inflexions in Northern England may well be due, not only to the Scandinavians, but also to the British who shifted their language earlier in the northern areas than in the west, where they were able to preserve their ethnicity longer
- the Northern Subject rule – that is, the use of an uninflected present third plural in cases where the verb is adjacent to the personal pronoun subject. This is a feature common only in Verb-initial languages, which includes Celtic. The rule did not apply in the western parts because it was helped along in the north by the fact that the ON -*a* ending also became zero (cf. White, 2002: 158–60; De Haas, 2011; Klemola, 2013)
- the twofold paradigm of the verb BE in OE (cf. Lutz, 2009; Wischer, 2010)

---

[21] Tristram (2002: 122, fn 17) notes that the dating of early Celtic texts is still disputed but that recent scholars prefer later ms dating, possibly even as late as the thirteenth century. Similar, but less severe, problems exist with respect to the dating of Anglo-Saxon mss.

[22] We ignore shared phonological features here which also exist (cf. the articles in Filppula *et al.*, 2002), but it must be clear that such features strengthen the idea of a Celtic substratum. We also ignore features typical of Irish English only, for such influence see Filppula (1999).

- the use of tag questions rather than straightforward *yes/no* answers (cf. Vennemann, 2009)
- periphrastic DO, first found in ME, also in affirmative clauses, in the (Brythonic) South-West (cf. Tristram, 2002: 126; Klemola, 2002; White, 2002: 160–61)
- the use of the 'expanded form' to express a continuous, repeated activity, which later developed into the progressive (possibly as a blend of the OE gerund and present participle, see Chapter 6) (cf. Tristram, 2002: 126; White, 2002: 161–64; van der Auwera and Genee, 2002)
- the external possessor construction in OE and ME where nowadays a possessive pronoun is used, as in *him bræcon alle þe limes* (*ChronE* (Irvine)1137; 'him [they] broke all the limbs'→'they broke all his limbs'; cf. Poppe, 2009)
- an identity of intensifiers and reflexive pronouns, in Europe typical for Celtic and English only, where *myself, yourself* and so on are used for both (cf. Poppe, 2009, Klemola, 2013); Poppe further suggests that the deviant behaviour in English in terms of the high frequency of verbs that are both causative and inchoative (e.g. *break*) may be related to this
- the use of *and* as a temporal, causal or concessive subordinator (in Celtic followed by a nominative pronoun in a non-finite clause; cf. Ronan, 2002)
- the use of cleft sentences (to convey emphasis), typical in Verb-initial languages and more prolific in English but with a provisional subject 'it' added (other Germanic languages, which are Verb-second, tend to put the emphatic NP in initial position followed by inversion of Subject and Verb – that is, Dutch *Máxima wil ik interviewen!* ['Máxima want I (to)interview'] versus English *It is Máxima that/who I want to interview* (Filppula, 2009)
- the use of embedded inversion, as in *She asked me why was he crying*, which according to Filppula (2000) occurs typically in regional dialects close to areas where Celtic has been or still is spoken

It is important to note that in many if not all of these developments, other system-internal factors may have played a role, as will become clear in discussions in subsequent chapters. For instance, with respect to cleft sentences, Ball (1991) has noted that the fixation of word order contributed to the sudden rise of these constructions in ME, and she also shows how a number of OE constructions, close to clefts in form, may have helped the development in providing a smooth, non-salient transition (similar arguments for a native development can be found in Patten, 2010; Los, 2012: 38ff.).

4.3.4   The Case of French

Most linguists seem to agree that the influence of French on English was mainly restricted to the lexicon (including the use of new affixes), to orthographic changes, and to changes in style including the use of meter and rhyme in poetry. Blake (1992: 16) writes that 'French vocabulary and syntax influence English', but gives no examples of the latter. Where there is influence on syntax, it seems to be restricted to translations (such as has been noticed for Dan Michel of Northgate's *Ayenbite of Inwyt* (fourteenth century), which follows the French original very closely) and to cases where the syntactic structure is based on French vocabulary items (this includes most of the influence on 'English phrasing' that Prins (1952) has noted, examples such as 'to take one's end' as a translation of *prendre fin*). In addition, quite a number of cases are cited where French influence may have reinforced developments in English syntax.

As to influence via French vocabulary, Fischer's (2004, 2006) studies on the position of the adjective in ME making use of a corpus of 1.3 million words, show that the use of post-nominal adjectives cannot be considered a result of French *syntactic* influence because it predominantly continues structures that were already common in OE.[23] Postposed adjectives occurred in OE when more than one adjective was involved (because adjectives could not be stacked as they can nowadays) and when the adjective conveyed new information (see Chapter 5). When these conditions were not observed, we may indeed find postposed adjectives in a 'French' fashion, but it is significant that these cases usually concern French adjectives, and quite often even complete French phrases (i.e. where both noun and adjective are French [as we still see in cases like *The Princess Royal*]). This makes the loan look lexical rather than syntactic.

Other cases for which French influence has been suggested concern mostly structures where a native development can also be discerned, and indeed where similar developments have taken place in other Germanic languages. One concerns the development of the *of*-construction that partly replaces the genitive, which may have been helped along by French *de*. However, Dutch and German developed similar constructions (with *van* and *von*, respectively), and they are part of a general replacement of cases by prepositions (cf. Fischer, 1992b: 226).

Another area concerns *wh*-relatives, which developed only in ME. The discussion of the available literature in Fischer (1992b: 298ff.) shows that a good case can be made for these relatives to have developed out of generalizing relatives, such as OE *swa hwa/hwilc swa* with loss of *swa*, as well as cases in which the interrogative pronoun *hwæt* was used in such a way that it could

---

[23] Nor is it likely to be the result of a typological shift like that of Greenberg, from a SOV to a SVO language, which would cause the reversal of Adjective Noun to Noun Adjective order, as suggested in Lightfoot (1979: 205ff.); because post-nominal adjectives constitute only a very minor pattern, which becomes increasingly less frequent in ModE.

be reinterpreted as an independent relative (*that* [*which*]), or indefinite pronoun (*whatever*; see discussion in Section 5.5.3). It is possible that this development was strengthened by French *qu*-forms, but the fact that *wh*-forms are also found in Dutch and German relatives is suggestive. In addition, *wh*-forms are found earliest in connection with a preceding preposition, and they may therefore also have been used to fill a structural gap because the most frequent ME relative, *þat*, could not be used this way. It is also not likely that the more formal use of the relative, *the which*, is an imitation of French *liquel* as its earliest occurrences are in Northern texts where French influence was slight. It is more likely that *the which* is a contamination of the OE generalizing relatives *se/seo/þæt þe* (which have a pronoun/determiner followed by the relative particle) and *swa hwilc swa* (see Fischer, 1992b: 303).[24]

Another interesting case is the occurrence of causative DO plus bare infinitive, which may have been modelled on French *faire* constructions as argued by Ellegård (1953: 90ff.; cf. (8)),

(8) *Vor he deþ ech þing praysi ase hit is be ri3te worþ*
   (car il fet chascune chose prisier selom sa droite value)
   (*Ayenbite*, Morris 1866: 152,17)
   For he causes praise each thing [each thing to be praised], as it is according to its right value

It is a fact that this use of causative *don* is not found in OE, the normal construction is a *þæt*-clause. Many of these *þæt*-complements became infinitival constructions in ME (cf. Manabe, 1989; Fischer *et al.*, 2000; Los, 2005), which may have also helped this development with DO. However, this construction with DO is rare in ME; normally *haten* or *leten* is used as a causative before an infinitive (cf. Denison, 1985a: 52). It is possible therefore that the DO variant was influenced by French but the analogy with existing *leten/haten* constructions may have been a stronger force (more on DO in Chapter 6).

Haeberli's (2010) study of Anglo-Norman influence on ME also comes to the conclusion that there is little evidence for such influence except possibly in some cases related to Subject–Verb inversion. He shows by means of quantitative evidence that the loss of 'then' as a distinctive trigger for inversion may be due to the fact that in Continental French and Anglo-Norman 'initial adverbs seem to be the weakest triggers of inversion in the thirteenth and fourteenth centuries' (*ibid.*: 151). He also believes French may be responsible for a 'temporary increase of inversion with subject pronouns' because this was 'entirely productive' in both Continental French and Anglo-Norman (p. 161). However, as argued in Section 4.3.2, this increase first occurred in the North

---

[24] Raumolin-Brunberg (2000) provides more information on the social and geographical use of 'the which' in late ME.

and is visible already in early ME (as Haeberli also admits), and it is therefore more likely that the koineization with ON is to 'blame' for this development, possibly further strengthened by French.

All in all, whenever a voice supporting French influence on syntax is raised, the arguments are usually not very persuasive, however much effort may have been put into proving the case. As an example we would like to finish with a consideration of 'the negative relative marker *but*' put forward by Moessner (1999) as a case of 'loan syntax' that became 'an integrated part of the structure of the target language' (1999: 67). It deals with examples such as the following:

(9) *ye shall never se thys shylde but ye shall thynke on me*
     you shall never see this shield but you shall think of me
     (*MorteDarthur*, Moessner 1999: 72)

based on the French:

(10) *cest escu ne verroiz qu'il ne vos doie souvenir de moi*
     this shield not you-will-see that it not to-you must remember of me
     'you will not see this shield without being reminded of me'

First, we note that the similarity between the two clauses is not very close as French uses *que* 'that' – which seems to be a complementizer rather than a relative, while English uses the conjunction *but*. Moreover, ME uses a semantically similar construction with the complementizer *þat* rather than *but*. These are earlier than the fifteenth-century Malory, and are also used outside texts translated from French, see (11).

(11) a *Was non of hem þat he ne gret*
        [there] was not-one of them that he did not weep (i.e. they all wept)
        (*Havelok*(Ld)2160, 13[th]c.)
     b *For wente nevere wye ... through that wildernesse/ That he ne was robbed.*
        'For there was never a man going through that wilderness [in such a way] that he was not robbed' (*PPlowman*,17.100, 14[th]c.)

There is no reason to ascribe the replacement of *þat* by *but* to French influence, instead it is a way of capturing the negative import of the subordinate clause in a stronger manner. The change to *but* can be said to form part of a much more general development towards a standard written language, in which we find 'more clarity and greater explicitness in the system of complex clauses' (Fischer, 1992b: 287).

Considering the situation of French in ME, the lack of syntactic influence is not very surprising because, as shown in Table 4.1, the influence took place via recipient-language agentivity, where the lexicon tends to be mostly involved, unless the contact is very direct and intense involving also the spoken channel, which Table 4.1 shows was not the case.

4.4   A Brief Conclusion

We have tried to show that syntactic borrowing is unlikely to have occurred as a result of contact with Latin and French unless an analogous construction was available in the target language, as was the case with the Latin *aci* construction and possibly French causative *faire*. In such a case the use of the native construction may have been given a boost, but the contact language hasn't really affected the native grammar system as such. In other cases, the similarity between the languages in contact may be accidental because it forms part of a natural native development, as can be shown in the case of relative *which* or the periphrastic genitive construction, which also occurred in other Germanic language that had no close contact with French. Only in the case of ON and quite possible also Celtic contact can we conclude that the syntax of English has been more deeply affected, but here too, not directly by imitation or borrowing, but by means of imperfect learning leading to a reduction of variant forms or to an extension (semantic or formal) of forms already possible in the native grammar.

5   The Noun Phrase

5.1   Introduction

The noun phrase [NP] can occur in various positions within the clausal unit depending on whether it functions as subject, as object (direct or indirect), as complement or as part of an adverbial or prepositional phrase [PP]. In PDE, the place of most clausal constituents is pretty much fixed (except for the Adverbial Phrase which enjoys more freedom), the most usual order being:

NP Subj. – Verbal group ([Aux] V) – [NP Indirect Obj.] – [NP Direct Obj.]
    – [Prepositional Obj.]

(the phrases in brackets are optional depending on the argument structure of the verb). However, the positioning of the NPs is not purely a syntactic matter; it also depends on genre and style and, more importantly, on the organization of the clauses within the larger discourse (i.e. on the role any NP constituent plays in terms of information structure), whether it conveys given or new information, whether it has focus or what its pragmatic function is within the clause. Generally, it can be said that in older English, position was more strongly determined by discourse-pragmatic factors than syntactic ones, resulting in greater positional variation. Thus, in OE, a subject (such as *se biscop* in (1)) could still follow the finite verb, and an object (*ðeosne* in (1)) could precede the verb of which it was an argument (*lædan*),

(1) *Ða   bebead   se biscop ðeosne to him lædan*
    Then commanded the bishop this   to him lead *(Bede, 5 2.388.20)*
    'Then the bishop commanded to lead this person to him'.

Similarly, it was also much more common to place a direct or indirect object, whether fully lexical or pronominal (i.e. *sinoð* in (2) and *him* in (3)), or an adverb(ial phrase) (*þær* in (2), *þurh benedictes gebedum* in (3)) earlier in the clause, even when they were not discourse-prominent or emphatic. In (2), the first time *sinoð* is mentioned, it is in first position to give it focus, while in the second clause in (2) it occurs in first position to indicate the continuation of the topic. In PDE this position would be strange in both cases: focus would probably be conveyed phonologically in the first instance, while the topicality of *sinoð* in the second instance would best be conveyed by making the clause passive, as indicated in our gloss, because in PDE the topic position is usually filled by a subject (see Chapter 9). Note also that PDE would not allow the subject, *Leo papa*, to follow the finite verb in a declarative clause. For the same reason the topicalized pronoun *him* in (3) is placed later in the clause in PDE.

(2) *Þær wæs se papa Leo & se casere, & **mycelne sinoð** þær hæfdon embe Godes*
There was the pope Leo and the emperor and great   synod there had   about God's
*þeowdom; **þone sinoð** foresæt sanctus Leo papa.*
serf-dom that synod fore-sat holy   Leo pope (ChronD(Cubbin)1050.52–53)
'Pope Leo and the emperor were there [i.e. in Rome] and they held a great Synod there about the divine service; the holy Pope Leo presided over the Synod'.

(3) *Þurh   benedictes gebedum **him wæs** se ungesewenlica draca æteowod.*
Through Benedict's prayers him was the invisible   serpent shown
(*ÆCHom.*II,103.390)
'through Benedict's prayers the invisible serpent was shown to him'

The changes that took place diachronically in the position of NPs will be discussed in Chapter 9. Here we will only be concerned with the internal order of elements within the NP.

Just as there are functional slots within the clause, there are similar slots within the NP itself (Quirk *et al.*, 1985: 1238–39; Bache, 2000). The central element within the NP is the head noun. When the head is a common noun, it may be accompanied by a number of modifying elements (with a pronoun head there are usually no modifiers, but see the discussion later in the chapter). When these elements accompany the noun, they usually occur in a specific fixed order in PDE, as shown in Table 5.1.

As far as the order of the slots is concerned, there has been very little change in English (i.e. the major functional slots have always been there).[1] What has in some cases changed, however, is the categorial content of these slots, and the possible combinations of slots that have been allowed at the various stages of the language.[2] In what follows, we look at the various formal categories that could occupy the slots and note changes in the way a slot is filled, 'combinatorial' changes and changes in the forms of these categories. While doing so,

---

[1] The only exception is the peripheral premodifier (e.g. *possibly* in *possibly the oldest church in England* or *even* in *even all the money in the world*), which emerged in the Modern period (Van de Velde, 2011).

[2] Another change, not further discussed here, concerns the increase in the use of premodification especially in the higher registers from the seventeenth century onwards, as noted by Biber and Clark (2002), – that is, the use of more than one premodifying adjective, and the greater use of adjuncts or noun modifiers. This increase may well be connected to the development of denser language use in written standardized prose in the course of time (cf. also Van de Velde, 2009: 354ff.).

Table 5.1. *Element order within the NP in PDE*

Predeterminer	Determiner	Postdeterminer	Premodifier	Modifier	Head	Postmodifier
quantifiers	articles, quantifiers, genitives, demonstratives, possessive/interrogative/relative pronouns	quantifiers, numerals, specialized adjectives	adverbials, some adjectives	adjectives, adjuncts	noun, proper name, pronoun	prepositional phrase, relative clause (some adjectives) (quantifiers?)
	the	*usual*			*price*	
	any	*other*		*embarrassing*	*details*	
	a		*potentially*	*unpleasant*	*encounter*	
half	*our*		*pretty*		*meetings*	*with the chairman*
	a			*decibel*	*level*	*that made your ears ache*
both	*these*	*two*		*criminal*	*activities*	

we will see that it is not always easy to distinguish between the various categories: adverbs, for instance, could look like adjectives (and still can in some cases), adjectives could be freely used as nouns, adjuncts and adjectives were not always distinguishable, quantifiers shared certain features with adjectives, and so on. When discussing these categories, we also sometimes point to features which do not strictly concern the internal make-up of the NP, but which are relevant to the category in question or which have undergone considerable change.

5.2   The Head of the Noun Phrase

The head of the NP is usually a common noun, but it can also be a name or a pronoun; the latter are mostly used by themselves, with all other functional slots left empty. Syntactically, there have been few changes here. Most of the changes that the noun has undergone concern losses, such as the loss of case endings and the loss of gender. These morphological changes, however, have had repercussions on the syntax. The loss of case, for instance, meant that, in certain constructions, the functional role that the head nouns play in the clause (i.e. that of subject or indirect object) had to be expressed by other means, such as a preposition or a fixed position (see Chapters 7 and 9, respectively); the loss of gender caused changes in the anaphorical or referential system. Thus, in OE, an anaphorical pronoun linked with the head of a NP would usually agree with the *grammatical* gender of that head noun:

(4) *Se hrof eac swilce   hæfde mislice heahnysse: on sumre stowe **hine man** mihte mid*
    the roof also likewise had various height: in certain place *him* one could with
    heafde geræcan, on sumre mid handa earfoðlice
    head   touch   in certain with hand barely (*ÆCHom*.I,34 468.101)
    'The roof likewise varied in height: in one place one could touch *it* with one's head, in another only just with one's hand'.

In (4), the masculine noun *hrof* needs to be referred to by the masculine form of the personal pronoun (i.e. *hine*). The same would hold for any anaphoric relative, demonstrative or interrogative pronoun. From ME onwards (somewhat earlier in the North than the South), we find *natural* rather than *grammatical* gender being used so that the reference to *roof* will be by means of *it* since *roof* is inanimate. In some cases, OE already made use of natural gender, especially for words which referred to male or female humans, such as *ænne wifman* [MASC] ... **heo** [FEM], 'a woman ... *she*' (*ÆCHom*.I,1 181.88). The demonstrative pronoun, however, being closer to the noun, would normally show grammatical gender in OE (i.e. *þæt wif*), rather than *seo wif*. It is interesting to see that the distance between noun and anaphor in the choice of gender also plays a role in modern Dutch and German (cf. Kraaikamp, 2017).

5.2.1. *Pronouns as Head*

Personal and indefinite pronouns can function by themselves as heads, while other pronouns such as relatives, interrogatives and demonstratives, can be either head or determiner of a nominal head.

Personal pronouns occasionally occur with a modifier in PDE, as in *poor old me*, *us girls*, and *he in the corner*. In such usages, they are in fact similar to referential nouns. Denison (1998: 106ff.), from whom the examples below have been taken, notes an interesting diachronic change in these forms when they function as subject or subject complement: the older nominative form in such combinations came to be replaced by the oblique form. This is a late ModE innovation, which affects not only modified pronouns (compare the earlier example in (5a) with the later one in (5b)), but also personal pronouns used emphatically (see (6)) or used as a subject (complement) not occurring in the usual subject position (see (7)).

(5) a That poor *I* must write helter-skelter (1832 Gaskell, *Lett.*2,p.2)
   b The miserable little *me* to be taken up and loved after tearing myself to pieces (1879 Meredith, *Egoist,*xlviii.606)

(6) a 'Not *she*,' said the Psammead a little crossly (1906 Nesbit, *Amulet*, viii,146)
   b 'Not *me*!' was Gerald's unhesitating rejoinder (1907 Nesbit, *Enchanted Castle*,I,26)

(7) a The children were as white as *he* (1906 Nesbit, *Amulet,*v.83)
   b for they are quite as well educated as *me* (1816 Austen, *Emma* I.iv.31)
   (spoken by the 'vulgar' Harriet Smith)

The change is quite recent; in the nineteenth century the oblique forms were still considered vulgar, but in our days they are normal even in educated speech. For some speakers, indeed, they are still a source of uncertainty, especially when coordinated, as in 'X and me/myself/I'.

5.2.2 *Adjectives as Heads*

When adjectives were still declined (in OE), showing case, number and gender, we frequently come across adjectives used substantively (i.e. as nouns), as the examples in (8) show.

(8) a he gehælde **untrume** on ðæs Hælendes naman, blinde and deafe
   he healed infirm[ACC.PL]in the Saviour's name, blind and deaf
   (*ÆLS*(Mark)45)
   'he healed sick people in the name of the Saviour, blind as well as deaf people'

b *Forþam   sona   gif he ænine **pearfan nacodne**   gemette, þone*
Therefore at-once if he any   needy   naked [both ACC.SG] met,   that-one
he scrydde
he clothed (*GD*.1(H)9.68.6)
'Therefore as soon as he came across a poor man who was naked, he would
clothe him'

These adjectives could be used generically to refer to a whole group, as in PDE
(*the French, the poor*), but they could also be used to refer to a specific subset,
person or thing, as is the case in (8b). This is now possible only with a small,
relic group of participial adjectives: *the accused, my beloved* and others. The
loss of non-generic usage is probably due to the increasing inflectional attrition
in the ME period. It is notable, in this respect, that in other Germanic languages
such as Dutch and German – where (some) gender and number distinctions (in
German also case) have been preserved – these substantival adjectives are still
possible, either via specific adjectival endings or via the form of the determiner.

Specific usage survived for a while, especially in poetry, but by the end of
the eModE period it had all but disappeared. In the meantime, the numeral *one*
(the element that came to be added to the adjective as a 'propword') had been
developing into an indefinite (personal) pronoun in the ME period, meaning
both 'a certain' as well as being used non-specifically, in the sense of 'someone' (e.g. *Þare cam on and seruede* 'there came [some] one and served', *Sleg*
(Ld)227: 282). Later in the fifteenth century, perhaps under the influence of the
Old French pronoun *on*, it also develops into a generic pronoun, used at first in
subject function, where it replaces the OE indefinite pronoun *man*.[3] At the
same time, also in ME, it begins to be used as an anaphoric pronoun, replacing
an earlier NP. This probably led to an extension from personal 'one' to general
'one', and hence to the prop-word 'one', which thus filled the gap that the loss
of adjectival endings had created.

The last phase of this development is described in detail in Rissanen
(1967: 73ff.). He shows that the future propword *one* first appears in the
thirteenth century in two different usages. It is found with an adjective, but
here two of the three instances found concern superlatives, and the third
instance involves *so*, making it likely that *one* is used as an intensifier. Next
to that, *one* is attested as an anaphor, but here it refers to a previous noun
without an adjective being involved, as in *He rents a house but I own one* (cf.
Rissanen, 1967: 63ff). In both these usages, *one* is first used only to refer to
people, not to things, and it is only as an anaphor that it begins to be used quite
soon also to refer to inanimate nouns. A more general use of *one* only becomes

---

[3] The loss of *man* as an indefinite pronoun is not connected to the rise of *one*, as Los (2002) has
convincingly shown, but the result of the loss of V2 (see Chapter 9), phonetic weakening,
homonymy with plural 'men', and the loss of number in verbs.

possible in the sixteenth century. An interesting fact is that all the early uses of *one* occur in indefinite NPs (i.e. *a good one* and not *the good one* – that is, it first appears in the least generic cases). Also noteworthy is that the earliest instances of adjective + *one* are found with superlatives. Presumably, this was done for emphasis because superlatives, which are by their very nature generic, can still even now occur without *one*.

5.3 Determiners

5.3.1 Articles and Demonstratives

The most common determiner in PDE is the article (definite *the* and indefinite *a(n)*). It is therefore perhaps rather surprising that in the very earliest stages of English there was no article at all, as is still the case in quite a number of languages (e.g. in Finnish, most Slavonic languages and Japanese). When a language develops an article system through a process of grammaticalization,[4] it usually does so using a limited number of sources: definite articles generally develop out of demonstrative pronouns, while indefinite articles stem from the numeral 'one', or sometimes from a quantifier (e.g. *sum* in OE, see (9b); cf. Heine and Kuteva, 2002: 109–10, 220–21). There is also a more or less fixed path of development for articles: the article first appears in positions in which the NP is presentational or referential – that is, it plays some role in the further discourse (see the examples in (9)), while it is slower to develop when the NP functions predicatively, as in (10), or generically, contrast (11a) with (11b), and slower still when the NP is in the scope of a modal or a negative element, as in (12).

(9) a *Đa wæs hwæþere **an** man rihtwis ætforan gode. se wæs noe gehaten*
   Then was still   a man righteous before God who was Noah called
   (OE, ÆCHom.I,1.185.181)
   'Still, there was then a man, righteous in the eyes of God, called Noah'

---

[4] Grammaticalization does not *explain why* an article system develops, as indicated in Chapter 3. Why it did so in some Indo-European languages (Germanic, Romance) but not in others (e.g. Slavonic) is still a matter of research. Sommerer (2015) points to factors such as inflectional loss, pattern analogy and phonotactic causes; these may have played a role already in OE. As to patterning, she notes on the basis of quantitative corpus evidence that most OE DPs [Determiner Phrase] have an initial slot filled by a determiner (a possessive or demonstrative pronoun, or genitive phrase), which may have led to a general $[[X_{determinative} + [Y_{common\ noun}]\ \text{HEAD}]\ \text{DP}\ _{definite}]$ schema becoming cognitively entrenched. For a discussion of whether OE already possessed a separate determiner category or whether the determiner should still be considered an adjective or pronoun, see Denison (2006). Breban (2012) shows how the generalization of the OE determiners into pure articles may, through functional shifts, have set the development of a determiner category in motion, which in turn may have led to other complex determiner types such as *the same* and *a certain*.

b ... & *þa sæt þær* **sum** *blind man be ðam wege:*
... and then sat there a   blind man by the way (OE, *ÆCHom*.I, 258.11)
'... and there by the wayside sat a blind man'

(10) a *Þa wearð   nerfa swiðe arfæst   man to casere   gecoren*
then became never Ø very honourable man as emperor chosen
(OE, *ÆCHom*.I,4 207.33)
'there was never then [a] very honourable man chosen to be emperor'
b ... *þat it is Ø meruaylle* ...
'... that it is [a] miracle ...' (late ME, *Mandeville*(Tit)104.17)
c ... *that were **a** greet merveille* (late ME, Chaucer,*Boece*,IV.1150–55)

(11) a *Brutus nom Ignogen, & into Ø scipe lædde* ...
'Brutus took Ignogen, and led [her] into [the] ship (on board)'
heo wunden up Ø seiles
'they hoisted [the] sails' (early ME, *Laʒ.Brut*(Clg)551–3)
b *Philotetes anon **the** sayle up droughe*
'Philotetes at once drew up the sail' (late ME, Chaucer,*LGW*.1459)

(12) *For 'of a thousand men,' seith Salomon, 'I foond o good man,*
'For among one thousand men,' Salomon says, 'I found one good one,
but certes, of alle wommen, Ø good womman foond I nevere.'
but certainly among all women, I never found [a] good woman.'
(late ME, Chaucer,*W.ofB.Prol*.1055)

In OE, therefore, (in)definiteness could still be expressed without articles. The standard way to express it was by means of weak and strong forms of the adjective (as is still the case in Modern German) although a demonstrative pronoun functioning as a kind of article usually occurred already in early OE prose to indicate definiteness in combination with the weak form of the adjective. Thus in (9b) and (10a), the adjectives *blind* and *arfæst* introducing indefinite NPs are strong ((10a) is also article-less), while in (13) the definite NPs are preceded by both a demonstrative and a weak adjective (*unspedigan, rican*),

(13) *Caseras   he geceas ac þeah he geendebyrde þone unspedigan fiscere ætforan*
emperors he chose and yet   he ranked   the unwealthy fisherman before
þam rican casere
the   rich   emperor (*ÆCHom*.I,38 508.34)

In ME, indefinite presentative *an* (as found in OE (9a)) becomes truly separate from the numeral *ān*, in that a formal distinction develops between the two. The OE numeral *ān* develops regularly into ME *oon*, with the long vowel remaining but becoming more back and close (i.e. [ɔː]); in the northern dialects the vowel becomes [aː], while the vowel in the article is reduced to short [a], and the word loses the final nasal when the next word begins with a consonant. This phonetic development is linked to the fact that the form *an* encroaches both on the territory of the zero article (cf. (10a)–(12)), as well as on the other indefinite marker *sum* (cf. (9b)) thus becoming more frequent and bleached of its original meaning (as typically happens in a grammaticalization process). *Sum* itself became specialized in ME, occurring mainly with plurals and nouns used generically, which is still its use in PDE.

The use of articles is somewhat variable in geographical names, names referring to places, diseases and body parts. In OE, ME and eModE, it was still usual for river names to be article-less (*yn Tempse* 'in the Thames'). Concerning places, an article is now often used when a specific building is referred to, so as to distinguish it from the general institution (*school, hospital,* etc.). There are still some interesting cases of article omission (or reduction) in present-day northern dialects. It is not quite clear whether this usage is a reflex of the OE situation or indeed a new development. What causes it also needs to be investigated further. Hollmann and Siewierska (2011: 32ff.), who provide a useful overview of the literature on this topic, suggest that it may be related to frequency, information structure as well as social identity. With body parts, OE usually had no article. Thus, the phrase *mid heafde* 'with head' in (4) lacks an article; in fact, there is only one instance of a phrase containing *heaf(o)d* with an article in the whole of the OE corpus: *ge scylan wyrcan rode tacen upp on þæm heafde* 'you must make the sign of the cross on *the* head' (*ÆLet*.3 (Wulfstan)2.6). From ME onwards the definite article (and later also a possessive pronoun) is the more usual option: *And with his fest he smoot* ['hit'] *me on the heed* (Chaucer,*W.ofB.Prol*.795). Use of the article with names of diseases seems mainly lexically determined; there has been no clear diachronic change here. For example, it is usually *the plague*, while with *flu* and *measles* both presence and absence of *the* are and have been possible; other, less widespread diseases have generally been article-less, presumably because these function more like proper nouns.

The deictic system, too, changed rapidly in the early ME period, with the simple (distal) demonstrative (OE *sē, sēo, þæt,* plur. *þā*) splitting out into the invariant article *þe* 'the' and the distal demonstrative sg. *þat* 'that' and pl. *þō* (*þat* also continued to be used as an article for a while, especially before the quantifiers *oon* 'one' and *oþer* 'other', still surviving in some northern dialects as *the toon* and *the tother*). The OE proximal demonstrative (*þes, þis, þēos,* plur. *þās*) kept its function. In ME, we find proximal *þes/þis* at first used indiscriminately in the singular and the plural (with Northern *þis* slowly replacing Southern *þes*). At first, we also find another plural proximal *þōs* (with the regular phonetic development of [ɑː] to [ɔː]), but because this form was rather similar to distal *þō* (the regular development of OE *þā*), these forms soon became ambiguous (also because the -*s* tended to be misanalyzed as a plural marker). The two forms therefore collapsed, and *þōs* 'those' became the new distal plural form. The origin of the present proximal plural 'these' is not clear; in later ME this plural is generally written with an <e> at the end, probably a diacritic to indicate the length of the stem-vowel. The vowel may be long on analogy of the OE plural *þās*, on analogy of the new ME distal plural, or it may be related to the OE feminine form *þēos*, which would give [e:] in ME.

5.3.2   The Genitive Phrase and Other Determiners

Other common determiners occurring all through the history of English are possessive and genitive phrases, interrogative, indefinite and relative pronouns, and quantifiers (as in '*his*' or '*Tom's* daughter', '*which* daughter did you meet?', you can take *what* book you like', 'the woman, *whose* daughter. . .', '*some* passers-by' respectively – note that the determiner-relative *whose* is in fact also a genitive phrase). Syntactically, not much has changed concerning the possessive, interrogative and indefinite determiners. Important categorial changes, however, have taken place in the relatives, which are dealt with in Section 5.5.3.

Most genitive phrases in PDE are functionally similar to possessive pronouns, but this was not always the case. There are two main developments to be noted in the use of the genitive phrase, a formal and a functional one; these are closely linked. Formally, the genitive case in nominal phrases gradually lost ground to a prepositional phrase with *of*. Mustanoja (1960: 75) shows how the *of*-phrase rose rapidly from barely 1 per cent of all genitives in the NP in OE, to roughly 85 per cent in late ME. Rosenbach (2002: 177ff.) has studied the development after 1400, noticing that there was a revival of the *s*-genitive after ME in certain functions (see the discussion later in this Section). The new *of*-construction itself is probably native (cf. similar developments in other Germanic languages) but may have been aided by the French *de*-phrase (cf. Chapter 4). The real 'culprit' in the diminishing use of the inflectional genitive was of course the general loss of inflections that marked the ME period. The genitive, although functionally one of the 'stronger' case-forms, gradually became eroded so that by late ME of all the variant OE forms (with inflections in -*an*/-*es*/-*e*/-*a*/-*ena*, depending on type of declension, gender and number) only the phonetically stronger -(*e*)*s* form remained, being analogically extended to all nouns and also doing duty for both the singular and the plural. Some OE nouns, such as *modor* 'mother', had the same form in the singular for nominative and genitive. For such nouns, it is possible that a zero-type of genitive survived in phrases like *mother tongue* (OE *Bæde þu forþi þinre modor spræce* 'oppress therefore your mother tongue', *ÆLS*(Julian&Basilissa) 3.5 353) although it is not unlikely that such phrases were looked upon as compounds already in OE considering the fact that we also find *modorcild* 'mother's child' and *modorcynn* 'mother's family, spelled as one word in OE. Whether *modor* itself is to be considered a genitive within such a compound is difficult to decide. After all, we find both genitive and nominative compounds in OE, cf. *dægeseage* 'day's eye' > daisy', *landmann* as well as *landesman* 'country ('s) man', *sunne beam* 'sunbeam' with nominative case as well as *sunnanleoman* 'sunlight' with a genitive.

The -(*e*)*s* form itself has undergone further formal change in that, in the course of the ME period, it stops behaving like a true case ending (for details see Allen, 2008: 152ff.). First, the genitive NP became fixed in prenominal position – that is, it could no longer occur after the head noun, as was still possible in OE (cf. *heretoga þæs folces* 'leader of-the people' (*ÆCHom*.I,12 (Pref)531.1) versus *þæs folces ealdor* 'the people's lord', (*Mald*.202)).[5] Secondly, the close link between noun and case inflection became loosened so that by the beginning of the ME period we begin to come across the so-called group-genitive. While in OE both name and rank would have to be inflected (*be Eadweardes cynges fullra leafe* 'by Edward[GEN] king[GEN] full permission', *Chr*.1478 24), in ME the genitive would simply follow the last noun in the group, *Þe laferrd Cristess karrte* 'the Lord Christ's chariot' (*Orm*.56). In later ME, by which time -*es* could be used with all nouns, the inflection could also be added to a descriptive PP following the head noun, as in *the god of slepes heyr* 'the god of sleep's heir' (Chaucer,*BD*.168), thereby loosening the link between case and head noun even further. Later still, even *of*-phrases referring to origin became part of the 'group' so that late ME *the kyng Priamus sone of Troye* (Chaucer,*T&C*.I,2) turned into *the king of Spaines armadas* (Camberlain 94, Rissanen, 1999: 202) in eModE, with a few examples already occurring at the end of the fourteenth century (cf. Allen, 2008: 153). This construction became the norm in the sixteenth century; the last examples of the earlier one (the so-called split-genitive) are found in the second half of the seventeenth century.

A third formal change concerns the appearance of the separate word (*h*)*is* for the suffix -(*e*)*s*, as in *Of Seth, ðe was adam is sune* 'Of Seth, who was Adam's son' (*Gen&Ex*(A)493, Allen, 2008: 223). This has often been interpreted as the replacement of the genitive case-ending by a possessive pronoun (rather like the development that took place in Dutch, German and Afrikaans, cf. Dutch *Anna/Daan d'r/z'n fiets* 'Anna's/Daan's bike', lit.: 'Anna/Daan her/his bike'), which then developed into a syntactic clitic (cf. Janda, 1980), which in turn made possible the development of the group-genitive discussed earlier (a

---

[5] An apparent exception to this rule is the so-called double genitive (i.e. the *a friend of John's* type), where we do find a genitive NP after the head noun (as well as an *of*-phrase). This type dates from the end of the ME period and may be a kind of ellipsis, not a true postnominal genitive. The earliest types can be read as partitives (but cf. Allen, 2002), as in *Gif ðu him lanst ani þing of ðinen* 'If you lend him anything [out]of your [things, property]' (*Vices&V*(1)(Stw) 77:21, Fischer, 1992: 232), with the final head noun left out.

syntactic clitic has a freer position than an inflectional ending, which must be tied to its head). Allen (2008: 223ff., summarizing her earlier work), however, shows that this scenario is unlikely since clear versions of the possessive pronoun (i.e. examples with *her* and *their*, which unlike (*h*)*is* are not ambiguous) only appear from the mid-sixteenth century onwards. It is much more likely that (*h*)*is* was at first simply a variant of the inflectional ending, which by the end of the fourteenth century developed into an invariant clitic making the group-genitive possible, and that this clitic was later occasionally misanalyzed as a possessive pronoun, an analysis which never took a firm hold in English.[6]

Apart from formal changes, there were also functional ones. The genitive in OE could express a wide range of meanings, but in ME the use of the *s*-genitive became more and more restricted to the possessive and the subjective function, as in *Alfred's book*, where *Alfred* is a possessor, and *the newspaper's attack on ...*, where *newspaper* is the agent of *attack* (and hence in a subject-like relation to its head noun). At the same time, objective and partitive genitives became rare. Thus, the OE objective genitive *saula neriend* 'souls' saviour' (*KtPs.*16), was replaced in ME by *the saviour of souls*, and the partitive *husa selest* 'houses' best' (*Beo.*144) became *the best of houses*. Many factors have been brought forward to account for these functional restrictions, conveniently summarized in Allen (2008: 158ff.).

In partitive expressions, the most usual order in OE was already head noun followed by genitive, as in *fela tacna* 'many [of-]signs', except with pronouns where both orders (*heora an/an heora* 'their one'/ 'one their' – that is, 'one of them') occurred.[7] The postnominal order became the rule in ME (cf. Rosenbach 2002: 178), but *of* was inserted because the only possible position for an inflectional genitive was now prenominal. Another possibility, especially after numerals and quantifiers, was to simply leave out *of* as an indication of case, so that *twa hund scipa*[GEN] became 'two hundred ships' (this was made even easier by the fact that the original case-forms in the plural had all become -(*e*)*s*, by analogy, so that in fact the genitive plural case looked like a bare plural).

The functional loss of most objective genitives may be related to the fixing of the *s*-genitive before the head noun in a different way: the general change in basic word order from SOV to SVO may have influenced the development. In possessive and subjective genitives, the genitive NP can be said to have a

---

[6] Allen (2008: 186ff.) compares the English situation with the 'possessor doubling' constructions in other Germanic languages, and shows convincingly that the developments are quite different on a number of crucial points (*ibid*: 218).

[7] The order *heora an* is about four times as frequent as *an heora*. The difference seems to be one of emphasis, *an heora* being used when *an* is more particularised while *heora an* refers to any person in the group no matter who.

subject-like relation to the head noun, either as possessor or as agent, and the order GEN-head noun therefore fits in well with the predominant SV order of both OE (predominant in main clauses) and ME. In the case of the objective genitive, the order GEN-head noun (as in *saula neriend* 'of-souls saviour') may have become less natural when the OV order (which in OE was still a regular order in subordinate finite and non-finite clauses) had changed to VO in the ME period. Mitchell (1985: §1281ff.) already noted the awkward ambiguity of objective genitives in OE, where *godes lufu* could refer to both 'God's love [for us]' and '[our] love for God', which some OE writers already disambiguated by using a prepositional phrase (*Cristes lufe on us, ÆCHom.* II,21 182.69) or a relative clause.[8] Rosenbach *et al.* (2000: 192–93) show that the *s*-genitive became increasingly associated with subjective genitives, and less so with objective genitives after 1500. Allen (2008: 167ff.), however, argues that other factors, such as the 'Affectedness Constraint' also play a role: the objective genitive is still usual with highly affected nouns as in 'the president's assassination', 'the queen's betrayers' or 'John's murderer'. The reasons for some of these 'exceptional' cases may well be different, however. A subjective genitive may be virtually impossible with 'betrayer' and 'murderer' because these nouns themselves mark an agent and so cannot have another (genitive) agent. In contrast, with a noun like 'assassination' the salient element is the person killed and not the killer, which is therefore likely to be the topical element for which first position is usual.

The more recent revival of the *s*-genitive (as noted in Rosenbach *et al.*, 2000; Rosenbach, 2002) is related to the narrowing of its use outlined previously. During ME, selection of an *s*-genitive over the periphrastic *of*-phrase comes more and more to depend on agency, animacy and topicality. Hence, it becomes the norm for the *s*-genitive to occur with all human possessors. Discourse factors also play a role in the choice; thus, when the human possessor is topical, the incidence of *s*-genitives is noticeably higher than when the possessor is not topical. In this way, after a quite general loss, the *s*-genitive slowly rehabilitates itself in a clearly defined niche. Next, Görlach (1999: 80) notes a subsequent 'large-scale extension to non-possessives', such as in 'the book's content', which he notes is 'predominantly a twentieth-century development' (although Rosenbach (2007) shows that the process starts in ModE). Here topicality and the emergence of a more formal academic style may both be involved. We see in Section 5.5.1 that discourse or information structure requirements also play a role in syntactic (word-order) changes involving adjectives.

---

[8] Jane Austen, with her archaic use of language, seems to have been among the last to use the objective genitive. Phillipps (1970: 163) notes her use of 'his sight' and 'his praise', meaning the 'sight/praise of him'.

5.3.3   Double Determiners

In PDE the determiner slot can only be filled by one element. This was not the case in OE, where we find combinations of demonstrative and possessive pronouns, and also possessive/genitive phrases and demonstratives, as in *se heora arwyrða bisceop* 'the their venerable bishop'(LS.25(MichaelMor)88) and *on Godes þa gehalgodan cyricean* (*HomU*.20(*BlHom*.10)66) 'in God's the hallowed church', respectively. Some examples are still found in early ME but they soon die out in common usage.[9] The reason is presumably that most genitive phrases (especially pronominal ones such as *his*, and *hiera*) came to be treated as definite determiners (which happened when a separate determiner/article system came into existence in ME); having a genitive as well as a demonstrative would therefore be tantamount to expressing definiteness twice. This development could therefore be seen as part of a larger development in which an explicit determiner system developed, but as Allen (2008: 98ff.) indicates, the situation is complex and not completely clear in that there are also indications that possessive/genitive phrases already functioned as definite determiners in OE. Allen (2012) furthermore notes that constructions with the order Possessive-Determiner always appear with an adjective before the noun, which is not necessarily the case with the reverse order, the Determiner-Possessive (which by the way is the one that can still be found, see Note 9). In addition, the Poss-Det order occurs only with the demonstrative *se, seo, þæt*, which also functioned as a definite article. Allen suggests that this construction was used in order to indicate that the adjective contained already known information (the usual role of the definite article) and hence was non-restrictive. Thus, in the phrase *þurh his þa halgan acenesse* 'through his the holy birth' (Allen, 2012: 259) referring to Christ's holy birth, possibly the definite article would have been used to draw *extra* attention to the non-restrictive adjective *halig* (non-restrictive because, from an information point of view, it was already known that Christ's birth was 'holy'). That the construction was lost in early ME may be connected according to Allen with the loss of the 'substantival' adjective in the same period (see Section 5.2.2), where the adjective was also preceded by a determiner.

---

[9] Rissanen (1999: 206) and Denison (1998: 115) notice leftovers of this usage in early and late ModE, but both remark that these are found only in archaic texts or texts of a legal nature. Both Denison (*ibid.*) and Traugott (1992: 173) also indicate that some of these examples may have to be read as NPs in apposition (e.g. interpreting *se heora arwyrða bisceop* as 'he / this one, their venerable bishop'). Demonstratives followed by possessives, also in apposition, is still a possible construction in PDE, as Allen (2008: 274) points out, but only it seems with proximal demonstratives, as in '. . . on this, his third NASA assignment'. For similar ideas on modifiers having originally developed out of appositions, see Van de Velde (2009).

Note finally that in PDE we can still have a combination of an article or demonstrative with a genitive, as in 'the plane's flight was smooth' and in phrases like 'these elegant women's watches'. In the former, the article is part of the genitive phrase, and does not directly modify the head noun, while in the latter the genitive functions as a classifier: 'women's' modifies 'watches' (i.e. it functions like an adjective and not a determiner).

5.4   Pre- and Postdeterminers

The predeterminer category is the least clearly defined category in the NP. The elements that can occur there (mainly quantifiers) very often also occur in other slots (e.g. *such* would be a predeterminer in 'such a to-do', a determiner in 'such people' and a postdeterminer in 'another such holiday'). Likewise *all* and *both* function as predeterminers in 'all/both the girls', but more or less the same meaning is also conveyed by the expressions 'all/both girls' (with *all* and *both* as determiners), and 'all/both of the girls' (with *all* and *both* as pronominals), and even 'the girls ... all/both'. Quantifiers, in fact, are generally mobile, both as regards position and function: they may function as pronominals (indefinite pronouns) as well as semi-adverbials (*all soaked he was*) and peripheral modifiers (*she was all gentleness*). It is not surprising therefore that they occur in many of the slots given in Table 5.1.

The quantifiers that can occur before the determiner are fairly restricted in PDE (only *all*, *both* and *half* occur here). In ME (with some instances already attested for OE) other quantifiers were found there too, such as *each* (OE *ælc an hagelstan* 'each a hailstone', *HomU*.36(Nap 45)51, ME *þurh out vch a toune* 'throughout each a town', *Horn*(Hrl)218), *some* (OE *sume þa englas* 'some the angels', *ÆCHom*.I,7 236.147, ME *some þe messagers*, *Glo.Chron.A*(Clg)2718), *(m)any* (ME *ony the other eyght*, Caxton's Preface, *Malory*,p.2), and in ME *all* and *both* could be combined (*alboth this thynges*, *Yonge S.Secr.*207.37–8). There seems to be an increasingly general tendency to insert *of* between a quantifier and the definite article. In PDE it is the rule with *some* and *any*, which are used without *of* in the OE/ME examples given here. The beginning of this development is in fact already visible in OE, where the noun following *sume* could be either in the same case as *sume* (*sume þa englas,*) or in the (partitive) genitive (*sume þara synna* 'some of-the sins' *Res.A*3.25,76). The new *of*-form is found already in ME after *some* and *any*, but has become current only much more recently with *all* and *both* (Denison, 1998: 117, notes that the *of*-less construction was still the most usual one in the nineteenth century).

Most of the changes concerning these quantifiers seem to be the result of the straightening out of the determiner system (with the quantifiers now acting as determiners themselves), which fully developed only in ME, and also of the gradual decrease in the floating positions of (some of) the quantifiers. In OE the quantifiers could still occur in almost any slot, so we could have *some the men ate .., the men some ate . . ., and also the men ate some . . .*'. When the number of slots decreased, probably due to word order becoming more and more fixed in ME, some of these quantifiers or their positions disappeared (e.g. *the men some* was lost but not *the men all*) while others became reanalysed (e.g. in *some the men,* the word *some* came to be seen as an indefinite pronoun and consequently *of* was added).

Other elements that can occur before an *in*definite article, apart from quantifiers such as *each* (in OE/ME, see earlier discussion), *such* and *many*, are the indefinite pronouns *what* and *which*. This usage with both quantifiers and *wh*-elements seems to have started in earnest in early ME, with only one or two examples found in OE (e.g. *hwylc an scep* 'which a sheep' *HomU*.42(Nap 52) 12) and *swylc an litel cicel* 'such a little cake', *PeriD*.20.13.30). The construction may have appeared as a result of inflectional *schwa*-endings being reinterpreted as the indefinite article (as argued for similar constructions in Dutch by Van de Velde and van der Horst, 2013). The same mechanisms can account for another construction that also first appears in ME, of the type *so hardy a here* 'so brave an army' (*Gawain*, 59). That these constructions possibly arose out of confusion need not mean that they are without function. Rissanen (1967: 252) states that the separation of predeterminer and noun makes the whole phrase more emphatic.

Postdeterminers in PDE are essentially also quantifiers, including ordinal and cardinal numerals, as in *the many girls, the two girls, the second girl*. Not many changes have occurred here except that again the floating possibilities of quantifiers and numerals have been reduced so that the postdeterminer position is now the most normal one. In ME, the group of postdeterminers was somewhat larger; for example, *both* could still occur here too, as in *his boþe armes* (*Gawain*, 582). Concerning position, the numerals and *other*, which are now restricted to postdeterminer position, could still occur as predeterminer in OE and ME (*oþre twegen þa fæmnan*, 'other two the women', *Mart*.5(Kotzor) Se, 16,A.17), especially before a superlative: OE *twa þa halegestan fæmnan*, two the holiest women (*Mart*.5(Kotzor)My,1,A.11), ME *Þre þe beste iles* 'three the best islands' (*Glo.Chron.A*.(Clg)34). These 'predeterminer-constructions became replaced by *of*-constructions, just as happened with *some* and *any* discussed previously. Again, it should be noted that in OE, we may find a (partitive) genitive after these numerals as well as a case-form that shows concord with the numeral. With the loss of cases, these now caseless forms went on to exist for a while until they came to be replaced by *of*-constructions.

An interesting diachronic development is the use of more and more adjectives as postdeterminers. An adjective like *other* was already in use as a cardinal numeral and postdeterminer in OE, next to a purely adjectival use in the sense of 'different in nature/quality'; similarly OE *ilca* 'same' functioned as a postdeterminer. Other adjectives have joined the group in the course of time. Davidse *et al.* (2008) sum up the circumstances under which this happens, involving a process of grammaticalization and subjectivization in which the original adjective slowly loses its syntactic and descriptive semantic properties – that is, they lose their gradeability (the comparative and superlative forms) and their use in predicative function, they form a unit with the determiner (sometimes even reflected orthographically, as in *another*, cf. Dutch *hetzelfde* 'the +same'), and they no longer modify the head noun, shifting from adjectives used in the propositional domain describing the external world, to adjectives used in the textual domain (in the sense of Sweetser, 1990). Adjectives that have followed this path include *different, opposite, complete, old, famous, regular* and *necessary* (some adverbs are also involved such as *then, late, sometime*). Often they can still be used both as postdeterminers and as adjectives, as in 'He goes out with a different girl every night' versus 'Her second book turns out to be very different from her first one', respectively. Davidse *et al.* (2008) illustrate the development for a number of adjectives, in which they show on the basis of quantitative corpus evidence how their fully lexical use is always diachronically earlier, and how the postdeterminer function encroaches slowly on the modifier one, steadily gaining in frequency over time. For instance, with respect to *similar*, they found that the postdeterminer use 'emerged as a small fraction (averaging less than 10 percent *vis-à-vis* lexical full uses) in lModE, but have increased in PDE to 30 percent of all uses': (Davidse *et al.*, 2008: 479). More in-depth discussion on some of these adjectives can be found in Breban (2010) and Ghesquière (2014).

5.5   Modifiers

5.5.1   *Central Modifiers*

Adjectives are the prototypical modifiers. Adjectives are also one of the most difficult categories to define. The reason for this is that they share many of the characteristics of the class of nouns and of verbs. Indeed, there are languages without an adjective-class, their function being performed by nouns and/or verbs. Van de Velde (2009: 169ff.) and others before him have argued that adjectives only became a separate category after the Proto-Indo-European stage, before that time functioning as nouns in apposition. Adjectives are interesting, therefore, from a diachronic viewpoint because they are less well-established as a category, making them a more likely target for change.

Adjectives in English have two distinct functions: they can be predicative (as in *the rhythm is important*) or attributive (as in *contemporary poetry*). In the former case they are closer to the verbal end of the continuum because together with the copula verb they form the predicate, and in the latter case they may (but need not) be closer to the nominal end of the cline. There are various formal means of distinguishing between these two functions: it may be done by position, by intonation or stress, or by inflection. In the history of English, there have been important changes in these formal means, which is the main topic of our discussion here.

Predicative adjectives are always non-restrictive that is, they give *extra* information about the head noun). From a discourse point of view they are often salient because they convey 'new' rather than 'given' information. It has been noted in discourse and in typological studies that the more salient exponents of a category tend to be more clearly or more explicitly marked (cf. Hopper and Thompson, 1984; Thompson, 1988); we see in the following discussion that this is indeed the case with non-restrictive adjectives, but that the ways in which they have been marked have changed in the history of English.

Attributive adjectives may be either salient or non-salient. When they are salient, as is often the case with an attributive adjective in an indefinite NP (because an indefinite NP is likely to convey new information), they have some stress in PDE, but when they are non-salient, the head noun receives the main stress; compare *She chose herself a rèd dréss* with *She spilled juice on her red dréss*. In the first case we are talking about a dress which has the important property of being red (the adjective here is similar to predicative adjectives, which are always salient); in the second case we are dealing with a *particular* dress – which happens to be red. In other words, salience or new information in adjectives in PDE can be conveyed by position (predicative adjectives follow the noun) or by the stress pattern within the NP, when position is not variable. In some cases, in PDE, the salience of an attributive adjective can be conveyed by position too, but these are rare; compare prenominal: **responsible** *people don't make mistakes like that* (BNC) with postnominal: *we cannot stand by and allow the people* **responsible** *to destroy the fabric of our society* (BNC). In the first example the adjective indicates what *kind* of people are the topic of the discourse; it qualifies the head noun. In the second example *responsible* separates one group of people from another; it distinguishes between two groups, but does not qualify the 'group' itself.

We will now look at what kinds of changes have occurred in the ways the different types of adjectives are marked. More work will still need to be done on the status of the adjective in OE and ME, but some distinctive features are emerging. The most notable differences between the OE and ModE/PDE systems (with ME as a period of transition) are: (i) the loss of inflections, including the strong/weak distinction, (ii) the different use of position, (iii) the way the more nominal and verbal uses of adjectives are differentiated and (iv) the development of 'stacking'.

(i) *Strong versus Weak Inflection* In OE the salient/non-salient distinction was made mainly morphologically in that predicative adjectives and adjectives in indefinite NPs were practically without exception strong, whereas definite NPs as a rule had weak adjectives (usually accompanied by a demonstrative article – an article system to distinguish between definiteness and indefiniteness was beginning to develop in OE, see Section 5.3.1). There are some exceptions to this rule, but interestingly enough, most of these can be understood from a discourse-informational point of view. For instance, in vocative phrases like *leofan men* 'dear men' and *ælmihtiga god* 'almighty God', adjectives are always declined weak, in spite of the fact that there is no definite determiner present. The reason for this is that these adjectives are part of the 'name' of the person addressed: they do not contain 'new' information and are therefore non-salient. Comparative forms are also always weak, even when used predicatively. They are typically lower in salience, in that they convey information that is already contextually present (for instance, as a property of some other discourse referent to which the comparison is made).

(ii) *Position* Position of the adjective was variable in OE (remnants of this can still be seen in ME, cf. Fischer, 2006). Syntactic position aligned with the morphological strong/weak contrast, and hence additionally marked the distinction between salient and non-salient adjectives. Therefore, only strong adjectives could occur in a postnominal position, either straight after the head noun or as part of the predicate, and these adjectives always conveyed 'new' or additional information. Bolinger (1952) has written on how the linear geometry of elements imposes certain relationships on those elements. Using this (essentially iconic) insight, he shows that pre- and postnominal adjectival positions are meaningful in many languages (e.g. Spanish, Italian, Modern Greek). When an adjective comes first in a linear sequence (i.e. precedes its head), it determines to some extent how the next element is going to be interpreted. When the adjective follows the head, it no longer has the possibility of 'changing' the head-noun, because it can only *add* to what is known already. Thus, in *genim þa reade*[WK] *netlan ufewearde*[STR] *hæbbende sæd* 'take the red nettle at-the-top containing seed' (OE, *Lch*.2.8.1.6), the weak prenominal adjective *reade* identifies the nettle as a specific type of nettle (i.e. the red-nettle), whereas the strong postnominal adjective, *ufewearde*, indicates which part of the nettle is needed (i.e. the top part with the seeds, which thus represents an *ad hoc* qualification of that nettle). In *nym betonican swa grene* [STR] 'take betony so green' (*PeriD*.63.45.24), it is not the 'green-betony' (as a different species) that must be used, but betony that is still green (i.e. fresh). It is for the same reason that referentially empty nouns like *auht* 'anything', *ælc wiht* 'anyone', *sum ðing* 'some-thing', always take an adjective postnominally in OE, as in phrases like *sum ðing digele* 'something secret (sometimes in the genitive

as in *auht godes* 'anything [of-]good'). This is because nouns without a referential function cannot be changed in 'quality' by an adjective.

In PDE, these differences are no longer expressed by position. Instead, position is more or less fixed (with the exception of a small number of adjectives like *responsible* discussed previously). The only adjectives that can still be postnominal are a number of well-defined groups such as those following the already mentioned indefinites (*something good*, etc.), some idiomatic 'French' (often quasi-legal) expressions (*The Princess Royal, heir apparent*, etc.), and adjectives that cannot be used attributively because they are too verbal or adverbial, such as *no person alive, the people involved, the music played* (all three groups can in fact be seen as historical relics, with the first and the third group still obeying the adjectival rules of OE).[10] In other words, with the increasingly fixed word order in the course of ME, the more frequent adjective position (i.e. the prenominal one) became the rule for both the salient (new) and the non-salient (old) informational function. Thus linear iconicity was replaced by phonological iconicity that is, stress rather than position has become the main distinguishing factor.

(iii)   The Link with Verbal and Nominal Usage   Because the OE strong adjectives were predicative in nature, as we have seen, it is not surprising that these strong adjectives were closer to the verbal end of the cline. We see then that some of the OE postnominal adjectives are now more easily translated adverbially or with an adverbial or relative clause rather than adjectivally, as with *ufewearde* in the example given earlier,, and *unsynnigne* and *lifigende* in (14),

(14) a *gif mon twyhyndne   mon **unsynnigne**[ACC] mid hloðe ofslea*
if one two-hundred man, innocent   with troop kill[SUBJ]
(*LawAf.*1.29)
'if a man worth two hundred shilling is killed innocently by a troop of robbers'
b *gif hwa   his rihtæwe **lifigende** forlæte*[SUBJ] *and on oðran wife on unriht*
if anyone his lawful-wife living leave   and an other woman unlawfully
gewifige[SUBJ]
take-to-wife (*LawNorthu.*64)
'if anyone leaves his lawfully married wife, while she is still alive, and takes another woman unlawfully'

---

[10] The beginning of this can already be traced in ME. Raumolin-Brunberg (1994) shows that 90 per cent of the adjectives that occur exclusively postnominally in the Helsinki corpus of ME are of French and Latin origin. This position is not likely to be a development from OE, but a 'loan position'. Native adjectives that occur postnominally usually do so in pairs (i.e. there is another adjective present that either appears prenominally, or both follow the noun combined by *and*). Single postnominal native adjectives are predicative in nature (for details, see the discussion later in this chapter, and Fischer, 2000, 2001, 2006). Such orders were preserved from OE times (see remaining discussion in this chapter) and not directly related to French influence (cf. Chapter 4).

Also adjectives that are derived from verbs (participles, see (15)) and adverbs (e.g. *ufewearde*, and other adjectives ending in *-weard*) occur more frequently in postnominal position than other adjectives, and the same is true for negative adjectives, as in (14a) and (15).

(15) *eft   wið   gefigon sceapes hohscancan **unsodenne** tobrec, gedo þæt mearh ...*
again against cimosis(?) sheep's leg   unboiled   break, do   the marrow ...
(*Lch.*1 2.23.6)
'in case of cimosis break an unboiled sheep's leg, put the marrow ...'

Negation is typically an attribute of the predicate, rather than of the nominal group; consequently it has its position usually close to the verb. Likewise, negative adjectives generally tend to be predicative, rather than attributive: when we want to express that an object is not large, we do not normally speak of an 'unlarge' or 'non-large object'. Another striking fact suggesting there is something verbal about strong adjectives and something nominal about weak adjectives is the total absence in OE of intensifying adverbs like *swiþe* 'very' preceding weak adjectives, and their high frequency before strong ones. Thus, a phrase like *the/this very old man* does not occur in OE (the equivalents of *a very old man* and *he is very old*, on the other hand, are frequent) and only begins to appear from the fifteenth century onwards.[11] Just as adverbs cannot modify weak adjectives in OE, one doesn't find inflected NPs or prepositional phrases and infinitives modifying a weak adjective. When an adjective governs a NP/PP, the whole phrase must follow the noun, and the adjective is strong:

(16) *gif hit ðonne festendæg sie selle mon wege cæsa ...   and mittan **fulne honiges***
if it   then fast-day   be, give one   wey of-cheese ... and measure full of-honey
(*Doc.*21a.16)
'if it is a day of fasting, then let a wey of cheese be given and a measure-full of honey'

Concerning infinitives, in PDE we can talk about *an easy dictionary to use*, and even *an easy-to-use-dictionary* but in OE this was out of the question; we only find *a dictionary easy to use* and even more frequently a predicative phrase, as in (17):

(17) *se x   niht   mona he is god to standanne mid æðelum mannum & ...*
the 10th night's moon, he is good to stand   with noble men and ...
(*Prog.*6.9(Foerst)10)
'the tenth day after the new moon, is a good day to mix with noble men ...'

Similarly we may now find temporal adverbs and even prepositional phrases fronted together with the adjective, as in *the still warm milk, this normally timid child, this by no means irresponsible action,* and so on. This is a

---

[11] But the construction type always remains uncommon, as shown by Vartiainen (2013).

development which could only take place after adjective position had become fixed.

In other words, what happened in the course of time is that the adjectival category became so closely associated with prenominal position that even where the adjective phrase is clearly predicative or discourse-salient, front position is preferred.

(iv)   The Development of Stacking   The positional options that existed for adjectives in OE were exploited to accommodate multiple adjectives inside one NP; this was necessary because they could not be stacked. It was virtually impossible to use adjectives one after another in a row (for some exceptions, see Fischer, 2000). Instead, the adjectives would be separated by *and*, or very often one adjective would precede and one follow the noun. The latter generally only happened when the adjectives were strong, as in *gyldenne wingeard trumlicne and fæstlicne* 'golden vineyard durable and firm' (*Alex.*1 107). When the adjectives were weak, postnominal position could only be used if the demonstrative was repeated, creating as it were an extra NP, as in *þæs swetan wætres and þæs ferscan* 'of the sweet water and the fresh' (*Alex.*1,338).[12] Why stacking did not occur in OE is probably due to the fact that adjectives were still closer either to the nominal or the verbal category (as mentioned earlier). Their situation in OE could be compared to the fact that we still cannot stack regular nouns or verbs in PDE without using a connector such as *and*. Weak adjectives in OE indeed seem in certain respects to form a compound together with the noun. This would also explain why *the very old man* does not occur in OE, just as in PDE we would not be able to say *the very grey-beard* when referring to an old man rather than a beard.

Apart from adjectives as modifiers, we also have modifying nouns, which in Table 5.1 we have termed adjuncts. Adjuncts as a rule stand closest to the noun, following the other modifying adjectives as in, *a warm black leather coat*. When there are two adjuncts, the most 'nouny' one stands closest to the noun; for example in *a leather dog collar*, *leather* comes first because it is more adjectival than *dog*, falling into a class which also contains true (albeit denominal) adjectives such as 'woollen', 'golden' and others. Such noun-modifiers together with their head noun can be premodified by adjectives in PDE, just as adjectives with their head noun can be premodified by adjectives; they cannot be premodified by adverbs, because they are noun-like (cf. **a very leather collar*). We saw earlier that in OE, weak adjectives behave very much like adjuncts in that they too cannot be modified by adverbs.

---

[12] For more information on the special status of the postnominal *and*-adjective construction and different views on their interpretation, see Haumann (2003, 2010) versus Fischer (2006, 2012).

5.5.2   Premodifiers

We have shown in Section 5.5.1 that adverbial premodifiers first only occurred
with predicative or strong attributive adjectives (i.e. discourse-salient adjectives). They only began to occur in ME with weak attributive adjectives once
adjective position became fixed to a position before the head, and the distinction
between weak and strong adjectives was lost. In ME, adjectives began to behave
more like present-day modifiers: they became less verbal and nominal. This
must also have led to a string of adjectives without the linking word *and*
becoming common, and an adverbial modifier becoming possible with formerly
weak adjectives. Both facts together would almost naturally lead to a situation in
which an adjective in a string could begin to modify the next adjective, just as an
adverb before an adjective could. In OE, it was not yet possible to build
sequences like PDE *a dirty old man*, where *dirty* modifies *old man* rather than
man because each adjective stood on the same level with respect to the noun:
there was no hierarchy in which an adjective could modify the whole adjective-
noun combination following it. When we wish to express in PDE that the man
was dirty as well as old, we would normally reverse the 'natural' order of
adjectives into *an old, dirty man*,[13] and add an intonation break (here represented by the comma) or indeed a connector (*an old and dirty man*).

It is difficult to determine when exactly the premodifying possibility of the
adjective became available, but that it did is clear from a development in which
formerly descriptive adjectives like *pretty* develop into premodifiers, which
cannot modify a noun, but only an adjective, as in *that was a pretty ugly
display*, where *pretty* clearly modifies *ugly*, and not *display* or *ugly display*.
Adamson (2000) has shown that, to trace such a development, one would first
have to ascertain when an adjective like *pretty* or *horrid* starts being used in a
row with another adjective, and secondly when *horrid*-type adjectives begin to
be predominantly placed in left-most position. No full answers to these
questions are available as yet,[14] but it is clear from the complete corpus of
Chaucerian (late ME) texts, that such a development with the now classic

---

[13]   For sequences of adjectives, most languages have a similar order (cf. Dixon 1982; Posner, 1986;
Plank, 2007: 61ff.), whereby the adjectives which are most like nouns such as those of colour or
material, are closest to the noun. In English, the usual order is roughly EVALUA-
TION>SIZE>COLOUR>ORIGIN, as in 'a beautiful big red woollen Swiss ball' (cf. Vandelanotte, 2002). This ordering does not apply yet to OE, which had no stacking but a flat structure
in adjectival modification (for a discussion of this 'stacking' development, and of the increasing
subjectivization of descriptive adjectives such as *lovely* into 'value-adjectives', see Adamson,
2000, and the discussion that follows below).

[14]   For instance, González-Díaz (2009, 2010) has shown in two studies on the development of *little*
and *old* from an objective descriptive into a subjective 'evaluative' adjective that this process
need not necessarily involve leftward movement. In the case of *little*, this is probably prohibited
by a stronger iconic principle (the proximity principle): placing *little* immediately left of the

value-adjectives *horrible/horrid* and *nice* had not yet taken place. *Nice* in Chaucer occurs only by itself. *Horrible* occurs by itself twenty-eight times; nine times there is another adjective. Of these latter cases, two instances have the connector *and* (*horrible and strong prison*, KnT.1451); one instance still has the adjectives draped around the noun (*sodeyn deth horrible*, FrlT.1010); five have two consecutive adjectives. Of these five, however, one has *horrible* not in leftmost position (*this false horrible boke*, RR.7132) in three, *horrible* is likely to be descriptive because the neighbouring adjectives describe feelings of horror too (*swollen, disordinate, dedly*), while the last double adjective construction, *horrible grete synnes*, is more likely descriptive too, because it is followed by *or smale* (ParsT.960). In other words there is no evidence yet in Chaucer of the adjectives having become premodifiers.

5.5.3   Postmodifiers

We have already discussed adjectival postmodifiers and what happens to them. Next to these there are finite and non-finite *clausal* postmodifiers. No changes of note occurred in the non-finite ones – that is, already in OE a head noun could be followed by an infinitival or a present participle construction:

(18) a *Ic hæbbe mete **to etenne** þone þe ge   nyton.*
        I have   food to eat   which   you not-know (*ÆCHom.*5.71)
        'I have food to eat which you know nothing about'
     b *Ða   ætywde   him drihtnes engel **standende on þæs weofodes swyðran healfe***
        Then appeareded him lord's   angel standing   on the altar's   right half (Lk(WSCp)1.11)
        'Then God's angel appeared to him standing on the right side of the altar'

The typical finite postmodifier is the relative clause. There were many changes here, mainly in the form of the element that served to introduce the clause. In PDE we distinguish two types of relative clauses, the so-called restrictive clauses and non-restrictive clauses, which differ in meaning in that the first narrows down the referent of the head noun, whereas the second gives extra information about the head noun. Formally, they are distinguished in that with the latter there is likely to be an intonation break (in writing indicated by the use of a comma), which is typically absent in the former. Another formal difference is that the relative pronoun *that* is typically employed with restrictive clauses, at least in standard English, while *who* and *which* can be used with either. In OE, we do not have any clear formal criteria to distinguish them,

---

head noun enables it to convey the affective value that diminutive affixes elsewhere in other languages display.

although there is a tendency for the particle *þe* to occur mainly in restrictive clauses. The following elements functioned as relatives in OE: the demonstrative pronoun *se, seo, þæt*, the undeclined particle *þe* and a combination of the two, see (19),

(19) a *he wolde adræfan anne æþeling* **se was Cyneheard** *haten*
    he would drive-out a nobleman who was Cyneheard called
    (*ChronA* (Plummer)755.6)
    'he wanted to drive away a nobleman who was called Cyneheard.'
  b *þu geearnast . . . þone stede þe se deofol of afeoll þurh ungehyrsumnesse*
    You earn . . .   the place which the devil from fell through disobedience
    (*ÆCHom.*I,181.79)
    'you will deserve the place which the devil fell out of through his disobedience'
  c *Se   wolde niman his magan to wife þæs cyninges dohtor. seo ðe wæs to*
    That wanted take his relative to wife the   king's daughter, who was to
    abbudissan gehadod.
    abbess   ordained (*ÆCHom.*II,277.152)
    'That one wanted to marry his relative, the king's daughter, who had been ordained abbess.'

Relative clauses may have had their origin in paratactic clauses (cf. Section 8.3.1). It is not difficult to see, for instance, how the type illustrated in (19a) with a demonstrative pronoun (*se was . . .*), may have developed out of a main (coordinate) clause:

(20) *þa sæde heo þam brydguman þæt heo gesawe engel of heofenum,* **ond se**
    then said she to-the bridegroom that she saw   angel of heavens, and that-one
    wolde *hyne slean myd færdeaðe, gif he hyre æfre onhryne myd unclænre lufon.*
    would him kill with sudden-death, if he her ever touched with unclean love
    (*Mart.*2.1(Herzfeld-Kotzor)22,A7)
    'then she said to the bridegroom that she had seen an angel from heaven, who would kill him swiftly, if he ever touched her in an unclean way'

Indeed in cases like (19a), where the demonstrative pronoun *se* by itself functions as a relative and where there is no clear indication of coordinateness as there is in (20) (*ond se . . .*), it is not clear whether the relative clause is subordinate or paratactic, especially because in OE there are no clear markers of punctuation, which might have helped settle the question.

Relative clauses that take a demonstrative pronoun as head as well as a particle, as in (19c), may have developed from an appositive construction, whereby the demonstrative originally was part of the main clause, as can be seen in a number of cases where the demonstrative pronoun bears the case-form of the antecedent in the main clause rather than the case-form of the function it reflects in the subordinate clause. Thus, in (19c), the demonstrative *seo* has nominative case because it functions as subject of the relative clause, while in (21), the demonstrative *þara* is in the genitive plural, like its antecedent *ealra*, in spite of the fact that it functions as subject in the relative clause,

(21) & *þu scealt wesan ealra bysen* **þara**   **þe**   *ðurh*   *þe on ðinne god gelyfað*
      and you must be   of-all example of-those who through thee in thy   god believe
      (*LS*.4(Christoph)57)
      'and you must set the example for all who, through you, believe in your God'

Another type of relative that is appositional in nature is the non-introduced relative clause,

(22) *Seo mægð asprang of   noes yltstan suna* **wæs gehaten sem**.
      This maiden sprang from Noah's eldest son, was called   sem (*ÆCHom.*I,186.222)
      'This maiden was the offspring of Noah's eldest son, (who was) called Sem'[15]

This was the only type of zero-relative clause possible in OE. The zero-relative that is the rule in PDE restrictive clauses when the relative element functions as (any kind of) object in the subordinate clause, as in *This is the book* 0 *I came to pick up*, is not found in OE. It first occurs in the ME period, interestingly enough in a *semantically* similar type of clause (employing the verb *clepen* 'to call') in which the zero-relative was usual in OE (and also still in ME),

(23) *And nameliche ther was a greet collegge/* **Men clepen** *the Soler Halle at*
      And particularly there was a great college, [that] people call King's College, at
      Cantebridge
      Cambridge (Chaucer,*Rv.T.*3989–90)

It is only after the ME period that the zero-object relative construction becomes common. This may well be related to the loss of *that* in complement clauses, which is also a ME development (see Chapter 8).

The greatest change in the ME period is the introduction of the *wh*-relative. In OE *wh*-pronouns (or rather their etymological equivalents in *hw*-) were used as interrogatives and as generalizing, indefinite pronouns, but never as relatives. The introduction of *wh*-relatives is partly a natural development (in many other languages interrogatives function as relatives), but its use may also have arisen due to the collapse of the OE relative system. *Þe* went out of use (probably because it was phonetically weak and identical to the new, unde-clined, definite article) in the early part of the ME period (a little later in the south), and was replaced by *that*, the only left-over of the original demonstrative series *se, seo, þæt*. The use of *wh*-relatives ([*the*] *which* [*that*], *whom, whose*) dates from the beginning of the ME period but became really frequent only in eModE. The earliest instances are with *whom* and *whose*,

---

[15] It is, of course, also possible that the second clause is another main clause with a null pronoun as subject (see Section 7.2), because punctuation marks were not clearly used yet.

possibly because, unlike *that*, they could indicate case. The development of interrogative into relative pronouns is natural when one considers their use in indirect questions such as *He wanted to know who did this*, where the interrogative could be said to function as an indefinite ('the one who') or generalizing ('whoever') pronoun. Already in OE interrogatives like *hwa, hwæt,* and *hwilc* were used as indefinites (sometimes indeed called 'free relatives'), as in (24a), and they frequently occurred in indirect questions of the type just mentioned, as in (24b),

(24) a *Ealle we sind gelice ætforan gode. buton* **hwa**   *oðerne mid godum weorcum*
     All   we are equal before god except who[ever] other   with good   works
     forþeo
     oppress[SUBJ] (*ÆCHom*.I,326.44)
     'We are all equal in the eyes of God except the one who oppresses another with good works'
   b *þa   cwæð hi to þan deofle: Ic wat   hwæt   þu þæncst*
     then said she to the devil: I know what[ever] you think
     (*LS* 14 (*Margaret* (CCCC 303)14.4)

For the 'free relative' to develop into a 'true' or strict relative, an antecedent is required, which in the free relative is missing (or one could say 'included'). The instance in (25), from early ME, shows how this could come about,

(25) *wham   mai he luue treweliche* **hwa**   *ne luues his broðer*
     'whom can he love truly   who[ever] [does]n't love his brother'
     (*Woo.Lord*,275.18)

Here, *hwa* can still be interpreted as a 'free relative', but at the same time it could function as a strict relative referring to *he*, because here *he* also has general reference.

The earliest instances of *wh*-relatives are mainly found in non-restrictive clauses and tend to be preceded by a preposition. Because the general relative particle *that* could not follow a preposition, this is perhaps not surprising. By the fifteenth century, *whose, whom* and *which* are frequent, but interestingly enough not *who*. The reason for this may be the fact mentioned previously – that is, *who* as a nominative form had no need of a preposition, and therefore this function could as easily be expressed by the usual form *that*, which was common with both animate and inanimate antecedents all through the ME period and far beyond (and still is in colloquial speech). Another possible factor was the original meaning of the *wh*-relative. As an indefinite pronoun or free relative, it occurred mainly in subject position; *who* may therefore have been too strongly generalizing still in ME to function as a mere relative. It is interesting to note in this respect that this 'lag of *who*' is also noticeable in German and Dutch, which even today do not allow nominative *who* (i.e. *wer* and *wie*, respectively) to occur as a relative, while both *wer* and *wie are* used as free relatives.

Finally, before we end this discussion of relatives, we should note the appearance of a new construction in ME: infinitival relative clauses of the following type,

(26) *She has no wight   to whom to make hir mone*
She has no creature to whom to make her complaint (Chaucer,*M.ofLaw.T* 656)

Such constructions do not yet occur in OE, but it is easy to see what could have given rise to them once the *wh*-free relative had become a strict relative:

(27) ... *seo leo bringð his hungregum hwelpum **hwæt**   **to** etanne*
... the lion brings his hungry   whelps   whatever [i.e. something] to eat
(*Or.*3,11.77.20)

Another quite likely source was the construction in (28),

(28) ... ***hwæt is to** cweðanne be ðam mænigfealdum smeamettum*
... what is to say   about the manifold   delicacies
(*HomU.*11(ScraggVerc.7)42)
'... what can be said/what to say about the manifold delicacies'

which began to be avoided in ME because of the awkward preverbal position of the object (see also Section 9.3). A way to replace it was by either using a passive infinitive or the new infinitival relative that, as it were, automatically appeared when the main verb *is* was left out.

5.6   Concluding Remarks and *More*

In this chapter, we concentrated on the major changes taking place within the NP, notably the development of a true determiner category, changes in the adjective group (as a result of both the loss of the strong and weak distinction and the increasing fixation of word order), new developments involving the genitive (changing from a case inflection into something that could loosely be called a clitic enabling the now uniform '*s* ending to appear in positions where it had not appeared before and at the same time reducing the function of the genitive to one expressing 'possession'), and finally new developments involving the relative clause and the way it was marked.

Naturally not everything that happened within the NP could be discussed here. As a final note, however, we would like to draw attention to the rise of the comparative marker *more*. For one reason, because two monographs dealing with the topic appeared, close to one another, not so long ago (González Diáz, 2008; Mondorf, 2009), but primarily because the case makes us consider syntactic change in general. Both studies show that, when one looks at a particular case of change or variation in great detail and with the help of extensive text corpora, the new construction is invariably the result of a complex interaction of factors. In the case of the rise of *more*, González Diáz first makes clear that the use of *more* is clearly a native development. It occurs regularly in OE with verbal participles, next to other markers such as *swiþor* and *bet*; but the rise of *ma* > *more* rather than the other two may have been helped by the calqueing of Latin *magis*, which may also have caused it to extend its use to adjectives, where it became more common in later OE. Similarly the entry of French on the scene may have been responsible for further spread, and it is indeed remarkable that in contact situations the more analytic form is often preferred, it being more salient. Mondorf (2009: 171ff.) indicates in this respect that *more* is more frequent in American English compared to British English. Both Mondorf and González Diáz point out additional factors leading to an increase in *more* usage, such as position (*more* is favoured in postnominal and predicative position and in coordinated adjectival phrases), the need for emphasis or clarity in complex clausal constructions (Mondorf, 2009: 63ff., shows that *more* is more common when the adjective is followed by a complement since this would ease parsing), or when adjectives are more abstract/figurative or less prototypical (e.g. weakly gradable adjectives tend to take *more*, *ibid.*: 96ff.). Phonology too may play a role. Mondorf refers to the 'Principle of Rhythmic Alternation' (*ibid.*: 18), which concerns the avoidance of successive stressed syllables. This would explain why *a próuder cándidate* with an iambic rhythm is preferred over *a móre próud candidate* because the latter has two consecutive stresses, and why adjectives like *bitter* and *sober* prefer *more* to avoid two unstressed adjectives in a row. Interestingly *clever* forms an exception again in this respect, which Mondorf (*ibid.*: 21) believes is related to its overall frequency (in other words, economy plays a role here). All in all, this case makes clear how complex change is, and that explanations may emerge from many different and sometimes unexpected directions.

6 The Verb Phrase

6.1 Introduction

The verb phrase [VP] is defined differently from one linguistic model to another. To some the VP consists of the verb and all its dependents, including arguments and adverbials, while to others it consists of just the verb and its auxiliaries if any are present. We follow the second, narrower definition here for practical reasons. As they constitute an inexhaustible area of change by themselves, this chapter deals with just the verbs and auxiliaries of English. Issues of argument realization are discussed in Chapter 9 ("Word Order"). Non-finite verb forms are dealt with in Chapter 8 ("Subordination").

In comparison to other branches of the Indo-European family tree, Germanic came down with a curiously impoverished verbal system. Set against the three voices, four moods and seven tenses of Ancient Greek or Sanskrit (Baldi, 1990: 46), the OE verbal system had little to boast of: a present and past tense, both with indicative and subjunctive mood, and an imperative. Those categories were expressed inflectionally. Of a system of auxiliaries, OE had only the rudimentary beginnings.

In contrast, what marks out the VP in PDE is exactly its rich repertoire of auxiliaries, neatly organized into a system that Denison (2000: 111) describes as being 'among the most systematic areas of English syntax'. In usage, this auxiliary system is rarely deployed to its full potential, but when it is, as in (1), the resultant VP is impressive.

(1) It is not without relevance that his views *would have been being formed* in the decade after the disastrous Second Jewish Revolt against Rome (GloWbE, IE)

Using various auxiliaries, a PDE VP can express modality, perfect tense, progressive aspect and passive voice – all together or in any combination, as long as the right sequencing is respected. In addition, PDE VPs feature the typological oddity of selecting a special auxiliary *do* in negative and interrogative clauses, as in (2). Remarkably, auxiliary *do* is in complementary distribution with the auxiliaries of modality, aspect and voice; where *do* occurs the other auxiliaries cannot and vice versa.

(2) Dimly he saw that she was holding something, but he *did not realize* what it was until she spoke again. (BNC)

This elaborate system comes on top of the tense contrast PDE inherited from OE. The only thing the VP was ever likely to lose is the subjunctive mood, but then again even the subjunctive is not quite gone yet; witness (3).

(3) Often his researches demand that he *visit* the far corners of the world. (BNC)

As far as syntax goes, then, the history of the English VP is mostly a story of gradual complexification. The following describes how the English VP developed from the limited system of OE with only a handful of inflectionally marked contrasts into the more elaborate and largely periphrastic system of PDE. Because the various changes involved are closely interwoven, any subdivision is somewhat arbitrary. The following sections simply follow the traditional distinctions into functional domains, dealing with modality (Section 6.1), aspect (Section 6.2), voice (Section 6.3) and tense (Section 6.4). A separate section is devoted to the rise of *do* (Section 6.5). Although it is also marked on the verb, this chapter does not deal with agreement (on which see Chapter 7).

6.2   Modality

Formally, modal expressions can be anything, ranging from verbal inflections and auxiliaries to adjectives, adverbs and particles. Common to all modal expressions is their meaning, though exactly what counts as modal meaning is hard to pin down. Generally, modal expressions say something about the state of affairs denoted by the rest of the VP by qualifying its ontological status. By one definition, they express 'a speaker's judgement that a proposition is possibly or necessarily true or that the actualisation of a situation is necessary or possible' (Depraetere and Reed, 2006: 269). For example, the speaker in (4) uses *may* and *could* to signal, with subtly varying confidence, that a state of affairs is potentially true.

(4) it *may* be epilepsy but it *could* be anything else (BNC)

Within the (narrowly defined) VP, modality can either be expressed inflectionally on the main verb, or it can be expressed by means of auxiliaries. The former type of expression is commonly known as 'mood'. English has three moods: the indicative, subjunctive and imperative. English also has a variety of auxiliaries expressing modal meanings, a subset of which is referred to as the 'modals' or 'modal verbs'. In PDE the modals make up a tightknit group of auxiliary verbs with some unusual syntactic properties. Its core members are *can, could, may, might, must, shall, should, will* and *would*. Apart from occupying the position of a finite verb in the clause, the modals are quite unlike any other PDE verbs. None of the modals have non-finite forms; none of them inflect for third person singular; their tense contrasts are more or less defunct; they can be inverted or negated without the help of *do*; and they can form tag questions. Next to the modals, PDE also has a more open-ended and arguably less bizarre class of so-called semi-modals, including auxiliaries such as *got to*, *have to*, *need to*, or *want to*. The major developments in the domain of modality, then, are the decline of the OE subjunctive mood, the rise of the modals and, later, the rise of semi-modals.

6.2.1   The Subjunctive

It has been claimed that if a language has a subjunctive at all, then that subjunctive will at least be used to mark low certainty or weak desirability (Givón, 2001: 313). Indeed, the OE subjunctive did just that, and some more. In main clauses the subjunctive typically signalled the desirability of a state of affairs, as in (5). This way, it contrasted with the indicative, which presented a state of affairs as factual.

(5) *ne* **beon**   *hi   æfre manslagan ne manswican ne mansworan ne* ...
    not be[SUBJ] they ever murderers nor traitors   nor perjurers   nor ...
    (*WHom.*10a,11)
    'They may never be murderers or traitors or perjurers or ...'

When combined with a second person subject, as in (6), the main clause subjunctive would offer a somewhat toned-down alternative to the imperative – the mood standardly used to issue commands.

(6) *ne þu huru   me fram þinum   bebodum   feor* **adrife**[SUBJ]
    not thou indeed me from thy   commandments far   off-drive (*PP5*(A5)118.10)
    'do not indeed drive me far away from your commandments'

In dependent clauses, the subjunctive would associate with situations that are desirable, conjectural or hypothetical. For example, OE adverbial *þæt*-clauses would take an indicative to construe a situation as an automatic outcome (result), but a subjunctive to construe it as an intended goal (purpose) (Visser 1963: 861). Compare the examples in (7).

(7) a *Ic þæt gefremme ... þæt ge min onsynn oft* **sceawiað**
      I that perform   that you my face   often behold (*Guth.*A.B.715)
      'I will ensure that you will often see my face'
    b *Ic sceal forð sprecan gen ymvbe Grendel ... þæt ðu geare* **cunne**..
      I must forth speak again about Grendel ... that you readily may-know ...
      (*Beo.*2069)'
      'I must speak again about Grendel so that you may clearly know'

In all, the OE subjunctive was in general use and alternated meaningfully with the other OE moods in many contexts.

What then caused the subjunctive's demise? Without a doubt, an important catalyst of change was the erosion of inflectional endings. Indicatives, imperatives and subjunctives increasingly coalesced formally, necessitating reliance on other forms to preserve functional contrasts. The exceptions may well prove the rule here, because where the subjunctive survived as an inflectionally distinct form, it would sometimes continue to be used. It is telling, for instance, that the OE first person adhortative, as in (8), was lost but main clause subjunctives in third person wishes continued in existence well into Modern English, as in (9). This is not all that surprising considering that the first person plural of the subjunctive inflection coalesced with the indicative (in the northern and midlands dialects, which became the standard form after the ME period), but the third person singular did not.

(8) *Men þa leofestan,* herigen[SUBJ]we *nu þone ælmihtigan Drihten &* **lufien**[SUBJ]
   Men the dearest,   praise   we now the almighty   Lord   and love
   we hine
   we him *(HomS.*33(Först)199)
   'Beloved men, let us now praise the almighty Lord and let us love him.'

(9) Some heavenly power *guide* us Out of this fearful country (1610, Visser, 1963: 797)

However, the loss of inflectional endings was probably not the only factor involved. While the OE subjunctive was clearly associated with modal meanings, the conjunction or matrix verb heading the subjunctive clause would often signal modality in its own right. In such cases, the subjunctive coded its modal meaning more or less redundantly, as in (10).

(10) *Ne bið <his> lof na ðy læsse, ac is wen þæt hit sie þy mare*
    not will-be his praise not the less, but is likelihood that it be the more
    *(Bo.*40.138.19)
    'his praise will not be the less, and it may, quite possibly, be greater'

Redundant contexts effectively rendered the subjunctive meaningless. Perhaps that is why even in OE some contexts saw competition between the subjunctive and indicative. For example, OE typically had the subjunctive in reported speech, but it occasionally allowed the indicative, as shown in (11), which has both moods in coordination.

(11) *Wulfstan sæde þæt he gefore of Hæðum, þæt he wære on Truso on*
    Wulfstan said that he went[SUBJ] from Hedeby, that he was[SUBJ] in Druso in
    syfan dagum & nihtum, þæt þæt scip wæs ealne weg yrnende under segle
    seven days and nights that that ship was[IND] all   way running under sail
    *(Or.*1 1.16.21)
    'Wulfstan said that he departed from Hedeby, that he reached Drusno in seven days and nights, and that the ship was running under full sail all the way'

Even where the subjunctive retained its meaning, it lacked the capacity of expressing finer shades of modal meaning without the support of other modal expressions. Particularly in main clauses, where there was no matrix verb or conjunction to guide interpretation, this may well have fostered the grammaticalization of the modals, as in (12).

(12) *Þa   ðe   bet   cunnon and magon.* **sceolon** *gyman oðra   manna*
    Those   who   better   can   and may   must   heed   of-other   men
    (*ÆCHom*.II,15 159.311)
    'those who have more abilities should take care of other men'

The rise of the modals probably dealt the subjunctive the final blow. By the end of the OE period, modals (often themselves in the subjunctive form) started appearing where earlier a subjunctive form would have sufficed, as in (13).

(13) *Forþon   us is nydþearf, þæt þa mynstru   of   þære stowe **moten**   beon*
    Therefore us is need   that the monasteries from that   place must [SUBJ] be
    gecyrrede to   oþre   stowe
    changed   to   other   place (*GD*.2(C)5.112.24)
    'it is necessary therefore that the monasteries will be moved from that place to another'

That the modals completely replaced the subjunctive is not true, however. Many subjunctive *that*-clauses were replaced by *to*-infinitives (Manabe, 1989; Los, 2005; see Section 8.2.1). And in some contexts verb forms that had lost their distinctive subjunctive endings simply continued functioning as indicatives, modality being coded elsewhere in the sentence anyway. Compare (14) to (10) above.

(14) it is probable that he then *left* them again (BNC)

By lModE and PDE the subjunctive has become a rare form, restricted to formal registers and very specific lexico-grammatical contexts. Even so, earlier grammarians who anticipated its complete disappearance have been proven wrong. The subjunctive is still attested in some formulaic wishes (*far **be** it from us to interfere*), and there is the past subjunctive form *were* in counterfactual conditions (*if I **were** you*). Finally, PDE has preserved the so-called mandative subjunctive following manipulative verbs (*I strongly request that the Minister **reconsider** the case*). Curiously, the latter has been making something of a comeback in American and Australian English, probably because it has acquired social prestige. The present-day state of the subjunctive, then, is aptly summarized in the words of Vaughan and Mulder (2014: 487): 'the subjunctive is alive and, if not kicking, it is at least wriggling a bit'. Compared to its use in OE, however, the subjunctive's role in the grammar of PDE is negligible.

6.2.2   The Modals

When it comes to great controversies in the field of English historical linguistics, the development of the modals is hard to beat. Lightfoot (1979) set the ball rolling with an encompassing theory, the upshot of which was that an entire grammar could undergo radical and abrupt change. The radical change in question was the introduction of a wholly new abstract syntactic category into the grammar of English. The category was AUX (for auxiliary) and its members were the modals. Because the event was sudden, Lightfoot could be quite precise about the timing: the watershed moment was sometime around 1600.

Lightfoot's story is, briefly, as follows. In OE and ME the core modals *willan* 'wish, want', *sculan* 'be obliged to', *magan* 'be able', *motan* 'be allowed' and *cunnan* 'know, be able to' behaved more or less as any other verbs did. Lightfoot, accordingly, does not call these verbs modals yet but 'pre-modals'. In the course of ME, the pre-modals were involved in a number of accidental and independent changes. Among other things, they lost the ability to take direct objects; their past-tense forms ceased to consistently signal past tense; and they failed to adopt *to*-infinitival complements as other verbs increasingly did. For example, OE *sculan* in (15) still takes both a direct and indirect object – something its PDE counterpart *shall* stopped doing sometime after 1500.

(15) *He cwæð þæt he **sceolde** him hundteontig   mittan   hwætes*
     'He said that he owed   him [a] hundred   bushels of-wheat' (*ÆHom.*17,26)

As another example, ME *might* in (16a) still functions as a past tense of *may*, expressing past ability, but in (16b) it expresses a potentiality that holds at the time of speaking.

(16) a *He was of grete elde, & **myght** not trauaile.*
       'He was of great age and was unable to travel' (*Langtoft's-Chron.*p.3)
     b *Come now, deth, I wile the calle, I wold þou **myhtest** myn herte cleue'*
       'Come now death, I want to call you, I wish[ed] that you might cleave my heart' (*Vernon-Ms,*688)

These and other changes gradually dissociated the pre-modals from other verbs to the point that they were no longer recognizable as verbs at all, forcing speakers to assign them to a different syntactic class altogether. With this, the modals were born. Their birth was marked by another set of changes, yet these took place suddenly and simultaneously. The modals shed all their non-finite forms (infinitives, present participles and past participles) and they ceased to occur in combination. This must have happened sometime around 1600, after which time the forms in (17) had all become ungrammatical.

(17) a [*Infinitive*]
   for he seyde manie tymis that ho so euer schuld dwelle at Paston schulde have
   nede **to conne** *defende hymselfe. (Past.Let.*I,p.27)
   'for he said many times that whosoever should live at Paston, would need to be
   able to defend himself'

   b [*Present participle*]
   And lo! a womman aȝen cam to hym, ... a chaterere, and vagaunt of reste,
   vnpacient, ne **mowende** *in the hous abide stille wih hir feet*
   (Wyclif,*Prov.*vii.11)
   'And look, a woman again came to him, a chatterer, one who is ever restless,
   impatient, and unable (lit. not maying) to stay in the house and keep her
   feet still'

   c [*Past participle*]
   For wel may euery man wite · if god hadde **wolde** *hym|selue, Sholde neuere Iudas*
   ne iuwe · haue Ihesu don on Rode (PiersPlowman(B-text)XV,258)
   'For every man may well know, if God had not wanted it himself, Judas or any
   other Jew would have gotten Jesus on the cross'

   d [*Consecutive modals*]
   ... that our broder Reynawde be well mounted vpon bayarde, whiche **shall maye**
   bere vs all four at a nede' (Caxton,*Four-Sons-of-Aymon,*IX,222)
   '... [let's do it so] that our brother Renard will be well mounted upon [the
   horse] Bayard, who will be able to carry all four of us if necessary'

According to Lightfoot, the simultaneous occurrence of the second round of
changes provides evidence that some more fundamental change had taken
place, situated at a deeper structural level of the grammar.

Unfortunately, there are quite a number of problems with Lightfoot's
story (see Plank, 1984; Warner, 1993; Fischer, 2007). Even in OE the
modals showed deviant behaviour. More precisely, the modals resorted
under the slightly bigger group of preterite-present verbs, including other
OE verbs like *witan* 'know', *durran* 'dare', *þurfan 'need' or *dugan* 'be
good'. The group had already formed in Proto-Germanic, containing mostly
verbs whose present tense had derived from Proto-Indo-European perfect
forms – an unusual situation, as the Proto-Indo-European perfect was primarily the source of the Germanic strong past tense. Their ancestry explains
their inflectional anomalies. Like strong past tenses, the OE preterite-present
verbs had no distinct third person singular ending. They also tended to lack
non-finite forms. These inflectional features already set the preterite-present
verbs, including the modals, apart as a somewhat separate group of verbs in
OE. Semantically, too, the preterite-present verbs had always been unusual
in that they typically had stative meanings, whereas most verbs have
dynamic meanings. Testimony to their status as a group is the fact that the
preterite-present verbs analogically attracted new members, notably *willan*,
and probably *motan and *cunnan* in Proto-Germanic times.

By treating them as ordinary verbs prior to 1600, Lightfoot's account downplays the exceptional position the modals already had in OE. This calls at least for a reassessment of his story. On the one hand, it becomes rather doubtful whether the changes to the modals before 1600 were really accidental and independent, because the modals were already behaving more or less as a group and had always cherished un-verblike behaviour. On the other hand, the changes after 1600 were less dramatic and abrupt than Lightfoot makes them out to be. In light of their preterite-present ancestry, the non-finite forms that the modals lost had never been a very integral part of their paradigms to begin with. In fact, some of the modals (*motan, *sculan) never had any non-finite forms, and for the others most attested non-finite forms were ME innovations. That those innovations failed to catch on may well be due to the development of the semi-modals (see Section 6.1.3), most of which had and still have non-finite forms. Note here also that, contrary to what Lightfoot claims, some modals actually continued to combine with direct objects until quite late – with can until 1652, with will until 1862 according to Visser (1963: 557–58). All of this undermines both Lightfoot's two-stage scenario and his claim of a radical and abrupt change.

The alternative picture that emerges is one of long-term incremental change. OE started out with a group of preterite-present verbs that were already somewhat exceptional, both formally and semantically. Some of the group's core members had developed or were beginning to develop modal meanings, along the familiar pathways of semantic change (Traugott and Dasher, 2002: 105–51). The grammaticalization process proceeded faster with some verbs than with others. *Sculan and *motan led, magan followed, cunnan and willan lagged behind (Denison, 1993: 336). But, together, the changes redefined and reinforced the functional identity of the group, which increasingly crystallized around the marking of modal meaning. In turn, this changing group identity promoted further changes. Erstwhile members that failed to adopt modal meaning, such as durran 'dare' or witan 'know', disappeared or shifted to normal verb behaviour, while some other verbs that displayed modal-like meanings, such as need, were (half-heartedly) recruited into the group of modals. To be sure, neither the gradualness of change, nor the idiosyncrasies of the individual items involved should belie the magnitude of the overall development. Together with the rise of the auxiliaries have and be (see Sections 6.3.2 and 6.4) and of operator do (see Section 6.5), the emergence of the modals gave rise to a very distinct class of grammatical markers and at the same time established a new functional and syntactic position in the English finite clause.

6.2.3   The Semi-Modals

As if the modals were not enough, English went on to grammaticalize another set of modal auxiliaries, which are sometimes referred to as the 'semi-modals'. The group is open-ended, but most will agree that it includes *be able to, be going to, (have) got to, have to, need to* and *want to*. The semi-modals developed not from the group of preterite-present verbs but mostly from ordinary main verbs combined with a *to*-infinitive. Formally, they are less distinctive than the modals, but functionally they do a very similar job expressing various shades of modal meaning. The examples in (18) illustrate two of the semi-modals – *have to* and *want to* – and some of their meanings. As is typical of modal expressions, many of the semi-modals developed complex polysemies within the modal domain.

(18) a [*Strong necessity*]
     Were things so bad between them that she just *had to* disappear? (BNC)
   b [*Strong certainty*]
     A shadow *has to* be cast by something (BNC)
   c [*Strong desire*]
     Look, can you give me another couple of hours? I *want to* try something. (BNC)
   d [*Weak obligation*]
     'Anyway, have you any news for me?' 'No, nothing of importance, except I think you *want to* keep an eye on Billy the welder.' (BNC)

The semi-modals form a much less clearly defined group than the modals. On the one hand, the category of semi-modals has no sharp external boundaries. That is because the semi-modals mostly developed from constructions involving more or less normal verbs. As a result, some semi-modal constructions are barely distinguishable from constructions involving main verbs, except on semantic grounds. On the other hand, the category of semi-modals is internally very heterogeneous. Partly that is because the semi-modals developed at very different times. Partly it is because they developed from syntactically diverse sources. For instance, *have to* developed from a combination of *have* with a direct object followed by an adnominal *to*-infinitive – a construction that at least implied modal meanings (though not necessarily of necessity) as early as OE, as shown in (19) (cf. Fischer, 1994a, 2015). In contrast, *want to* originated as a combination of *want* with a *to*-infinitival complement clause, whose first desiderative uses date only from the eighteenth century, as in (20) (Krug, 2000). *Need to, be going to* and *got to* derived from yet other source constructions (for more on *be going to*, see Section 6.2.2).

(19) **hæfst**   ðu   æceras   **to erigenne**
     'Have   you   acres   to plow?' (ÆGram.135.2)

(20) Cheats mingle the Flower or Seed among the Food of those whom they want to defraud. (1751, OED)

If we also consider other candidate members of the category, such as the modal expressions illustrated in (21), internal heterogeneity only increases.

(21) a I *got to* get batteries to go with it though (BNC)
  b The manufacturers *are bound to* have sent samples to other people, not just us. (BNC)
  c The hot drink *was supposed to* be tea but tasted awful. (BNC)
  d Someone *had better* go down and have a word... (BNC)
  e Don't cause any trouble and don't insist if they *look like* objecting. (BNC)

In this light, one may in fact wonder whether there really is such a thing as a category of semi-modals. Interestingly, however, some more or less consistent group identity seems to be emerging in PDE (Krug, 2000: 238). It is striking that most semi-modals are formed with a *to*-infinitive. It is also striking that most have obtained phonetically reduced variants that are disyllabic and end in a schwa (sometimes with a conventionalized form in spelling, too):

['gʌnə]	*gonna* < *be going to*
['gɒtə]	*gotta* < *(have) got to*
['hæftə]	*have to*
['wɒnə]	*wanna* < *want to*
['niːtə]	*need to*
['betə]	*had better*
['spəʊstə]	*be supposed to*

This may be a coincidence or it may point to the existence of an emergent category of semi-modals. On the latter interpretation, the semi-modals, like the modals, may be caught up in a complex dynamic, involving grammaticalization at the level of individual expressions and analogical alignment to an emergent class.

6.3   Tense

Tense markers serve to situate a process in time, either with respect to the time of speaking or with respect to another process. In English, the basic distinction is between present and past tense and is marked inflectionally. In (22) the present tense form *is* signals that the state of affairs described by the main clause holds at the time of speaking. The past tenses *grew up* and *inherited* situate a state of affairs in a time before the time of speaking.

(22) My house – not the one I *grew up* in, but this one, the one I *inherited* from
my grandmother – *is* a shrine to her conventional, turn-of-the-last-century
taste (COCA)

The present/past distinction was inherited from Germanic and its core function
has been essentially stable since OE. At the margins, however, changes have
occurred.

The present and past tenses themselves have developed a few new uses that
arguably have little to do with tense marking at all. The past tense took over
some of the uses of the OE subjunctive, as illustrated in (23).

(23) a *Iohannes: cum   to me tima is þæt ðu   mid   þinum   gebroðrum*
    John: come to me time is that you   with   your   brothers
    wistfullige   on minum   gebeorscipe
    feast[PRES.SUBJ]   in my   banquet (*ÆCHom*.I,4 214.246)
    'John, come to me, it is about time that you and your brothers attended one of my
    feasts'
  b Mrs Edwina Currie claimed that many pensioners were well-off ... 'We are in the
    age of the 'woopy' the well-off old person and it is about time we all *recognised*
    that fact ...' (1988, OED)

Scholarship further agrees that OE had no historic present (Mitchell,
1985: 241–44), so the use of a present form to describe a past situation, as in
(24), must be another innovation. Its function is to render past narratives more
vivid and to foreground the peak events in the narrative.

(24) *And by the welle adoun she **gan**[PAST] hyre dresse. / Allas, Than **cometh**[PRES] a
wilde lyonesse / Out of the wode, withoute more arest, / With blody mouth, of
strangelynge of a best, /To drynken of the welle there as she **sat**[PAST]. (Chaucer,
LGW.802–11)*
    '... and she was only just kneeling down by the well. Alas, then a wild lioness
    comes out of the wood, without any delay, with a mouth bloody from strangling a
    beast, to drink from the well where she was sitting'

More importantly, English also developed a more fine-grained carving up of
temporal space. Situations occurring in the future increasingly came to be
marked with dedicated markers – especially the future auxiliaries *will*, *shall*
and *be going to*. Situations occurring in the past but with relevance to the
present came to be marked by the so-called perfect. Both these tense categories – the future and perfect – have links to other functional domains. Some
would count future markers as modal elements, or see the perfect as an
aspectual category (de Haan, 2010). They are treated under tense here because
their development in English primarily impacted the functional range of the
inflectional past and present tenses. The following sections discuss the development of future auxiliaries (Section 6.2.1) and the history of the perfect
(Section 6.2.2).

6.3.1   The Future

PDE has no shortage of ways to express future meaning – witness the examples in (25).

(25) a The next guard *arrives* at 12.15. (BNC)
   b I have to go. My mother *is leaving* tonight. (BNC)
   c I've got some news for you. I*'m about to* sell the house... (BNC)
   d Whatever you advise I *shall* do my humble best to concur. (BNC)
   e Mrs Duncan *will* take you up to your rooms. (BNC)
   f You*'re going to* become a poet, Shih Hammond. (BNC)

The PDE examples represent a historically layered system. The simple present with future reference in (25a) – though today much more restricted in use – is an OE inheritance, as shown in (26).

(26) *Ic **arise** of   deaðe on ðæm þriddan dæge*
      I arise from death on the   third day (*ÆCHom.*I,10(259.27)
   'I will rise from the dead on the third day'

The use of a present tense to express future meaning is cross-linguistically widely attested (Dahl, 2000). This makes sense, because situations holding at the time of speaking often in one way or another extend into the future – or conversely, future situations are often somehow prefigured at the time of speaking. The natural link between present and future at once explains the progressive with future meaning in (25b), whose emergence was a corollary of the rise of the progressive in lModE (see Section 6.4.1). In much the same way, the *about-to* future in (25c) developed from a construction expressing ongoing activity, as illustrated in (27).

(27) *Þat þis fend namore me dere, Lord, y praye þe! For he **is abouten** me to traye*
      'that this Fiend may harm me no more, I pray thee Lord, for he is plotting to betray me' (1230, *Alt.Leg.*323–5)

The histories of the other three future markers – *shall*, *will* and *be going to* – are more complex. *Will* and *shall* belong to the class of modals discussed earlier (Section 1.2) and their future meanings developed from earlier modal meanings (Traugott, 1989). For *shall*, the future meaning probably developed from deontic obligation. In (28), for instance, the decree of providence spells out a necessary future. For *will*, several pathways are possible. Future meanings are often implied when the verb is used to mark intention, as in (29a), but they may also have developed from generic uses, as in (29b).

(28) *Đu   eart eorþe, and þu **scealt** eft   to eorþan weorðan*
  You are   earth and you shall again to earth   become (*Blickl.Hom.*l.123,9)
  'Dust you are, and to dust you will return'

(29) a *Ne þearf   nan man þæs   wænan, þæt hyne   ænig man mæge alysan fram*
  not ought-to no man of-that think   that him-self any man can   save   from
  *helle wite gif he sylf **nele**   his synna betan   ær   his ende*
  of-hell pain if he self not-will his sins   repent before his end
  (*HomS*.6(Ass.14)49)
  'Nobody should think that anyone can save him from the pain of hell if he
  himself does not want to/will not repent of his sins before his death'
  b *ælc wyrt & ælc wudu **wile** weaxan on þæm lande selest þe him best gerist*
  each plant and each tree   will grow   on that land best that him best suits
  (*Bo*.34.91.13)
  'Each plant and each tree will grow best in the land that suits it best'

The division of labour between future *will* and *shall* has been something of an
issue ever since seventeenth and eighteenth-century grammarians saw the need
to regulate usage. It is difficult to work out to what extent their prescriptive
statements shaped, followed or simply misrepresented historical reality. The
careful study by Fries (1927) shows that the prescriptive rules were and are part
fictitious. Nevertheless his evidence suggests that they were not completely off
the mark. The choice between *will* and *shall* to some extent depended on the
person of the subject and the illocutionary force of the utterance. There has
always been variation, however, and over time *will* gradually supplanted *shall*.
In PDE future *shall* survives only with first-person subjects, and (for some
speakers) in second-person interrogatives (Huddleston and Pullum, 2002: 195).

The history of the *be-going-to* future is a classic of the grammaticalization
literature (Hopper and Traugott, 2003: 1–3, 88–89). Verbs of motion commonly develop into tense markers and so did English *go*. It is generally
assumed that *be going* initially expressed purposeful motion and would combine with a *to*-infinitive functioning as a purpose adjunct. Later, purpose
meaning was lost, what was originally an implied future sense remained as
coded meaning, and the whole sequence was rebracketed as an auxiliary-verb
combination. A possible problem with this account is that future meaning is
already the dominant sense in the very first generally accepted example of *be
going to*, given in (30). If *be going* expressed purposeful motion here, one
would not expect a passive *to*-infinitive (cf. Hopper and Traugott, 2003: 89).

(30) *Thys onhappy sowle . . . **was goyng to** be broughte into helle for the synne and
  onleful lustys of her body* (1482, *Monk-of-Evesham*,43)
  'This unhappy soul was going to be brought into hell for the sins and unlawful
  lusts of her body'

Another open question is why it was *be going to* that developed into a future
marker and not just *go to*, which was more common (Visser, 1963: 1399–1400).

These little mysteries notwithstanding, the later development of *be going to* is consistent with the assumed shift from purposeful motion to future. Hilpert (2008: 118–22) finds evidence of the hypothesized pathway in the verbs *be going to* combined with. At first, these were typically verbs denoting intentional actions, such as *say*, *fight* or *give*, but then collocational constraints were gradually loosened as *be going to* developed into a pure future marker.

6.3.2 The Perfect

Along with articles, periphrastic passives and various other grammatical constructions, periphrastic perfects are a defining feature of Standard Average European. Drinka (2013) shows how periphrastic perfects developed historically across a large area of Europe, which she refers to as the 'Charlemagne *Sprachbund*'. Perhaps because it sits at the periphery of this *Sprachbund*, English followed the European trend but with some peculiarities.

In PDE the perfect is expressed by *have* and a past participle, as in (31a). It is generally assumed that this construction must have developed from a pattern with lexical verb *have*, meaning 'possess', a direct object and a past participle that somehow modifies the direct object – in short, something analogous to (31b).

(31) a He *has overshot* the landing strip again. (BNC)
    b The museum also *has* a section *devoted* to the Harlem Renaissance (Google)

Curiously, examples that match the syntax of (31b) are not readily forthcoming in OE (Mitchell, 1985: 293), even though examples that look like proper perfects are already attested, as shown in (32), where *have* clearly cannot mean 'possess'.

(32) *Soð ic eow secge, ðæt an is mid eow þe me hæfð gesealdne.*
    Truth I you say   that one is with you that me has sold
    (*HomS*(Schaefer)19,29)
    'I tell you truly the one that has sold me is amongst you'

In other respects, however, the behaviour of *have*-perfects during OE fits with the hypothesized source construction. The typical OE *have*-perfect had a direct object, betraying the original status of *have* as a transitive verb. Moreover, as the glossed endings in (32) show, the past participle would sometimes agree with the object, indicating that the object once (or still) was its syntactic head, rather than its dependent. Only by the end of OE did *have*-perfects begin to appear with non-accusative objects (which must be dependent on the participle), as in (33a), or even without objects altogether, as in (33b).

(33) a *biδ   hit swutol ... Ðætte on oðre wisan sint to manienne ða   ðe **gefandod***
Will-be it clear   that   in other way are to instruct those who explored
habbaδ   ðara   flæsclicra synna[GEN],
have   of-the fleshly   sins (*CP*.52.403.7)
'It will be clear ... that the ones who experienced the sins of the flesh have to be
instructed in another way'
   b *þin   folc   **hæfð gesyngod***
'your people   have sinned' (*ÆHom*.21 47)

As these examples show, the order of *have*, object and past participle varied in
OE. The PDE word order of the *have*-perfect, with *have* immediately preceding
the participle and any object following, was one of various possible orders. The
PDE order was fixed only in the course of ME, bringing the *have*-perfect fully in
line with the emergent [S V$_{aux}$ V$_{lex}$ O] template (see Section 6.5).

Like its continental neighbours, English not only developed a *have*-perfect but
also a *be*-perfect, as in (34). *Be* appeared with intransitive verbs but, as (33b)
shows, it always competed with *have* and was eventually driven into obsolescence.

(34) *Þe folk þanked god echone, Þat þe dragun aweye **was gone**.*
'The people all thanked God that the dragon had gone away'
(ME, Brunne, *HC*,p.58).

Another remarkable difference between English and other European languages
is that the perfect actually remained a perfect – that is, a marker of past events with
relevance to the present. It did not develop into a marker of pure past tense. Then
again, such a change may still be on its way. Engel and Ritz (2000) show perfects
alternating with past tenses in colloquial Australian English story-telling. An
example is (35). The function of such perfects is reminiscent of that of the historic
present. The past tenses serve to set the scene, providing background, while the
perfects are important for the story line, advancing the plot. Whether the pattern
will spread beyond these contexts remains of course to be seen.

(35) ... a guy in Mexico, he *said* ... 'I reckon we should go to the zoo, but we shouldn't go
there when it's open, we should go there when it's night time. ...' And so he*'s jumped*
the fence with a few friends, and *went* over to the lion enclosure and he*'s dropped*
his mobile phone into the lion enclosure. ... Now the funny thing is ... that he just
jumped the fence, *went* into the lion enclosure to get his phone, he*'s walked* up to his
phone and the phone *has started* ringing. ... (Engel and Ritz, 2000: 134)

6.4   Voice

Voice contrasts offer different ways of assigning the central participants
associated with a verbal process to the different slots of clausal syntax. It is
generally assumed that the only voice contrast grammatically encoded in English is the opposition between active and passive (but see the discussion that

follows below). In the active voice, the agent(-like) and patient(-like) roles of a verbal process are assigned respectively to the subject and object slots of the clause. In the passive voice, the patient(-like) role is assigned to the subject slot, while the agent(-like) role is left unexpressed or demoted to a prepositional phrase. The contrast is illustrated in (36). Of the two voice categories, passive voice is the one that is formally marked in English. Its main marker is the *be*-passive, consisting of the auxiliary *be* and a past participle, illustrated in (36b).

(36) a [*Active voice*]
    later a car bomb *blew up* his Cadillac in Caracas (Google)
   b [*Passive voice*]
    later his Cadillac *was blown up* by a car bomb in Caracas

In PDE, the *be*-passive has a close look-alike in the adjectival passive (Huddleston and Pullum, 2002: 1436). The adjectival passive combines copular *be* and a past participle to describe a resultant state, as in (37a). In this construction, the past participle behaves like any adjective following copular *be* (e.g. in allowing modification by the intensifier *very*). The *be*-passive, by contrast, is dynamic in interpretation, as in (37b). Its past participle is the actual main verb of the clause, which is most obvious when it comes with an additional argument role (as in *A Victorian jug on the mantelpiece had been given **him** by Louise one Christmas* (BNC)). Ambiguity between the two constructions is very common, as in (38).

(37) a My emotional reserves had been depleted. .... In retrospect, I *was shocked*, dazed, confused and not able to cope. (BNC)
   b whenever the leg touched the liquid an electrical circuit was completed and the cockroach *was shocked* (BNC)

(38) I think he *was shocked* to find his new Professor of English staying in a cheap pension. (BNC)

PDE ambiguity still hints at a historical development from the adjectival passive to the *be*-passive. While this is plausible enough, the change had already happened by OE times – witness the dynamic interpretation in OE examples like (39).

(39) *Þæt tacnade þæt on his dagum sceolde* **beon geboren** *se se þe*
    that showed that on his days should be born that that who
    us ealle to anum mæggemote gelaþaþ
    us all to one meeting summons (*Or*.5,14.131.9)
    'That showed that in his days the man would be born who would summon us all to one meeting'

After OE, the *be*-passive underwent a number of changes, notably the emergence of the indirect and prepositional passive (see Chapters 7 and 9), and its extension to infinitives (see Chapter 9). But it is fair to say that a proper periphrastic passive was in place already in OE (cf. Denison, 1993: 416–23; Warner, 1993: ch.5).

Two other passive auxiliaries are worth mentioning here, the first of which is notable for its disappearance. OE could mark passive voice using *weorðan*, as in (40). Testifying to the link between passive auxiliaries and copulas, *weorðan* was also used as a copula in OE, meaning 'become'.

(40) *Heo hine freclice bat.*   *Ða*   **wearð** *heo sona*   *fram deofle* **gegripen**
     She him heavily beat   then   got   she suddenly from devil seized
     (*GD*.1(C)(4.31.1))
     'She beat him heavily. Then she was/got suddenly seized by the devil'

The cognates of *weorðan* developed into the exclusive markers of dynamic passives in Dutch and German. Not so in English, however, where *weorðan*, despite a promising start, simply disappeared. Explanations of this curious disappearance have invoked Scandinavian influence, phonotactic anomaly and competition with the *be*-passive. Petré (2014: 25–38) reviews the various accounts and proposes a radical alternative. He argues that *weorðan* was closely associated with verb-second syntax (see Chapter 9). The typical use of *weorðan* was in a past tense main clause with initial time adverbial and inverted verb and subject (cf. (26)). When verb-second declined, *weorðan* was largely lost with it (Petré, 2014: 157–59), after which, its uses outside verb-second contexts dwindled and succumbed to competition with other constructions.

The other auxiliary is *get*, which developed into a marker of passive voice in lModE. Because the development is recent, we can this time actually trace the various steps of change. In light of the preceding discussion, it is unsurprising that a copular use was involved, but the whole development, starting from the transitive verb *get* 'obtain' was considerably more complex – so much so that Gronemeyer (1999) describes it as a case of 'polygrammaticalization'. The various constructions that are likely to have contributed to the PDE passive use are illustrated in (41a–d). The actual passive auxiliary *get* is illustrated in (41e).

(41) a [*Intransitive motion verb*]
       Many ... [were] apprehended before they could *get to the castel*. (1548, OED)
     b [*Copular verb*]
       How to *get cleere* of all the debts I owe. (1599, OED)
     c [*Copular verb with past participle*]
       A certain Spanish pretending Alchymist ... *got acquainted* with foure rich Spanish Merchants. (1652, OED)
     d [*Causative verb with past participle*]
       The first thyng that he ought to doo, is to *get described*, and *payncted oute* all the countrie. (1562, OED)
       '... to get all the country described and painted out'

e [*Passive auxiliary*]
    I *got supplied* with bread, cheese and a pint of wine. (1814, OED)

Note that the *get*-passive sometimes differs from the *be*-passive in that its subject unites agent and patient-like qualities, as in (42).

(42) for Christ's sake let's *get married* and turn on the telly and have some peace.
    (BNC)

Indeed, Mitkovska and Bužarovska (2012) argue that the *get*-passive not only covers the functional domain of passive voice but also that of middle voice, encoding 'intentional activities of a human subject referent that affect the same referent' (2012: 204). In that light, the *get*-passive (if the term is still appropriate) filled an open niche in the English voice system.

6.5   Aspect

Of the four functional categories of mood, tense, voice and aspect, it is aspect that most closely interacts with a verb's lexical semantics. Any verb denotes a process that unfolds over time. What an aspectual marker does is highlight one or other phase of that process (Croft, 2012: 53–56). The main aspectual marker in the PDE VP is the 'progressive', which presents a process as a temporary state, usually by defocusing its begin and end point so that it comes to be seen as 'ongoing', as in (43). The progressive is a distinctively English feature. Its use in PDE is more extensive and more systematic than the use of semantically similar constructions in the other Germanic languages.

(43) Wider and wider, the dragon *was opening* its mouth. (BNC)

Another distinctively English feature is the existence of an array of verb particles such as *up*, *out*, *on* or *about*. Although their use is limited to specific verbs and often conveys additional lexical meanings, verb particles, too, have been argued to manipulate the aspectual profile of the verbs they accompany (Brinton and Traugott, 2005). *Up* in (44), for instance, specifies the process of drinking as being 'telic' – that is, it signals the existence of a natural end point. Its aspectual function is mixed up with lexical meaning, however. In the case of *drink up*, *up* equates the natural end point with an emptied glass, cup, bottle, or the like.

(44) So I'll be obliged if you two gents would *drink up* and leave. (BNC)

The following two subsections discuss the emergence of the progressive and the history of verb particle constructions.

6.5.1   The Progressive

There are two chief constructions from which the progressive may have developed. One is the combination of *beon/wesan* 'be' and a present participle, as in (45). This construction, which is attested with remarkable frequency in some OE texts, syntactically resembles the PDE progressive. The OE construction itself may have emerged as a blend between three different syntactic structures: adjectival participles, as in (46a), adverbial participle clauses, as in (46b), and the now-obsolete use of the present participle as an agentive noun, as in (46c) (Nickel, 1967: 271–72).

(45) *þa   ic   wæs   Dryhten   byddende æt neorxnawanges geate,   þa*
      when I   was   Lord   praying   at of-paradise   gate   then
      ætywde me Michael se   heahengel
      revealed me Michael the   archangel. (*Nic*(A)19.1.7)
      'When I was praying to the Lord at the gate of paradise, Michael the archangel
      revealed himself to me'

(46) a *Næs   him   cild   gemæne: for þan ðe   elisabeð wæs   untymende*
        not-was   them child   in-common because   Elizabeth was   unteeming
        (*ÆCHom.*I,25 379.7)
        'They did not have a child together because Elizabeth was barren'
      b *Þa   wæron hydras   on ðam earde   waciende ofer heora eowde*
        then   were   shepherds in that region waking   over their flock
        (*ÆCHom.*I,2 190.21)
        'There were shepherds then in that region watching their flock'
      c *Ne beswice eower   nan   oðerne on cypinge, forþon God his bið   wrecend.*
        Not deceive of-you none other in trading, because God of-it will-be avenger
        (*ThCap*.1(Sauer)35.373.8)
        'No one of you should deceive another in business because God will avenge it'

The other putative source of the progressive is the combination of *be* with *in* or *on* followed by a gerund, as in (47). This second construction is marginally attested in OE but more common in ME. If it is to be a source of the PDE progressive, the construction must have somehow lost its preposition. That may have happened through phonetic reduction, as is suggested by the existence of what looks like an intermediary stage, with an *a-* prefixed to the *-ing*-form, as in (48).

(47) *The kynge is gone on huntynge, certayne*
      'The king has gone out hunting, for certain' (*Beves-of-Hamtoun*,2051)

(48) *John Cheynye is owt a hawkyng, as sone as he comyth home I shall delyver yowr
      letter*
      'John Cheynye is out hawking, as soon as he comes home I will deliver your letter'
      (*Stonor-Lett*.287)

It is impossible – and probably pointless – to try to restrict the progressive's ancestry to either one of these constructions. More likely, both contributed to its development (Kranich, 2010: 78–79). Importantly, however, in function neither the participial construction in (45) nor the gerundial construction in (47) behaved exactly like the PDE progressive. The OE participial construction, while sometimes allowing translation with a progressive (cf. (45)), often occurred in contexts where PDE would not use the progressive at all. For example, Killie (2008: 80) finds that it would sometimes have bounded meaning, viewing an event 'as a whole' and being used to rhetorical effect, to 'mark peaks in a narrative', as in (49).

(49) *Her   cuom micel sciphere   on   Westwalas,   &   hie   to   anum*
     In this year came great ship-army into West-Wales and   they   to   each
     gecierdon &   wiþ   Ecgbryht   West seaxna cyning   winnende   wæron
     turned   and with   Ecgbryht   West Saxon king   fighting   were
     (*ChronA*(Bately)835.1)
     'In this year a large (Viking) army arrived in western Wales and they turned to each and every one and fought with Egbert, the West-Saxon king'

The gerundial construction, by contrast, usually allowed translation by a PDE progressive but was largely restricted to 'absentive' contexts. It was used to say that someone is absent while engaged in some activity, typically an outdoor one like hunting or fishing, as in (47)–(48).

Exactly when the progressive emerged as we know it today, in form as well as in function, is hard to tell. Petré (2015) shows that the crucial semantic change started in ME. At the beginning of the ME period, he finds, the progressive was usually fully stative. Its typical use at the time is illustrated in (50a), where it ascribes a stable quality to a non-agentive subject. In the course of the period, the progressive came to be increasingly used to present a situation as ongoing. Often it would appear in a subordinate clause to 'frame' the foregrounded event in the main clause, as in (50b). By the beginning of eModE, marking ongoingness had become the construction's dominant function – as it still is today.

(50) a *Now I wryte a sang of lufe, þat þou sal delyte in when þow ert lufand Jhesu Criste*
       'Now I write a song of love, that you will delight in if you love Jesus Christ'
       (Rolle, *Ego-Dormio*,p.60)
     b *Reynawde slewe the neuewe of kynge Charlemayne wyth a ches borde, as they were playnge togyder at the chesses*
       'Reynard killed the nephew of king Charlemagne with a chess board as they were playing chess' (*S.ofAymon*,ch.2)

But that is not the end of it. Throughout eModE and much of lModE, the progressive still failed to be used in contexts where it is obligatory today. Consider the examples from Shakespeare in (51), or the lModE examples in (52), which Denison (1998: 143) judges 'odd to my ears'. Such examples suggest a process of gradual obligatorification that continued well into the nineteenth century.

(51) a Why how now Captaine? what *do* you in this wise Company. (*Tim. of Ath.*II,1)
    b Por. Is Caesar yet gone to the Capitoll?—Sooth. Madam not yet, I *go* to take my stand, To see him passe on to the Capitoll (*Jul.Caesar,* II,2)

(52) a Now I will return to Fanny – it *rains* (1818, Denison 1998: 143)
    b How is Mr. Evelyn? How *does* he *bear up* against so sudden a reverse? (1840, *ibid.*)

Moreover, it was only in LModE that the progressive developed a formally marked passive, as in (53). Arguably, before that time, the progressive had not been fully integrated into the verbal paradigm of English.

(53) I scream as if I *was being killed* (1783, CLMET3.0)

Much as we saw in other changes, then, the development of the progressive has been a protracted affair, with neither an obvious starting point nor a clear point of completion.

What is remarkable, however, is that the English progressive has been so much more successful than semantically similar constructions in other Germanic languages. One wonders whether this might have some deeper system-internal cause. In other constructions, too, English is fond of construing processes as backgrounded states, often using verbal -*ing*-forms – for instance in absolute constructions (van de Pol and Petré, 2015: 220–23) or premodifying participles (De Smet and Vancaeyzele, 2014: 152). Los (2012: 41–42) suggests that this typifies English as an unbounded language, as opposed to its West Germanic sister languages. She goes on to raise the intriguing possibility that the unbounded character of PDE is a consequence of the loss of verb-second (see Chapter 9).

6.5.2   Verb Particles

OE had a large set of verbal prefixes. Deriving from Proto-Indo-European preverbs, these prefixes had grammaticalized into unstressed bound elements by the time they appeared in OE. This means they attached directly to the verbal stem and could not be separated from it. The meanings of the prefixes had been spatial in origin, but many had developed additional functions, mostly related to aspect. For example, the prefix *þurh-* clearly has a spatial meaning in *þurhcreopan* 'creep through' or *þurhfleon* 'fly through'. But in verbs like *þurhetan* 'eat through, eat out' or *þurhgeotan* 'pour over, fill, saturate' it allows both a spatial and aspectual reading. In a verb like *þurhlæran* 'persuade, lit. teach-through' no spatial meaning is left – here, *þurh-* simply marks completeness or thoroughness (Brinton, 1988: 205). Some other common prefixes were *a-, for-, forð-, ge-, of-, to-* and *ymb-*. Of these, some still occurred in OE with predominantly spatial meanings, such as *ymb-* 'around' in *ymbcirran* 'revolve round' or *ymbgurdan* 'gird about', whereas others had highly abstract meanings, most notably the elusive *ge-* prefix, which among other things had grammaticalized into a marker of past participles in OE.

Most verbal prefixes appear to have been already on the decline in the OE period, and many disappeared almost completely after ME. The causes of their decline are undoubtedly complex – Brinton (1988: 189) lists as many as eight factors from the literature, including Scandinavian influence, word-order change, advanced semantic bleaching, phonetic reduction in unstressed syllables and the 'general analytic tendency of English'. Whether it was as another cause or as a consequence or both, the rise of verb particles was likely bound up in the process, too (see also Chapter 7).

Some of the English verb particles derive from the same Proto-Indo-European preverbs as the prefixes. They differ from the prefixes, however, in being free morphemes, separable from the verbal stem, and in being stressed elements. According to van Kemenade and Los (2003), they functioned as secondary predicates. Thus, in (54) *forð* is separated from the verbal stem by an intervening negative element *ne*, showing that *forð* is not a prefix here. It is positioned where an OE secondary predicate is expected to be positioned (preceding the verb in a finite subordinate clause, cf. Chapter 9), and it transparently denotes a resultant state of the verbal process. Some other common OE particles were (*a*)*dun* 'down', *of* 'off', *onweg* 'away', *up* 'up' and *ut* 'out'.

(54) *forðæm   hio   nanne   swetne   wæsðm   forð   ne   bringð*
      because she   no   sweet   fruit   forth not brings (*CP*.45.341.22)
      'because it does not produce any sweet fruit'

Co-occurrence of prefixes and particles suggests that the particles were sometimes used to reinforce the bleached meanings of the prefixes, as in (55), where the particle *of* 'away' reinforces the prefix *a-* 'away, out'.

(55) *On naman þæs   ælmihtigan Godes ic þe   ofslea   &   þe   þine teþ   of*
      In name of-the almighty   God   I you hit   and you your teeth away
      abeate
      down-beat (*Med*.1.1(deVriend)1.2)
      'In the name of the almighty God, I will strike you down and knock out your teeth'

Even so, the particles started going down the same path as the OE prefixes: they began to develop aspectual overtones. The particular semantic changes involved still constitute an underresearched area in the history of English, but at least for *up* a detailed picture is available from Denison (1985b). Compare *up* in (56a), where its meaning is spatial, to its use in (56b), where it highlights the telicity of the verbal process. Some examples of other particles with aspectually-laden meanings are given in (57).

(56) a *Þa **ahof** Paulus **up** his heafod.*
     'Then Paulus raised up his head' (*LS*.32(Peter&Paul)303)
   b *The grace of humanyte is not **dreyed vp** in the.*
     'The grace of humanity has not dried up in you.' (1484, OED)

(57) a You will hardly be quite at rest till you have *talked* yourself *out* to some friend (1764, OED)
   b The surest way to try the merit of any disputed notion is, to *trace down* the consequences such a notion has produced (1759–67, CLMET3.0)
   c Laughter, he read and believed, was a sign of good moral health, and he *laughed on* contentedly, till Lilia's marriage toppled contentment down for ever. (1905, CLMET3.0)

The result is a subsidiary aspectual system, with a broad range of markers, each of which interacts in specific ways with the lexical semantics of the verbal stems it combines with.

6.6   The Verb *Do*

As a lexical verb, PDE *do* is a highly general activity verb, roughly meaning 'perform, act'. This is a function *do* already had in OE, as shown in (58).

(58) *Ða   dyde Eadric ealdorman swa he oft   ær   dyde*
    Then did Eadric alderman   as   he often before did . . . (*ChronF*(Baker)1016.24)
    'Then prince Eadric did, as he had often done before, . . .'

There is nothing unusual about general activity verbs grammaticalizing. Among other things, they are particularly prone to becoming causative markers, emphatic elements or pro-verbs (Heine and Kuteva, 2002: 117–20) – indeed, all of these are functions that English *do* fulfilled at some point or other. But what *do* does in Standard PDE is, both from a Germanic and from a typological perspective, more remarkable (Van der Auwera, 1999: 461–62).

PDE *do* is obligatory in negative and interrogative clauses when there is no other auxiliary present. In such cases *do* appears to be an empty 'operator', simply required by the syntax of the negative or interrogative clause. The PDE system is illustrated by the examples in Table 6.1. Essentially, *do* does in clauses without another auxiliary what the auxiliary does in clauses with one: in negative clauses it carries the negator *not* and in interrogative clauses it inverts with the subject.

Table 6.1. *Distribution of* do *over PDE clause types.*

CLAUSE TYPE	*Without other auxiliary*	*With other auxiliary*
Declarative	We saw a unicorn.	We will see a unicorn.
Negative	We **did** not see a unicorn.	We will not see a unicorn.
Interrogative	**Did** we see a unicorn?	Will we see a unicorn?

In contrast, the system inherited from Germanic did not require *do* in negative or interrogative clauses without other auxiliary. As shown in (59), the lexical verb itself would carry the negator and would invert with the subject.

(59) a *whanne þou* **wenest** *not I schal reproue þe*
    'When you do not believe me, I shall reprove you' (Wyclif, *Aug.*Ch.XX)
  b *hwerof* **chalengest** *þu me.*
    'What do you accuse me of?' (*Anc.Riwle*,1,II.44.403)

Do started grammaticalizing into an operator during the ME period. Input to this process may have come from various source constructions. The most promising candidate is probably the causative use of *do*, as in (60a). Most OE and ME causative verbs, notably *hatan* and *lætan*, could leave the subject of the infinitive unexpressed. This use is attested for *do* as well, as shown in (60b). However, while this brought causative *do* syntactically very close to the later operator, its use with a subjectless infinitive was very uncommon (Denison, 1993: 257–58).

(60) a *and* **deþ** *hi* *sittan,* *and* *he* *gæþ* *sylf* *and* *hym* *þenað.*
    and does them sit, and he goes self and them serves
    (*ÆHom.*26.1 8)
    'and (he) makes them sit down, and goes himself and serves them'
  b *Ðis* *hali* *mihte* *ðe* **dieð** *ilieuen* *ðat...*
    this holy virtue that causes believe that... (*Vices&Virtues*, p.27)
    'This holy virtue which causes one to believe that ...'

Another construction that may have played some role in the development of operator *do* is the resumptive pro-verb use, as in (61). While the causative was syntactically closer to the later operator construction, the pro-verb uses resembled the operator semantically, in being practically empty of lexical content.

(61) *and hit þær forbærnð þæt mancyn, swa hit her ær* **dyde**.
    and it there burns-up that mankind as it here before did (*HomU.*35.1(Nap 43)9)
    'and it will burn those people to death, as it has done here before'

The question of the sources of operator *do* is further complicated by the possibility of Celtic influence. A balanced appraisal of the evidence is given by van der Auwera and Genee (2002), who conclude that the contact hypothesis is equally hard to prove as to disprove.

Whatever its sources may have been, there is another riddle to the history of operator *do* that has puzzled commentators. The first examples did not function like today's operator. Ellegård (1953: 56) reports the first operator-like uses of *do* in the thirteenth century, but they occurred in declarative clauses, as in (62). The first examples in negative and interrogative clauses – which is where *do* prevails today – only appeared in the late fourteenth century.

(62) *Ʒif þe Devȝ is . . . a-doneward i-falle al-so And þare come*[SUBJ] *a þicke myst, and a cold forst þer-to; þanne freost þe þicke Myst . . . And þarof comez þe Rym-forst, ase þilke Mist **deth** fleo.*
'If the dew has thus fallen down and [if] a thick mist comes, and also a deep frost, then the thick mist will freeze up . . . and from that the rime arises as that same mist does disappear' (*S.Engl.Leg.*617–21)

It therefore looks like the operator must have had a somewhat different function in early ME than in PDE. What that function was, however, remains uncertain. The explanation that first comes to mind is that *do* might have been an emphatic marker. But in light of the actually attested examples, such as (44), that is not very plausible. For one thing, in metrical verse *do* is typically found in unstressed positions (Ellegård, 1953: 121). Probably, Denison's, (1993: 281) suggestion that *do* for a while expressed perfective meaning is more consistent with the evidence.

The following stage in the history of *do* is marked by major frequency increases. As Ellegård (1953: 162) demonstrates, the increases mainly occurred in negative and interrogative contexts, so that from late ME onwards these were the contexts *do* began to be increasingly associated with. The association was further cemented in eModE, when the use of *do* in declarative clauses began to steadily decline. Clearly, these are the developments that eventually led to the PDE system. The interesting question is what caused them.

In at least one respect, the rise and redistribution of *do* makes good sense. Denison (1993: 467–68) observes that in ME texts, the majority of negative and interrogative clauses had an auxiliary – be it *be, have* or one of the modals. It follows that the rise of *do* systematized an existing statistical trend that already distinguished negatives and interrogatives from declaratives. Moreover, *do* also made the system of negative and interrogative clauses more internally uniform, by extending the dominant pattern to all negative and interrogative clauses (cf. Table 6.1). Perhaps this explains why the system of negative and interrogative clauses was reorganized in this particular way. That said, it probably does not explain why the system needed reorganizing in the first place. Although interpretations vary in their technical details, most accounts agree that the changes to *do* starting in ME must have been additionally triggered by the changes in English word order taking place around the same time (e.g. Kroch, 1989; Warner, 1993: 226–34).

To get an impression of the factors involved, first consider *do* in interrogatives. Verb-subject order had been common in English both in declarative and in interrogative clauses, until the loss of verb-second caused a massive decline in the incidence of verb-subject order in declaratives (cf. Chapter 9). As the dominant order became subject-verb, inversion in interrogatives turned into an isolated exception. Also, it became more and more unusual for a verb to be separated from its object by an intervening subject. Against this background, *do* may have served to bring interrogatives back in line with an increasingly strict SVO grammar. Schematically, the change was as follows:

V	S	O		V-aux	S	V-lex	O
Saw	*we*	*a unicorn?*	⇨	*Did*	*we*	*see*	*a unicorn?*

Its effects were twofold. On the one hand, *do* allowed inversion to mark a clause as interrogative, without having the subject follow the lexical verb. On the other, *do* still allowed the object to be positioned immediately following the lexical verb. One piece of evidence supporting this explanation is that interrogatives with a direct object were quicker to adopt operator *do* than interrogatives without (Ellegård, 1953: 203).

As to negatives, the crucial change may have had to do with adverb placement. In the course of ME, the position between the subject and verb became a favoured position for adverbs, particularly so for light adverbs expressing modality or degree, like *never*, *hardly* or *almost* (cf. Quirk *et al.*, 1985: 493, for PDE). The negative adverb *not* naturally belonged to this class but had of old resisted positioning between the subject and verb, especially in main clauses (Haeberli and Ingham, 2007, give figures for early ME). It is conceivable that *do* was again exploited to solve this tension between opposing tendencies. Schematically, this is what happened:

S	V	Adv	O		S	V-aux	Adv	V-lex	O
We	*saw*	*not*	*a unicorn.*	⇨	*We*	*did*	*Not*	*see*	*a unicorn.*

In other words, the change put *not* where it liked to be (i.e. following a finite verb), but at the same time manoeuvred it into the favoured position for light adverbs (i.e. before the lexical verb). One observation to back this interpretation is that, for a while, *do* did the same thing for other adverbs that resisted positioning between subject and verb (Ellegård, 1953: 186).

To what extent the history of operator *do* can be explained only in system-internal terms is an open issue (Stein, 1990). Even so, there is a certain compelling logic to the interactions between word-order change and the rise of *do*. Moreover, there can be no doubt that the rise of *do* had a profound impact on the grammar of the English VP. It constituted the final rift between lexical verbs and auxiliaries as two distinct grammatical classes. It also further consolidated the division of labour within the VP, with most functional categories being encoded by auxiliaries preceding the lexical verb.

6.7   Concluding Remarks

From OE to PDE, the English verb phrase underwent a complete makeover. Remarkably, however, most of what happened over this long stretch of time followed the same basic recipe. One after another, biclausal constructions with a finite verb (*be, have, will, do,* etc.) or a verbal complex (*be going, have got,* etc.) and a non-finite form (a participle, gerund or infinitive) fused into monoclausal structures, with the original finite form developing into a grammatical modifier to the lexical verbal head. The result is an accumulation of relatively similar structures. In a way, it is surprising that English should have chosen the same path again and again, especially as alternative grammaticalization paths are well-known from other languages. For instance, the potential of verb particles for marking grammatical meanings seems – in comparison – underexploited (see Section 6.5.2). Similarly, English has paratactic structures as in (63) but contrary to what happened in other languages, these do not or scarcely develop grammatical uses.

(63)   Yes, you can *sit and peel* the potatoes. (BNC)

No doubt, more than one explanation is conceivable here, but it is perhaps not implausible that once a certain structural path has been taken, this constrains possible future developments. Different linguistic theories will express this idea in different ways (cf. Chapter 3). In a constructionist or usage-based approach, the phenomenon can be interpreted as a manifestation of analogy, with changes being more likely if they result in structures that resemble already existing patterns in the language.

7   Clausal Constituents

7.1   Introduction

In this chapter we discuss diachronic developments involving the various clausal constituents. The emphasis here will be on arguments (subjects, direct, indirect and prepositional objects) and negation, concentrating on the changes they have undergone in terms of function and expression. Changes in the behaviour of adjuncts are discussed in Chapter 9 ("Word Order"), as these mostly have to do with their position in the clause. We first discuss internal developments in the expression of subjects and objects (Sections 7.2 and 7.3), followed by changes in the relations they enter into with each other and with the finite verb, which involve the loss of impersonal constructions, the active/passive relation and agreement (Sections 7.4 to 7.6).[1] Finally, we turn to changes in the expression of clausal negation (Section 7.7). For each constituent, we start with a description of the basic historical developments, followed by a discussion of how these developments can be understood when viewed in the context of other changes taking place in the language, such as the effect of the large-scale introduction of loanwords and other types of linguistic contact, the loss of verbal and nominal inflections, the concomitant rise of periphrastic constructions, and changes in word order.

7.2   Subjects

Throughout its history, English has had a stable system of grammatical functions in active clauses that contain an agent expression: the agent of the clause functions as the subject, the theme or affected entity functions as the direct object, and the recipient or experiencer as the indirect/prepositional object, while other roles, such as instrument or source, or references to time and location, have adjunct status. In (1), we give two present-day examples in which semantic roles and grammatical functions are linked in this way.

---

[1] For changes in the *form* of the passive, see Section 6.3.

(1) a He   promised us   an answer by Saturday evening.
    AGENT   RECIPIENT THEME TIME-ADVERBIAL
   b I   bought the books from Amazon with my mother's credit card
    AGENT   THEME SOURCE   INSTRUMENT

However, even within this basic clause type, certain variations and alternations are possible, and there have been several changes in the types of elements that can function as specific clausal constituents. As far as subjects are concerned, the principal changes have to do with 'empty' and 'dummy' subjects, and a widening of semantic roles in subject position (see further Sections 7.5 and 7.6, and Chapter 9).

First, let us look at empty subjects, as in PDE (2) and (3). We use the symbol Ø to mark the empty subject.

(2) Ø seems he was involved in some sort of scandal (BNC).

(3) Mmm. Ø Did not know Giles but Ø think advice was quite good
    (Helen Fielding, 'Bridget Jones's Diary', *Daily Telegraph*, 2/5/1998)

The sentence in (2) illustrates the omission of a dummy *it*, which has no referential meaning but is present simply to fill the subject slot in clauses containing a subordinate argument clause; we will use the label 'null dummy subject' for this phenomenon. The sentence in (3) is different, because the empty subject position has to be interpreted as *I*, a meaningful pronoun. In PDE, the distribution of these two types of empty subjects is not exactly the same: *it*-omission as in (2) appears to be characteristic of informal speech, while pronoun-omission of the type seen in (3) (for which the term *pro*-drop is sometimes used) is typical of diary-style (see Haegeman 1997). Both types are more usual in main clauses than in subordinate clauses.

We first discuss the first type: *null* dummy subjects. These subjects are plentifully attested in OE texts; an example is (4). The corresponding example in (5) makes clear that use of an overt dummy subject with *hit* 'it' was also possible (sometimes also *þæt* is found here, but this is infrequent).

(4) *Swa þonne is me nu   swiþe earfeðe hiera mod   to ahwettanne*
    So then is me now very easy   their mood to whet (*Or.*4,13.113.7)
    'In the same way then it is now easy for me to whet their appetite'

(5) *hit bið   swiðe unieðe ægðer to donne*
    it will-be very   uneasy either to do (*CP.*46.355.19)
    'It won't be easy to do either'

In ME texts, the two options (i.e. null and overt dummy subjects) continue to exist side by side; an example with a null dummy subject from this period can be seen in (6).

(6) Acc *himm   wass lihht to lokenn himm/ fra   þeʒʒre laþe wiless*
    But to-him was   easy to keep   himself from their   evil wiles *(Orm.*10316)
    'But it was easy for him to protect himself against their evil tricks'

After 1500, however, only the variant with overt dummy *it* survives in the
written records, becoming, therefore, correspondingly more frequent. Some
suggestions have been made about the possible causes for this development —
the increasingly fixed subject-verb order being one of them, but the existence of
informal spoken examples like (2) in PDE must make us hesitant to declare null
dummy subjects dead and buried by 1500. Rather, the development appears to
have been from general use of null dummies in OE to restricted use in PDE. It is
quite likely that standardization also played a role with *it* becoming compulsory
in written language.

Besides the use of *it* as a dummy subject, the word *there* can also be found as
a dummy or expletive subject in PDE existential sentences – that is, in intransitive clauses with an indefinite 'logical' subject, as in *There is a shift in the
political wind* (BNC). This usage likewise goes back to OE times, but at that
period the *there*-construction was only one of several competing variants (and a
rather minor variant to begin with). Thus in the relevant sentence types, the use
of *there* (7a) alternated with *hit* (7b) and the absence of a dummy subject (7c).

(7) a ... *þæt þær nære   buton twegen dælas: Asia & þæt oþer Europe*
      ... that there not-were but   two   parts: Asia and the other Europe
      (*Or.*1,1.8.11)
      '... that there were only two parts: Asia, and the other one, Europe'
    b *Is hit lytel tweo ðæt ðæs wæterscipes welsprynge is on hefonrice*
      is it little doubt that the watercourse's spring   is in heaven-kingdom
      (*CP.*Ep.6)
      'There is little doubt that the source of the watercourse is in the heavenly kingdom'
    c *Sum   rice man wæs*
      some rich man was (*ÆCHom.*I,23 366.44)
      'There was a rich man'

It is during the ME period that these other variants fall out of use, and the PDE
situation establishes itself with expletive *there* becoming the rule. In late ME,
dummy *there* is actually used somewhat more widely than in PDE, as it
sometimes appears even in transitive clauses (Tanaka, 2000). This construction
is found especially in cases where the logical subject is a negative word like
nobody or *nothing*; as in (8).[2] The construction disappears soon after 1500.

---

[2] A connection has been posited between the late ME occurrence of such 'transitive expletive'
constructions with a negative subject and the occurrence in the same period of the divergent
object-verb word order in clauses with a negative object (see Ingham, 2000, 2002). Both
phenomena instantiate the general tendency, attested in many languages, for negative clauses
to show special syntax (cf. e.g. Van der Wurff, 1999; Moerenhout and Van der Wurff, 2000).

(8) *Ther shal no thyng hurte hym* (*Past.Letters*,643.24(1461))

We now turn to the history of *pro*-drop in English, the second type of omitted subject illustrated in (3). The usual account of the development holds that *pro*-drop was possible (but never very frequent) in OE, and disappeared well before the present time. It was probably an archaic remnant from earlier prehistoric times, and indeed most of the examples are found in *Beowulf*, a poem that is known to have preserved more archaic syntax overall (cf. Fulk, 2014). An OE example of the phenomenon is given in (9).

(9) *Se halga ða   het   him bringan sæd. Ø wolde on ðam westene wæstmes tilian*
    The saint then ordered to-him bring seed. Ø wanted in the wasteland plants grow
    (*ÆCHom.*II.10.86.176)
    'The saint then ordered seed to be brought to him. He wanted to grow a crop in the wasteland'

Again, as with the null dummy subject, the development seems to have been from somewhat wider (but not very frequent) use in OE to very restricted use in PDE, but a more accurate account of this can only become possible when more data have become available on the exact distribution of *pro*-drop over the stylistic spectrum at each individual stage of the language (including PDE).

For the OE period, more detailed work has been done recently on this phenomenon by Walkden (2013) (an analysis based on the tagged Penn-Helsinki corpus), and Van Gelderen (2013). But even when corpus evidence is used, there are problems. Lass (2004: 26–28) notes with reference to an example of *pro*-drop with the first person plural in the early OE text of *Caedmon's Hymn* (i.e. in *Nu Ø sculon herigean heofonrices weard* 'Now [we] must praise the heavenly Lord') that most editors of the early mss of this poem have inserted the OE pronoun *we*, even though the pronoun only appears in tenth-century or later versions (where it was indeed sometimes inserted by scribes), thus obscuring (possibly) relevant linguistic evidence. A problem here is that the corpora are usually based on edited texts and not on mss (cf. also Walkden, 2013: 156).

Still, on the basis of these two recent studies, it is possible to identify a number of structural factors and contexts that seem to have promoted the occurrence of *pro*-drop in OE. One factor that has clearly played a role is person features: first and second person pronouns are omitted far less often than third person ones (the example in (9) is typical in this respect). Walkden (2013: 165) shows that in the texts that robustly allow *pro*-drop, its occurrence in first and second person never rises above the level of 4 per cent, while in the third person (both singular and plural), it may amount to as much as 80 per cent. It is likely, because all these texts are based on Latin, that *pro*-drop use will have been influenced by the source text, but the fact that it is infrequent in the other two persons counts against this as a crucial factor. Rather, the distribution may show that the omission of the third person was in itself a native phenomenon, unlike that of the other two persons.

The two studies further note that *pro*-drop is far less frequent in subordinate clauses; the context promoting *pro*-drop usually involves a sequence of main clauses with identical subjects (as can also be seen in (9), and one subordinate example can be found in (10)). Walkden (2013: 172) refers in this respect to the availability of 'aboutness topics' – that is, the subject can be left out when the topic that the null pronoun refers to is already known, and situated on the same discourse level. This would link it to the regular absence of a subject pronoun in *coordinated* clauses, with or without a conjunction, where of course the null subject is still regular even in PDE (as in *They won their opening match by 51 runs, but Ø lost the second by four wickets* (BNC)). It should also be remembered in this connection that the distinction between main and coordinate clauses was not always so clear in OE texts. Finally, there are two factors that may be more controversial or more difficult to prove. Walkden suggests that the phenomenon may have been dialectal since it occurs more often in Anglian texts, which, themselves being rare, also would explain the rarity of *pro*-drop itself, while Van Gelderen (2013) argues that rich inflexional agreement was responsible for *pro*-drop, connecting its later loss to the loss of overt agreement with the first and second person pronouns. We agree, however, with Walkden (*ibid.:* 168) that this cannot be a crucial factor because *pro*-drop is regular also in the third person plural, even though the plural had no inflexional person-distinctions in OE. More generally, there seems to be no correlation between the distinctiveness of a verbal ending and the incidence of *pro*-drop.

Other examples of pronoun omission in OE are more clearly different from what is possible in PDE. They concern cases where the omitted subject is identical to a *non*-subject in an earlier clause, as in (10)–(11). In (10) the empty subject is understood to refer back to the dative *him* in the preceding clause. Examples like (11) are attested more frequently since here the dative NP occurs in an impersonal construction with the dative functioning notionally as a subject (see further Section 7.5),

(10) *ah hie   a motan mid him gefeon, þær Ø leofað & rixað a   buton   ende*
but they ever may with him rejoice, there Ø lives and rules ever without end
(*HomU*.18(Bl.Hom.1)188)
'but they may rejoice with him forever, where he lives and rules for ever without end'

(11) *Ða gelicode þam   gedwolum þæs bisceopes dom,   and wacodon þa   þreo*
Then liked to-the heretics   the bishop's proposal, and watched then three niht
nights (*ÆLS*(Basil)336)
'Then the heretics liked the bishop's proposal and watched then for three nights'

Pronoun omission of this type continues throughout the ME period and is still sometimes found in the sixteenth century, as in example (12), but then disappears from written texts.

(12) *that done they ledde hym faste bounde in chaynes of yren in to Babylone and there Ø was set in pryson (Fisher, Rissanen, 1999: 249)*

In ME, we occasionally come across another (and apparently new) context allowing subject pronoun omission. It consists of clauses with a topic phrase introduced by a prepositional element and an empty subject that is understood to be identical to this topic; an example is (13).

(13) *As for Thomas Myller Ø   wyll do nothyng in thys mater*
     As for Thomas Myller, [he] will do nothing in this matter
     (*Cely Letters*, Fischer *et al.*, 2000: 70)

However, this is a short-lived innovation, as it does not seem to survive the ME period.

A final context for *pro*-drop that we mention here is the use of a second person singular verb in -*(e)st*, which sometimes lacks the subject pronoun *thou*. We saw in the prior discussion that *pro*-drop of a second person pronoun is somewhat rare in OE, but it is not unusual in ME and it continues in eModE, until the pronoun *thou* and the associated verbal form cease to be used altogether. A Shakespearian example is given in (14).

(14) *Hast thou neuer an eie in thy heade? Canst Ø not heare?* (*1Henry IV*.ii.1)

It is in cases like this that English comes closest to what may be called standard *pro*-drop languages like Spanish and Italian, where the rich verbal inflection suffices to identify the person and number of the empty subject (i.e. a clause like Spanish *Te quiero* cannot mean anything else than 'I love you', due to the -*o* ending). However, even with the eModE verbal form in -*est*, it is much more usual to find overt *thou* rather than a null subject. Quite possibly this omission has a phonetic cause. We know from other evidence that the pronoun *thou* could be assimilated to the verbal ending in -*(s)t* in ME constructions, which resulted in forms like *canstu,* further reduction could then lead to *canste* (with a schwa) > *canst*.

7.3   Objects

To begin the discussion of objects and the changes that they have undergone, we may first consider some cases of object omission. In PDE, this phenomenon can be found in various types of sentences, some of which are illustrated in (15a-c).

(15) a His friends were eating/He was reading
     b I see/You know
     c Grill for five minutes/Handle with care
     d The trumpets are blowing

The examples in (15a) feature verbs that can be used transitively, but in their use here they appear to be used intransitively, with no syntactically active object being present at all. The precise nature of such transitive-intransitive alternations is still a matter of debate, but their historical development is not particularly spectacular: they are found from the earliest period onwards. The instances in (15b) are different: they feature verbs of cognition like *see*, *know*, *understand*, or *imagine*, whose empty object is always interpreted as referring to the topic currently being discussed or considered (hence, they cannot refer to a concrete entity: *You know* can be equivalent to *You know what I mean* or *You know what he/she/it is like*, etc., but not normally to *You know him/her/it*). Some of these cases can be regarded as semi-frozen expressions, resulting from a process of grammaticalization. Thus, Thompson and Mulac (1991) show how the subject-verb-object sequence [*I think* + *that*-clause] may have given rise to the epistemic marker *I think*, which has shed its clausal object (via an earlier loss of the complementizer *that*) as a result of repeated and predictable use in discourse. Crucial in Thompson and Mulac's scenario is the loss of the complementizer *that* before the object clause. Fischer (2007: 297ff.) shows that this creates a problem with dating: *I think* is already attested as an epistemic marker before *that* was lost. She suggests, referring to evidence from other Germanic languages, that epistemic *I think* developed out of earlier formulaic, independent clauses, later strengthened by the scenario sketched by Thompson and Mulac (see also Chapter 8).

In both (15a) and (15b), the absence of an overt object is lexically restricted: the choice of another verb can make the construction odd or impossible (**His friends were making*; **?I discovered*). The only productive use of empty objects in PDE is found in imperative clauses, in particular in instructions of the type seen in (15c). It is also only in these cases that an overt pronominal object can be inserted without causing an appreciable change in meaning, making them comparable to the cases of subject *pro*-drop discussed above. This type of 'object *pro*-drop' can already be found in the earliest texts; an OE example is given in (16).

(16) ... **nim** *marubian*   *sæd, mængc wið wine, syle   drincan*[INF]
     ... take of-white-horehound seed, mix   with wine, give   drink
     (*Med*3(Grattan-Singer)28.1)
     '... take the seed of white horehound, mix (it) with wine, and give (it) (to them) to drink'

In this sentence, the empty object of *mængc* and *syle* is coreferential with the overt object in the preceding coordinated clause **nim** *marubian sæd*. This is in fact a context in which object *pro*-drop is found more generally in OE and ME, also when the verb is not imperative. Ohlander (1943) and Visser (1963–73: 525–27) give many examples like (17), with the pattern [verb + overt object *and* verb + empty object].

(17) *He [. . .] clupte   him and keste   kyndeliche   ful ofte*
     He   embraced   him and kissed (him) affectionately very often
     (late ME,*Wil.ofPalerne*,1587)

After 1500, this construction disappears, 'almost suddenly and for no perceptible reason', as Visser (*ibid.*) puts it. However, it may be possible to view PDE imperatives like (15c) as survivals of the somewhat wider options for object *pro*-drop existing at earlier stages of the language. These wider options also licensed sporadic examples outside imperatives or coordinated clauses. An example is: *Gerueys answerde, 'certes were it gold, Or in a poke nobles al vntold, Thow sholdest haue'* (Chaucer,*Mil.T.*3780, 'Gerveys answered,' certainly, if it was gold, or nobles [gold coins] in a bag, all uncounted, you would get (it/them)'.

As regards the sudden disappearance of structures like (17), it is quite possible (but more research is necessary) that this development is related to word-order changes. Note that when the object precedes the finite verb, as was the case with (clitic) pronouns in earlier English before 1500, then one pronoun would have sufficed: *He him clupte and keste,* a structure still found in OV languages like German and Dutch in subordinate clauses. Possibly (17) functioned as a bridge construction between the old and the new orders.

(15d), finally, presents an interesting case of a verb, originally transitive, which acquired intransitive properties in the ME period. This development is probably related to word-order changes, affecting the role of the subject in the structuring of information in the clause (see Chapter 9).

When it comes to overt objects, there are several changes in their nature and marking to be noted, mainly as a consequence of other changes in the language (for changes connected to position, see Chapter 9). To begin with, the loss of case distinctions had an effect on the marking of the direct object. In OE, the canonical case for direct objects could be said to be the accusative, but some verbs governed a dative and a few took a genitive. Examples are given in (19).

(19) a *He sende þone halgan gast*[ACC] *to eorþan* (*ÆCHom.*I,22 360.168)
       He sent   the   Holy   Ghost   to [the] earth'
     b *he wolde gehelpan [. . .] þearfum*[DAT] *and wannhalum*[DAT]
       he wanted [to] help [the] poor   and [the] sick (*ÆLS*(Oswald)272)
     c *Uton for þi   brucan þæs fyrstes*[GEN] *þe us god forgeaf*
       let-us for that enjoy the time   that us God gave (*ÆCHom.*I,40 530.186)
       'Let's therefore enjoy the time that God has given us'

It may be possible to see a semantic difference correlating with the choice of the case form, with the accusative marking complete and direct affectedness of the object, the dative incomplete or indirect affectedness, and the genitive some sort of partitive meaning (cf. the discussion of transitivity in Hopper and Thompson, 1980). In particular for verbs that show *variation* in the case form of their object, some kind of semantic differentiation seems plausible. The OE pairs in (20), for example, may express antagonistic or more direct action in (20a) and a less directly oppositional action in (20b) (for more discussion, see Plank, 1983; Fischer and Van der Leek, 1987).

(20) a i *and ða   folgode   feorhgeniðlan*[ACC]
          and then followed deadly-foes (*Beo.*2928)
          'and then he pursued his deadly foes'
       ii *Ongann ða Augustinus mid his munecum to **geefenlæc**enne þæra*
          Began then Augustinus with his monks   to imitate   of-their
          apostola lif[ACC]
          apostles life (*ÆCHom.*II,9 78.205)
          'Then Augustinus with his monks began to imitate the life of the apostles'
     b i *Him*[DAT] *folgiað fuglas scyne*
          him   follow birds bright (*Phoe.*591)
          'Bright-coloured birds will follow him'
       ii *pater fæder ... and patrisso ic **geefenlæce** minum fæder*[DAT]
          pater father ... and *patrisso* I look-like   my   father (*ÆGram.*215.3)

However, the difference is not always clear-cut, and for many verbs allowing only one case option, the specific form taken was probably to a large extent conventional rather than semantically motivated (though the respective roles of convention and semantic motivation need not have been the same for all verbs or verb classes); Mitchell (1985: §1082) gives a convenient overview of the semantic classes that verbs governing the dative and genitive tend to fall into. Whatever the exact system in OE may have been, the disappearance of the formal accusative-dative distinction in all nouns and pronouns after the OE period meant that contrasts as in (20) could no longer be made. Instead, it became the rule for any object to have the objective form (i.e. the base form of any ordinary noun and the object-form of the personal pronoun). In some cases, the *semantic* distinction was maintained with the help of French loanwords; for example, the OE verb *hieran* could mean either 'hear' (when governing an accusative) or 'obey' (when governing a dative). In ME, the distinction came to be expressed by using the separate (French) lexical item *obey*. Similarly, the different cases with *folgian* and *geefenlæcan* seen in (20) can now also be expressed by means of a loan (*persecute, imitate*) being used next to native *follow, look like*. Note that, even though the genitive survived as a formal category (though more clearly in the singular than in the plural), it nevertheless ceased to be used for object marking, perhaps because it was not very frequent in that function in OE anyway. The genitive did of course retain its function as a 'possessive' marker in noun phrases (see Chapter 5 for more detailed discussion).

From the early ME period onwards, verbs increasingly came to be used in various types of larger multi-word idioms, including prepositional verbs, phrasal verbs and light verbs (Brinton and Akimoto, 1999). The rise of such expressions, in some cases, affected also how objects are expressed or how they function in the clause. For a start, there was an increase in the use of verb and prepositional complement collocations where OE might have had a verb-object collocation. Thus, the OE verb *ofsendan* seen in (21a) has disappeared from the language, but its function has been taken over by the prepositional verb *send for*. In a similar way, *forweorpan* in (21b) has been replaced by a verb plus particle (or again a French equivalent):

(21) a *& ofsænde   se cyng Godwine eorl*
        and sent-for the king Godwine earl (*ChronE*(Plummer)1048.35)
        'and the king sent for earl Godwine'
    b *Forþan þe þu eart strencð min hwi **forwurpe** þu me*
       Because   you are strength my why out-throw you me
       (*PsGlI*(Lindelöf)11,42.2)
       'Since you are my strength, why do you throw me out /reject me?'

In ModE, this development has continued to the point where there are systematic pairs like *hit/stab/poke* versus *hit at/stab at/poke at* or *live/feed/subsist* versus *live on/feed on/subsist on*. A similar development, involving the emergence of multi-word verbal expressions, is seen with the so-called phrasal verbs – for example, verbs like *to swallow down, to mail off, to give up*, accompanied by an adverbial particle or preposition, which increased enormously in eModE, as Hübler (2007) has shown (see also Chapter 6). He relates the rise of these to a general cultural change starting in courtly society, arguing that a drift appeared toward an increased use of lexical means of expression at the expense of gestural means, because the latter began to be seen as rude or uncivilized.

It is highly likely that the increase in the use of prepositional and phrasal verbs was helped along by contact with ON (cf. Hiltunen, 1983). Phrasal verbs often express distinctions that were made in OE by means of prefixation to the verb (thus OE *geotan* means 'to pour (sth.)', but *begeotan* means 'to pour (sth.) over (sth./sb.)'). The ON pattern came in useful since many OE prefixes got lost in the later ME period. In other cases, the loss of prefixed verbs could be compensated for by Romance loanwords; thus, the semantic content of the verbs *ofsendan* and *forweorpan* used in (21) came to be expressed by *summon* and *reject* respectively. The changes in this area are therefore most profitably viewed as consisting in a shift in general methods of meaning-making rather than the replacement of individual forms by others.

The reason why such replacements occurred much more frequently in English compared to other Germanic languages, is twofold. First, as already mentioned, contact played a role: the easy availability of French loans followed later in the Renaissance by more Latin loans, and the ON pattern with phrasal verbs. Secondly, another development, in itself also related to contact, was that OE not only lost many of its inflexional affixes but also the majority of its derivational ones. Where Dutch and German and the Scandinavian languages have preserved their prefixal system more or less intact (e.g. OE *begeotan* and *forweorpan* have remained as Du *begieten* / Grm *begiessen* / Swed *begjuta* and Du *verwerpen* / Grm *verwerfen* / Swed *förkasta*, respectively), English lost it. Because of this, it was easier in many cases to adopt French words or follow ON patterns rather than to try and preserve affixes which had become unproductive. In some cases native OE prefixes were kept as in PDE *beset/behead/ belittle/ behave/become* and *overhear/overflow/oversee*, but most of these prefixes are no longer productive, and in many cases the verbs are fully lexicalized, with the derivation no longer transparent.

Another long-term development in meaning-making involving the object concerns the use of combinations like 'take a look', 'do a somersault', 'make an attempt', 'have lunch', and so on, where the meaning of the combination appears to be located primarily in the indefinite object NP rather than in the verb (hence, they are sometimes called 'light verb combinations'). Some combinations like this are attested in OE (e.g. *andan habban* 'to have envy', *rest habban* 'to take rest' and *blod lætan* 'to let blood'); more appear in ME, also with nouns preceded by the indefinite article, such as 'take a nap', 'make a leap' (see the data in Iglesias-Rábade, 2001; Moralejo-Gárate, 2001); and from 1500, there is a further steady increase in the types and tokens of these collocations (Claridge, 2000; Trousdale, 2013). Their high frequency in PDE is therefore the result of a gradual process stretching over a period of more than a thousand years.

It is not only direct objects that underwent change. The loss of the accusative-dative distinction also had an effect on the marking of the indirect object. In OE, this constituent was always in the dative case (usually without a preposition), as in (22), but from ME onwards it had what came to be called 'objective case', as in (23), making it formally indistinguishable from the direct object.

(22) & sealde ðam fixum[DAT] sund &   ðam fugelum[DAT] fliht
      and gave the fishes swimming and the birds   flight
      (*ÆCHom*I,1 182.106)
      'and he gave fish the ability to swim and birds to fly'

(23) *Wolle we sullen Iosep þis chapmen þat here come?*
      'Shall we sell Joseph to these merchants that are coming this way?'
      (*Jacob&Joseph,*118)

(Note that (23) is a relatively unusual example where the direct object is also human.) Perhaps as a reaction to this reduction in overt marking, another option developed for the indirect object: the *to*-phrase, as in (24).

(24) *Betir is that Y 3yue hir to thee than to another man*
    'It is better if I give her to you than to another man' (Wycliff,*Gen*.29.19)

Until quite recently it was believed that the *to*-phrase in these ditransitive constructions was quite rare in OE, both in traditional philological works (cf. Mustanoja, 1960: 95ff.; Visser, 1963: 637) and in a number of generative studies (e.g. McFadden, 2002; Polo, 2002). De Cuypere (2015: 5) has shown, however, that this is not really the case; he found that *to*+dative already occurs in OE in 15 per cent of the ditransitive cases. He concurs with Allen's (2006) findings that one cannot really maintain that the *to*-phrase replaced the dative indirect object as a result of the loss of morphological case. As Allen (2006) notes, there was a broad correlation between the rise of the *to*-phrase and reduced morphology and increasingly fixed word order, but no direct connection. Rather, the already existent OE *to*-indirect object spread slowly to more and more verbs in the ME period as a good alternative (especially when the order of the two objects used was accusative-dative); this in turn may also have been advanced by a prepositional French construction frequently seen in ME texts translated directly from the French (cf. Allen, 2006: 214–15).

    Whether there was any difference in meaning between the two options (dative or *to*-PP) at this time is difficult to say. Whereas a great deal of effort has been spent on the 'dative alternation' in PDE involving Indirect Object–Direct Object versus Direct Object–*to*-Indirect Object (see, for example, Thompson, 1995; Davidse, 1996; Bresnan and Ford, 2010), so far little work has been done on this question for historical stages of the language. A study by Wolk *et al.* (2013) investigates the factors governing the dative alternation for lModE. The factors governing the choice are found to be essentially the same as in PDE, but their relative impact has changed over time. De Cuypere (2015) tested the variables used by Bresnan and Ford (2010) (pronominality, word length, definiteness and number) on the order of the two objects in OE (irrespective of form). In addition, he checked the OE forms against two extra variables, namely date of composition and influence from Latin source texts. De Cuypere established that the order in OE is again motivated by the same factors that motivate it in PDE. As far as the difference between the use of a bare dative or a *to*-PP is concerned, he found that the PP only occurs in OE after verbs of communication (e.g. *cweðan* 'to say', *tellan* 'tell') and cause-motion (e.g. *bringan* 'bring', *feccan* 'fetch'), but not yet with verbs of 'transfer of possession' like 'to give'. However, unlike McFadden (2002) he does not find clear evidence for grammaticalization of the preposition *to* from a more concrete 'goal' function to one of 'recipient'.

7.4   Impersonal Constructions

We have seen so far in this chapter that changes affecting the subject as such and the object as such have not been spectacular. However, when it comes to alternations involving subjects and objects together, there have been some major changes, both losses and gains. The losses have mainly affected the class of constructions usually labelled impersonal (discussed here), while the gains have been in the passive (discussed in Section 7.5). It is quite probable that these gains and losses are related. Passives and impersonal constructions share the absence of an agentive subject, so that the loss of one construction may lead to the use of another. See also the discussion later in this Section for cases in which a passive replaced an impersonal.

In OE, there was a well-developed system of grammatical marking for verbs expressing various kinds of sensation and emotion – for example, verbs with meanings like 'be ashamed', 'regret', 'be hungry', 'like', 'detest' and so on (the class as a whole is sometimes called 'psych' verbs, bringing out their shared concern with psychological states). Concentrating on verbs involving an experiencer and a source (or cause) of the relevant sensation/emotion, we can summarize the grammatical patterns in OE as in (25).

(25) a EXPERIENCER   SOURCE
       nominative   genitive/PP
     b SOURCE   EXPERIENCER
       nominative   dative/accusative
     c EXPERIENCER   SOURCE
       dative/accusative genitive/PP

The alternation between experiencer-as-subject and source-as-subject (both can occur in the nominative) is in itself remarkable enough; it is complemented by a third pattern which has no overt subject at all, and oblique marking of both experiencer and source. Example sentences with the impersonal verb *ofhreowan* 'to pity/repent', corresponding to the structures given in (25a-c), are given in (26a-c).

(26) a *se mæssepreost*[NOM] *þæs mannes*[GEN] *ofhreow*
       The mass-priest   of- the man   was-pity (*ÆLS*(Oswald)262)
       'The priest felt pity for the man'
     b *Đa ofhreow*   *þam munuce*[DAT] *þæs hreoflian mægenleaste*[NOM]
       Then was-pity to-the monk   the leper's   feebleness
       (*ÆCHom*I,23 369.139)
       'Then the leper's feebleness arose pity in the monk'
     c *him*[DAT] *ofhreow þæs   mannes*[GEN]
       to-him   was pity of-the man (*ÆCHom*I,13 281.12)
       'He felt pity for the man'

Not all OE impersonal verbs occur in all three constructions, and some verbs show a clear preference for the one or the other pattern, but these differences appear to be lexical rather than grammatical.

In cases where the EXPERIENCER is in the dative and the SOURCE is itself a clause, dummy *hit* sometimes fills the subject slot (compare Section 7.2), as shown in (27), although the empty subject variant, as in (28), is much more usual.

(27) *hit ne gerist nanum ricum   cynincge*[DAT] *þæt* [...]
it not befits to-no powerful king   that (*ÆLS*(Augurius)257)
'It does not befit any powerful king to...'

(28) *Ne gedafenað bioscope*[DAT] *þæt* [...]
not befits   to-bishop   that (*ÆCHom*II,10 81.14)
'It does not befit a bishop to...'

What happened to this OE system of impersonal verbs? In ME, the system survives but it shows signs of a slow loss of productivity. Several of the relevant OE verbs, such as the ones used in (27) and (28), are lost from the language, and the remaining ones tend to become restricted to the one or the other nominative pattern, with other lexical items, often from French, filling in the gaps; for example, OE constructions with the verb *lician* meaning 'to have/give pleasure' split into constructions with the verb *like* and the new French verb *please*, *like* being used in construction (25a) and *please* replacing *like* in (25b) and (25c) (accompanied by *it*) from about 1350 onwards. In principle, therefore, the three patterns of (25) are all still attested but without any formal distinction between accusative and dative, without genitive marking of any arguments (sometimes a PP was used), and mostly with a dummy subject added when there was no complement in the form of a clause or infinitive and only one lexical argument present. Interestingly, there were also some new additions to the class of impersonal verbs. These include the native English modals *ought* and *must*, as in (29a), but also loans from French such as *marvel* in (29b).

(29) a *Us*[OBL] *moste putte oure good in aventure*
'We   must put our goods in the hands of fortune'
(Chaucer,*Can.Yeo.Tale*,946)
b *Me*[OBL] *mervayleth mykel of þis sight*
me   marvels   much of this sight (*Alteng.Leg*.500)
'I greatly wonder about this sight'

By the end of the ME period, however, the patterns of (25) cannot be said to be characteristic of the class of impersonals any more. The empty subject option (25c) was lost from the language altogether (compare Section 7.2) and individual verbs had mostly become restricted to the pattern of either (25a) or (25b). Some continue to show dual behaviour for a while in the sixteenth century, the verb *like* being the most prominent example; compare *the lykor liked them so well, that they had pot ypon pot* (Harman, Rissanen, 1999: 251), with a source-subject, and *I liked well his naturall fashion* (More,*Letters, ibid.*), with an experiencer-subject. They also became involved in alternations in ways that varied from verb to verb; compare the sentences with the verbs *remember* and *shame* in (30)–(31), which, next to the old impersonal types (30a–b) and (31a), now also show reflexive (30c) and passive constructions (31b), as well as constructions with a nominal element (31c):[3]

(30) a *Whan she remembred his unkyndenesse* (Chaucer,*M.ofLaw.T.*1057)
      b *But lord crist! whan that it remembreth me . . .* (Chaucer,*W.ofB.Prol.*469))
      c *. . . I wol remembre me alle the yeres of my lif* (Chaucer,*Pars.T.*135)

(31) a *Or ells/ he shal shame hire ate leeste* (Chaucer,*Fkl.T.*1164)
      b *And weren ascam[ed] sore for þan o[n]wreaste deade*
         'and were sorely ashamed because of that evil/wretched death'
         (*Laȝ.Brut*(Otto)29608)[4]
      c *. . . he/ that hath shame of his synne* (Chaucer,*T.ofMel.*1776)

One of the reasons for the ultimate demise of the system of grammatical marking for impersonals may be the influx of French loanwords, which might have 'impersonal' meanings but resist full-scale integration in the system of impersonal syntax, thus introducing all kinds of exceptional behaviour into this verbal class. Other causes may also have played a role. Thus, it has repeatedly been suggested that instances of (25b) with a preposed experiencer could have been reanalysed as instances of (25a), with the experiencer functioning as subject. The standard (but invented) example given to illustrate this is (32) (cf. Lightfoot, 1979: 231):

(32) a *þam cyninge*[DAT] *licodon*[PL] *þa peran*[NOM PL] (OE)
         the king   liked   the pears
      b the king liked the pears (ME)

In (32a), the phrase *þam cyninge* is unambiguously recognizable as a dative, and the verb *licodon* is clearly plural, showing that the plural noun *peran* is the subject of the clause. In (32b), however, the relevant formal markers have disappeared and the sentence would therefore be liable to reanalysis, whereby *the king* would become subject (in accordance with the increasing fixation of subject-verb word order in ME) and *peran* object. It has been objected that the very frequent sentence-type *Him liked pears*, where the case of the experiencer is unambiguously objective, would be counterevidence to such a reanalysis, but this observation itself has been countered by arguments to the effect that

---

[3] For connections between passives, impersonals and reflexives, see below and Light and Wallenberg (2015).

[4] The parallel but more archaic Caligula ms still has the active voice here with a dative experiencer: *heom sceomoden wel sære* 'shamed them very sorely'.

preposed dative experiencers had several subject properties anyway, even in OE (see especially Allen, 1995).[5]

As the systematic OE alternations involving impersonal verbs were thus becoming eroded, some individual impersonal expressions survived as lexicalized or even fossilized units. A good example is the phrase *methinks*, now obsolete but fully alive in the eModE period.[6] Its origin lies in the OE impersonal verb *þyncan*, which means 'to seem'. In the ME period, this verb was still used productively with various kinds of experiencer argument; in (33), the experiencer is third-person singular, and in (34) it is third-person plural. (Note that the verb *þinken* in (34) is plural, suggesting that the preposed experiencer *hem* 'them' indeed has subject status in spite of its case marking).

(33) *and as he paste beyonde the castel/ hym thought he herde two bellys rynge* (Malory,*MorteDarthur*,205)

(34) *For hem þinken þat þei wolden ay be to-gydere*
     'For to them, it seemed that they would always be together' (Hilton,*MED*)

In addition, it was also possible for the experiencer argument to follow the verb, as in the phrase *It thynketh me good* (Caxton,*Reynard* 57) 'it seems good to me'. After 1500, however, the verb soon became restricted to the single collocation *me thinks*, with a first-person singular experiencer preceding the verb. At the same time, the phrase loses its verbal status and comes to function as a single-word adverb, as shown by the spelling *methinks*, the absence of a past tense form, and its increasing mobility inside the sentence. We thus have here an erstwhile verb slowly grammaticalizing (or lexicalizing) into an epistemic adverb (on the difficulty of assigning this to either lexicalization or grammaticalization, see Wischer, 2000).

7.5   Passive Constructions: Gains and Losses

A construction that has undergone considerable development in the history of English is the passive. The sources from which the passive developed were discussed in Chapter 6 and its subsequent success in English may be related to the changing functional demands placed on the subject, as discussed in Chapter 9. Here, we deal with changes in the realization of the arguments of

---

[5] Also note that, from late ME onwards, the pronoun *you* is no longer unambiguously objective, as it comes to be used in subject function as well. In expressions such as *if you like(th)* and *if you please(th)*, there could therefore well have been reanalysis of *you* from object to subject. Lutz (1998) in fact suggests that reanalysis in polite phrases like this was not a consequence but a cause of the replacement of the earlier subjective form *ye* by the form *you*.

[6] It seems, however, to have been recently revived through usage in the *Star Wars* film so that it is nowadays quite often found at the end of a clause to sound 'cool' or to convey a sense of idiocy. The Dutch cognate *medunkt,* also archaic, has likewise acquired an emotional function, used as a kind of pragmatic marker at the end of the sentence.

the passive verb in a finite clause. We shall first distinguish three types of passives in PDE, as shown in (35).

(35) a He was arrested   *direct passive*
     b He was given a reprimand   *indirect passive*
     c This was frowned upon.   *prepositional passive*

The labels in (35) reflect the status that the passive subject would have in the corresponding active clause: direct object in (35a) (*they arrested him*), indirect object in (35b) (*they gave him a reprimand*) and object of a preposition in (35c) (*they frowned upon this*). Of these three types, only the first one goes back to OE times; the other two came into existence in the ME period.

The indirect passive is first found towards the end of the fourteenth century; an example is (36).

(36) *whan he was gyvyn the gre be my lorde kynge Arthure*
     'when he was given the prize by my lord King Arthur'
     (Malory, *MorteDarthur*, Denison, 1993: 125)

Its rise has generally been attributed to the coalescence of the dative and the accusative,[7] and the increasing fixity of word order to SVO has also often been said to play a role (cf. Denison, 1993: 103ff.). The first factor would have the effect of making the indirect object of an active clause formally indistinguishable from the direct object: both would have the same objective case (i.e. the indirect object of an active clause would then be just as eligible as a direct object to become the subject of a passive clause). The second factor would allow an *initial* dative object to be reinterpreted as subject.

A problem with this scenario is, as Allen (2001: 54) has pointed out, that dative fronted passives had died out *before* the new indirect passives arrived. Allen shows on the basis of a detailed corpus investigation that the change involving the development of the indirect passive took place in separate steps, and that no *direct* relation can be postulated therefore between the loss of dative case and the emergence of the new indirect passive. Allen argues, instead, that there *is* a direct relation between the loss of the dative fronted passive (*The student was given a book*) and the fronted dative in *active* sentences (as in *The student I gave a book*). Owing to this positional loss (of the fronted element), the original dative and accusative NPs (Allen does not include the pronouns in this story because they still had distinct case forms for subjects and objects) came to be used side by side immediately after the finite

---

[7] As done for instance in Lightfoot (1991: 104ff.; 1999: 127ff.), where the new passives are attributed to the change taking place from an overt morphological case system in OE to one of structural Case in ME, which collapsed dative and accusative into one Case governed by the verb.

verb (*I gave the student a book/I gave a book the student*). It was only when the *recipient* object came to be fixed in the first position after the verb, that it became reanalysed as an *object*. This fixed position is what enabled the indirect passive to occur: because of the reanalysis to object, a subject position in passives became possible.

Other accounts (cf. Denison, 1993: 113ff.) of the change focus, unlike Allen, on passive clauses already in existence. Compare the Old English example in (37) with the similar ME one in (38).

(37) *Ðæm scipmannum*[DAT] *is beboden gelice &   þæm landbuendum*[DAT][. . .] *þæt*
     To-the sailors   is ordered likewise and to-the landdwellers   that
     hig Gode[DAT] *þone teoðan dæl agyfen*
     they to-God   the   tenth   part give[SUBJ] (*ThCap.*1(Sauer)35.375.12)
     'The sailors and likewise the farmers are ordered to give the tenth part to God'

(38) *ech bischop* [. . .] *is ordeyned* [. . .] *that he offre 3iftis and sacrifices for synnes*
     every bishop   is ordered   that he offer gifts and sacrifices for sins
     (Wyclif,*Hebr.*5.1)
     'For every bishop is ordered to offer gifts and sacrifices to atone for sins'

In OE, (37), the initial NP is clearly marked as a dative, and the clause has an empty subject, just like the example in (4). In ME, (38), however, the initial NP would have become liable to reanalysis as a subject, because it had lost its case marking and it occupied the canonical subject position (a reinterpretation analogous to that of the structure in (32), *The king liked the pears*). This account, however, suffers from the same problem (i.e. the fact that these passives only occur long after the demise of morphological case on common nouns).

A fact that is left unexplained in the regular accounts, where the rise of the indirect passives is directly related to changes in the morphological case system, is the extreme slowness of the spread of the indirect passive. Only a handful of clear examples have been found in fifteenth-century texts, and several run-of-the-mill PDE instances were still considered odd (or characteristic of careless usage) in the early twentieth century. The sentence in (39), for example, was still held up in Jespersen (1909–49: III,309) as an unacceptable indirect passive.

(39) He was sent a note

Nowadays, however, this and other tokens of the construction are quite unexceptionable. It therefore appears that lexical and analogical factors have played a major role in the development, with certain verbs accepting the new construction long before others. This would tie in well with the idea, proposed by various scholars over the years, that passives (or at least certain types of passives) involve a lexical rather than syntactic rule (i.e. that the spread involves an increase in schematic macro-construction types).

Prepositional passives as in (35c) are somewhat older than indirect passives: they start appearing around 1200. In their rise, a crucial role is played by word-order change, and their history is therefore dealt with in Chapter 9.

To set off against these gains in the possibilities for passive formation, there is one type that existed in OE but disappeared early in the ME period. This is the passive of a verb that did not take an accusative object. We saw in (19b) that *help* was such a verb; a passive with it is given in (40).

(40) *and wæs ða geholpen ðam   unscyldigum huse*[DAT]
     and was then helped   to-the innocent   house (*ÆCHom*.II,39.1 293.178)
     'and then the innocent house was helped/was given help'

Here, the passive has an empty subject, and the only argument of the verb is the object – it is marked by dative case, just as it is in the active clause in (19b). The passive operation in OE therefore appears to have worked as follows: if the active clause had an accusative object, it would be promoted to subject of the passive (this is the direct passive); if the clause had no accusative object, the subject would remain empty or its position would be filled by the dative indirect object, the so-called dative-fronted passive, see (41). If the object was a clause, the subject position in the passive was sometimes filled by dummy *hit* (42a), sometimes by a fronted dative, see (42b) and (37), but the position could also remain empty (42c).

(41) *and sæde þam   arleasan hu   him   geandwyrd wæs.*
     and said to-the wicked   how to-him answered   was (*ÆLS*(Edmund)94)
     'and told the cruel man how he had been answered.'

(42) a *Eac hit awriten is, ðæt sunne aþystrað ær   worulde ende*
        also it written is that sun   darkens   before world's end (*WHom*.3 41)
        'It is also written that the sun will be eclipsed before the world's end'
     b *Him*[DAT] *wæs geandwyrd. þæt hi   angle genemnode wæron*
        Him   was answered   that they angels called   were
        (*ÆCHom*.II,9 74.67)
        'He was told that they were called angels'
     c *Næs nanum men forgifen þæt he moste habban* [. . .] *his agen fulluht*
        'not-was no man granted that he might have   his own baptism
        buton Iohanne anum
        but   John   alone (*ÆCHom*.II,3 25.206)
        'It was granted to no one to perform his own baptism except to John'

As with other impersonal and empty subject constructions, the option in (42b, c) disappeared (from written texts, at least) in the course of the ME period; compare the discussion in Sections 7.2 and 7.3.

We also briefly mention here a phenomenon that is somewhat similar in effect to the passive as far as meaning is concerned. It consists in the suppression of the agent argument of a verb and conversion of its direct object to subject status, but without the attendant introduction of a passive auxiliary. In studies of PDE, the construction is sometimes called the 'middle' or 'medio-passive'; two examples are given in (43) and (44).

(43) This car drives like a dream.

(44) This book won't sell.

In PDE, the middle use of verbs is systematically different from the simple active use in requiring either a manner adverbial or a modal. This type of alternation is already found in eModE, but it becomes really frequent only in texts from the past two hundred years. The causes of its rise in popularity, and the pathway that it has followed, still need to be fully investigated. The development as such is no doubt connected with the fact that, throughout the history of English, individual verbs have sometimes allowed both transitive and intransitive uses; examples are the verbs *grow* (*the potatoes grew/they grew potatoes*), *heal* (*the wound healed fast/he healed the wound*), *fly* (*he flew his kite/the kite flew*), and many others. Next to this, more transitive verbs acquired an intransitive use in ME, related to word-order developments, as mentioned in connection with (15d) above. Dreschler (2015: 371ff.) further notes a link with changes in information structure, when subjects become the preferred way to express old information, which she believes also furthers the use of middles (see also Chapter 9).

The overall result of the increase of all these alternations is that the subject position in English has come to be associated with a wide variety of functional roles: whereas the subject in OE active clauses was strongly associated with the role of agent – except in one of the variants of the well-defined impersonal system and in passive clauses where it had the role of theme – at later stages the subject of an active clause can be not only the agent but also a theme or experiencer, while in (medio)-passives the only role it cannot bear is that of agent.

7.6   Agreement

Having discussed changes in the nature and use of subjects and objects, it is now time to look at the kind of relations these two constituents enter into with the finite verb and how they are referred to anaphorically in discourse. This falls under the heading of agreement or concord. Next to agreement *between* clausal constituents, there is also agreement inside the NP. In OE adjectives and determiners would agree with their head noun in terms of case, gender and number. With the loss of the inflectional system, however, this type of agreement disappeared in the course of the late OE and early ME period. Here we will concentrate on clausal agreement. There is agreement between subject and finite verb, between subject and subject complement, and between NPs and their anaphors.

When we look at agreement between subject and verb, or subject and subject complement, we note that this was to some extent more loosely structured in the older periods than in PDE. In OE, ME and also still in eModE, both syntactic and semantic considerations play an important role, while in the later periods syntactic factors became more prominent in avoiding what is seen as 'number-mismatch'. A good deal of what was considered to be more 'logical' found their origin in rules laid down by prescriptive grammarians and schoolmasters in the sixteenth century and after. This 'logical' attitude was no doubt furthered by the development of a written standard and the influence of general education, as we see that many of the loose constructions found in the older periods are still quite common in spoken and non-standard language today. Evidence for this has become more easily available since the development of spoken next to written corpora, such as the spoken parts of the BNC corpus (for a good discussion of the various possibilities in subject-verb agreement, and the factors that influence it, see Keizer 2007: 12–17 and *passim*).

In general, concord or the lack of it seems to depend on the following four parameters: (i) the semantic and syntactic nature of the NP triggering concord; (ii) the relative positions of finite verb and subject NP in the clause; (iii) the animacy principle; (iv) the presence of a specific context (presentational or generic).

Concerning (i), nouns, when collective, occur both with singular and plural verbal inflections, many of which are determined lexically. This is true for PDE (e.g. *people* and *police* take a plural, *herd*, *committee*, *meeting* and others are usually followed by a singular verb, and nouns such as *team*, *army*, *government* may take both, at least in British English), but there was somewhat more variation per individual noun in the older periods, no doubt because of the absence of a standard language, in which pre/proscriptive attitudes play a role. For instance *people* occurred with both a singular and a plural verb in ME (see (45)), while *folk* tended to occur with a plural verb.

(45) a *Unnethe myghte the peple that was*[SG] *theere / This newe rachel brynge fro his beere.* (Chaucer,*Prior.T.*625)

  b *Thus seyn*[PL] *the peple and drawen*[PL] *hem*[REFL.PL] *apart* (Chaucer,*Sq.T.*252)

When the NP is complex, the inflection of the verb depended and depends on whether the NP as a whole is seen as a semantic unity (or not) in the case of a coordinate NP, see (46), or on which part of the NP acts as the head in the case of *of*-adjuncts (47).

(46) a *Whereof Supplant and tricherie/ Engendred is*[SG] (Gower,*CA*(Frf)ii.2840–1)

  b *so þat rightwisness ne vengeance han*[PL] *nought to don amonges vs* (*Mandeville*(Tit)192.1)

(47) a *Also ther is*[SG] *a kynde of small beastes no bigger than a pigges of a moneth*
       olde (Roger Barlow's *A Brief Summe of Geographie, c.*1541)
    b *Þere ben*[PL] *also in þat contree a kynde of Snayles* (*Mandeville*(Tit)128.36)

Concerning the examples in (46), there is also still variation in PDE but here a complex NP coordinated by *and* usually takes a plural, and one coordinated by (*n*)*or* a singular verb. With reference to the examples in (47), an interesting development has been and still is taking place with phrases like *kind of, sort of, type of.* Plurality has become a stronger force here as is evident from the fact that, particularly in spoken varieties of PDE, we now often come across utterances such as *those sort of courses* rather than *this sort of courses* (cf. Keizer, 2007: 171). It is possible that these phrases are grammaticalizing into post-determiners, so that they no longer form the head of the construction, with the result that the *of*-phrase determines the agreement rather than the original head (for a synchronic analysis see Keizer, 2007: ch.7; more details on their historical development can be found in Traugott, 2008, and Brems and Davidse, 2010).

Anaphoric elements (demonstrative, personal, relative pronouns) usually agree with their antecedent NP in number and gender (in OE there was grammatical gender, which becomes natural gender in ME), but again, as with subject-verb agreement, parameter (i) plays a role here, as can be seen in the examples of (48):

(48) a *the meynee*[SG] *of the Soudan, . . . þei*[PL] *ben*[PL] *aboute the souldan with*
       swerdes drawen (*Mandeville*(Tit)24.26–8)
    b *Vor harpe & pipe & fuȝeles [song]/ mislikeþ ȝif hit*[SG] *is*[SG] *to long*
       (*Owl&N*(Clg)343–4)

Concerning position (parameter ii), lack of agreement occurred more often when the plural subject followed the verb, as in (49a), while the verb tended to be plural when the last part of the subject NP that precedes it contains a plural noun, as in (49b):

(49) a *In that cytee was*[SG] *the sittynges*[PL] *of the .xij. tribes of Israel*
       (*Mandeville*(Tit)71.17–8)
    b *. . . where the Arke of god with the relikes*[PL] *weren*[PL] *kept longe tyme*
       (*Mandeville*(Tit)70.20–1)

The animacy parameter (iii) was already shown to be relevant for the emergence of natural gender in anaphoric relations. It also comes more and more to the fore in the treatment of collective and coordinated NPs. Thus in (48a), the household or private army of the Sultan, being human, is referred to as *they*, while the coordinated plural in (48b), being inanimate, has *it* as an anaphor. This trend continues in the modern period. It is noticeable, especially in British English, that collective nouns referring to humans, tend to take a plural rather than a singular verb, in spite of still strong prescriptive norms.

In presentational contexts (parameter iv), where some new element is introduced onto the scene, the verb either agreed with the dummy subject *there* or *it*, whether overt (50a) or not (50b), or with the subject complement (50c). In PDE, the rule is for the verb to agree with the 'logical' subject and not with the dummy subject.

(50) a *And all aboute þer is*[SG] *ymade large nettes*[PL] (*Mandeville*(Tit)141.26–7)
   b *Hyllys, wodes and feldes wyde*[PL]/ Ø *Was*[SG] *in that cuntre on euery side*
      (*G.ofWarwick*,6023)
   c *Hit ben*[PL] *þe Shirreues men*[PL] *þat hider ben*[PL] *comen.*
      (Chaucer,*Gamelyn*,583)

While on subjects and agreement, we may also note a relatively minor change in the form of subject complements, which nevertheless has given rise to a great deal of heated prescriptive comment. It is seen in sentences like (51).

(51) a The person responsible is I / It is I who is responsible
   b The person responsible is me/ It is me who is responsible.

In earlier English, the form of the pronoun in this presentational sentence type would always be the nominative, as can be seen in (52a-c)

(52) a *Ic hit eom* (*ÆCHom*.I,15,301.50)
   b *it am I* (Chaucer,*Kn.T.*1736)
   c *I it am* (*Town.Plays,Conspiracy*,372)

Note, however, that it is the finite verb here that agrees with the personal pronoun, turning the pronoun into more of a subject, hence the use of the nominative. This is also seen in other clauses introduced by (*h*)*it* followed by a plural subject (complement), as is clear from the OE example in (53), and also ME (50c).

(53) *ealle hit sindon godes æhta.*   & *na diofles*
   all   it   are   god's properties[NOM PL] and not devil's (*ÆCHom*.I,11,269.96)
   'they are all God's properties and not the devil's'

In OE, only the order given in (52a) is attested, while in ME the order shown in (52b) is the norm, (52c) is rare. It looks as if both the development of cleft sentences to convey emphasis, using the construction *it* + BE, and the fact that subjects became more and more fixed in initial position immediately followed by the finite verb, have led to this development with the result that, *ic hit eom* > *it am I* > *it is I*. The last stage, *it is me*, with the oblique pronoun, probably arose to give the pronoun extra emphasis, and the development may also have been promoted by semantically ambivalent contexts with zero-relative constructions like *It's me you fear*, where *me* is – at least semantically – the patient argument of *fear* (for details see

Lange and Schaefer, 2008).[8] The first examples of the 'modern' construction are attested in the sixteenth century. A Shakespearian example is: *Oh, the dogge is me, and I am my selfe* (*Two Gentlemen of Verona* ii,3). In the following centuries, this sentence type becomes very common. That the older form, (51a), has managed to survive at all is in fact surprising; prescriptive condemnation of (51b), misguided though it appears from a historical-linguistic point of view, may have been influential.

Finally, we look at anaphora used in generic contexts after indefinite pronouns such as *anyone, everyone*, and so on. In OE, these pronouns are still rare (cf. Rissanen, 1967: 246), but when they occur, the original numeral *an* 'one' still has individualizing force (it is written separately from the quantifier), and a singular anaphor is therefore the rule. In ME, usage becomes looser presumably because the indefinite pronoun acquires a more generic sense, now often written as one word: the singular form is still the rule but plurals are now also found, as can be seen in (54)

(54) *For scham ilkan   þat werk   þai*[PL] *left* (*Curs.Mundi*(Cotton)2263)
     For shame each-one, that work, they   left

Later prescriptive grammars advocated the use of a singular pronoun, as being the logical option, while the more 'neutral' pronoun *he* was used in cases of gender uncertainty. The question of the appropriate style for using pronouns to refer to such generic antecedents became politicized in the 1970s, however, and remains a matter of substantial dispute. Traditional grammarians and guide-books stick to the 'logical' rule, objected to by feminists and others who are looking for social justice. Uncertainty as to what is right is clearly present in practice, judging from the many variants that are found, with most people using the plural anaphor in order to avoid offence, as in *Each one gets thirsty, so they drink*. This plural form sounds more awkward, however, when the anaphoric (possessive) pronoun occurs within the same clause, as in *Every boss should treat their staff well*. Other solutions being reverted to are the employment of a plural noun in the first place, as in *Bosses should treat their staff well*, or using *he or she* (*his/her*) or *(s)he*, but these latter options are often felt to be clumsy and awkward, particularly when the anaphor needs to be repeated a few times (for more details on the usage of anaphors such as *nobody ... they* between 1500–1800, see Laitinen, 2004).

---

[8] Yet another factor is suggested by Sapir (1921: 170), who argues that oblique pronouns became increasingly associated with post-verbal position due to the fixation of word order. Because of that tendency, the clause type *it is I* would have become increasingly anomalous.

7.7   Negation

A final clause-level structure to be discussed in this chapter is negation. In OE, negation was expressed by the negative marker *ne*, which immediately preceded the finite verb, as in (55). With some verbs (notably *be*, *have* and some of the pre-modals as well as some of the other preterite-present verbs), *ne* cliticized to the verb, as illustrated by *nolde* (from *ne wolde*) in (55).

(55) *Þeah ðe   eall   mennyssc   wære   gegaderod.   ne   mihton   hi   ealle*
     although   all   mankind   were   gathered   not   might   they   all
     hine acwellan. gif   he   sylf   nolde
     him destroy   if   he   self   not-wanted (*ÆCHom*.I,1 188.269)
     'Even if all of mankind were gathered together, all of them would not be able to
     destroy him if he did not want (it) himself'

Sometimes – and increasingly so towards the end of the OE period – negative clauses would have multiple negation or so-called negative concord. Two negatives did not cancel each other out (as present-day prescriptive grammar would have it) but simply reinforced one another (as they indeed still do in colloquial speech and in many dialects of English). The typical pattern was for *ne* to be accompanied by another negative marker, especially *not*, as in (56).

(56) *and   þæt   fyr   ne   derede   naht   þam   ðrim   cnihtum. ðe   on   god*
     and   that   fire   not   hurt   nought the   three   youths   who   in   God
     belyfdon.
     believed (*ÆCHom*.II,1 9.241)
     'and that fire did not hurt the three youths, who put their faith in God'

In origin, *not* was a negative pronoun meaning 'nothing', which had developed from a compound noun *na-wiht* (lit. 'no thing/creature' – that is, a thing of no value). It survived in its pronominal function into PDE in the form *nought*. Its OE pronominal use is illustrated in (57). As (56) shows, however, by OE times *not* could already be used as a negative adverb as well.

(57) *7   þa   git   þa   he wæs ymbhringed mid   his feondum he   nawiht on hand*
     and then yet   when   he was surrounded   with   his enemies   he   nothing in hand
     nyman wolde   buton his agene gyrde anlipie.
     take   would   but   his own   staff   only (*Bede*3(O)14.208.26)
     'and even when he was surrounded by his enemies, he would not take anything in
     his hand with the exception of his own staff'

In ME, negation by *ne* continued in use, but reinforcement by the negative adverb *not* became more and more common while *ne* itself came to be increasingly omitted. The only circumstances in which unsupported *ne* still occurred (even up to the eModE period), was in subordinate clauses after inherently negative main clauses, such as after an interrogative or negative clause, after the adverb *but*, and verbs such as 'deny' and 'doubt' (cf. Fischer, 1992b: 282), as in (58),[9]

(58) a *ffor ther **nys no creature** so good / that hym **ne** wanteth somwhat of the perfeccion of god / that is his maker* (Chaucer,*Boece,*2270–1)
    'for there exists no creature who is so good that he doesn't lack something of the perfection of God, who is his maker'.

    b *'Denyestow'quod sche, that alle schrewes **ne** ben worthy to han torment?'*
    (Chaucer,*Boece,*BkIV,pr4, 225)
    'Do you deny', she said, 'that all wicked people deserve to suffer?'

As a result of the loss of *ne*, *not* became virtually obligatory in negative clauses as the default negative adverb. Its typical position would be following the finite verb, as in (59), though occasionally it would slip into the old position of *ne*, as in (60). This situation eventually settled into the PDE system, the last major change being that in the course of late ME and eModE negative clauses would more and more often have either a modal, or the auxiliaries *be* and *have*, or operator *do* as finite verb (cf. Section 6.6). As a result, *not* nearly always follows one of a relatively small set of verbs, leading to a handful of highly frequent combinations. It is therefore hardly surprising that new patterns of contraction developed, as in (61).

(59) *the othir ij. ostis of the Frenshemenne cam **not**, for thay lay longe tyme in the hauene of Scluys, abidyng wynd and wedir* (Chronicle,*Richard II,1378–9*)
    'The other two armies of the French did not come, because they lay still a long time in the harbour of Scluys, waiting for the right wind and weather.'

(60) I *not* doubt He came aliue to Land. (Shakes.*Temp.*II.i.122)

(61) But I *shan't* take up your valuable Time with my Remarks
    (1731, Lillo,*The London Merchant*)

The development from *ne* over *ne* . . . *not* to *not* as default negator has become a classic example of what is called Jespersen's Cycle – though Van der Auwera (2009) argues it should in fact be known as Gardiner's Cycle. The cycle is a cross-linguistically recurrent pattern of change, whereby a negative marker first gets to be reinforced but is eventually replaced by its reinforcement. For English, the cycle is well documented in Jack (1978) and Iyeiri (2001).

In itself, this negative cycle did not completely do away with patterns of negative concord in English. *Not* was never the only element that could

---

[9] Denison (1998: 244) notes that such negatives still occur in PDE, as in 'There were doubts that it would *not* be possible'; he comments: 'a negative implicit in the semantics of the higher verb . . . is made explicit as an otiose *not* in the lower clause'. It is noteworthy that in standard Italian and French such 'otiose' negatives are still common in similar situations.

reinforce *ne*. For example, NPs in negative clauses might take the negative determiner *no*, as in (62).

(62) *Whan any of hem sike were, to him he wolden a-non, / And arst ar he hem*
*blessede, **nane** fot fro him nolden gon. (S.E.Leg.VitaBlasii,73,11)*
'When any of them fell ill, they would immediately go to him and unless he gave them his blessing, (they) would not move an inch from his side (lit. they would not go no foot from him)'.

As *ne* disappeared, the negative determiner *no(n)* could either become the only marker of negation in the clause, as in (63a), or *ne* could be replaced by *not*, leading to a new negative concord pattern with *not...no*, as in (63b).

(63) a *Also I beseche ʒow þat ʒe willyn speke to John Martyn as towchyng þe mater of*
*Chertone þat he wolde take **non** distresse (Stonor.Lett.1425)*
'I also ask you that you would speak to John Martyn with respect to the matter of Chertone, so that he would not be distressed (lit. take no distress).'
b THEY SCHALL ***not** go in **no** wise to **no** dishonest festis dyners or sopers*
(Third Order St.Franceys,Ch.vi)
'In no way shall they go to any dishonourable feasts, dinners or suppers.'

The latter pattern eventually disappeared, however, possibly due to standardization and the example of Latin, which had single negation. If negative clauses needed reinforcement, this was increasingly done by means of non-assertive forms such as *any* or *ever*, as in (64),[10] even though outside the written standard language negative concord continued to thrive, as illustrated by (65).

(64) I shall *not* declare vnto you *ony* parte of the epystle. (1509, Fisher,*Wks.i.2*)

(65) Ca*n't* see *no* bloody parachute on there! (BNC)

A final remark about changes taking place in the negative system concerns the phenomenon of 'negative raising' as found in (66), were the negative of the lower clause ('we should *not* take a bus') is as it were raised into the higher clause.

(66) I *don't think* we ought to take a bus because we were very badly treated when we did that (BNC)

There is no evidence for negative raising in OE. The only cases that look like negative raising are cases such as (67),

---

[10] The use of *any* rather than *no* in explicit negative clauses (as in (63a)) was uncommon in ME (cf. Fischer, 1992b: 284, and the examples in (57), (62) and (63b)). Only in eModE (cf. Rissanen, 1999: 272), do *no* and *not any* come to be used in variation (but expressing different emphasis), as we still see in PDE cf. 'he *would take no advice* of that sort' (BNC) versus 'Of course he *wouldn't take any notice* of you' (BNC).

(67) *ac he ne   com   na to demenne mancynn . . . ac to gehælenne*
       but he not came not to judge   mankind . . . but to heal (*ÆCHom*.I,22 320.5)
       'but he didn't come to judge mankind but to save them'

But it is more likely that these are cases of 'forward-looking' negative concord (cf. Traugott, 1992: 271). Fischer (1999) notes that the OE cases all concern instances like (67) where a contrast is expressed, which makes the use of the negative in the first clause more natural (i.e. 'he did *not come* to judge but he *did come* to save'). She finds evidence for negative raising only in eModE mostly with the verb 'seem' where there is also subject raising (68), or in cases with a small clause (69), which makes it different from true negative raising, which crosses a clause boundary.

(68) so that it seems this Creature has no very good foresight: *It* [the creature] does *not seem* to have any eyelids (Hooke,13.5,211; Fischer, 1999: 66)

(69) *I don't think it lawful* to harbour any Rogues but my own (Farquhar 8, *ibid*.: 76)

The first examples which truly look like raising are instances like (70), but note that this still does not involve raising from a full subordinate clause but from an infinitival one.

(70) when his spirits were so low and spent, that he could not move nor stir, and he *did not think* to live an hour (BURNETROC 21, *ibid*.: 75)

Cases like the one illustrated in (66) are slow to develop and only become more frequent, also spreading to other verbs such as *believe* and *expect* in lModE. Interestingly, it is most common in PDE when the complementizer *that* is lacking (see (71), and Note 11) suggesting that there is still no real clause boundary, and that verbal forms like *I don't think/expect*, etc. function more like pragmatic markers than independent main clauses in these cases (cf. Sections 7.3 and 8.3.1).

(71) a *I don't think that he* himself would see it as a failure at all (BNC)
     b *I don't think he'll* eat them (BNC)[11]

7.8   Concluding Remarks

The changes discussed in this chapter are somewhat more disparate and less dramatic than some of the changes discussed in the other chapters. Nonetheless, they illustrate some of the typical features of language change. Much of what happened to the expression of clausal constituents in English happened as a result of other changes. The loss of inflectional case markings and the

---

[11] (71a) in this particular form occurs 6 times in the BNC, while the exact same form without *that* occurs 404 times.

fixation of word order undoubtedly contributed to the increasing obligatoriness of the subject slot, the loss of impersonal constructions, the decline in dative objects and the rise of passives (see further discussion in Chapter 9). Such knock-on effects are typical of syntactic change. Another recurrent characteristic of change is the interaction between syntax and the lexicon. It is not uncommon for syntactic changes to have lexically gradual implementation, constructions with different lexical heads being affected at different times. For instance, the loss of impersonal constructions, the loss of dative objects and the loss of prefixed verbs all have been long drawn-out processes, with different verbs affected at different times. Compensation strategies, too, may take a rather piecemeal shape – such as the borrowing of French alternatives to English prefixed verbs.

8   Subordinate Clauses

8.1   Introduction

In Chapter 7, we discussed changes taking place in clausal constituents consisting of NPs. In this chapter, we look at clausal constituents that themselves take the form of a clause, either finite, as in (1a), or non-finite, as in (1b). Traditionally, such clauses are known as subordinate clauses, while the clauses they are part of are main clauses.

(1) a Every piston moves *because every little cog plays its part.* (NC)
     b *Having the collision* was the easy part. (BNC)

The relation between subordinate and main clauses is asymmetrical. In the purest case, the subordinate clause cannot occur alone while the main clause can; the subordinate clause receives special marking of its subordinate status; it depends on the main clause for aspects of its interpretation; and it contains backgrounded information while the information in the main clause is foregrounded. Clauses can be linked without such asymmetry, as in (2). When clauses are connected with roughly equal status and without one being part of the other, they are said to be coordinated.

(2) Either *it was the brandy* or *it was the heat* (BNC)

In various ways, the traditional characterization of subordination is less straightforward than it seems. In part, definitional issues arise because of how subordinate clauses historically develop and what may subsequently become of them – such 'problems' form much of the substance of this chapter. But in part, they also relate to an idealized notion of the sentence that developed with written standard languages. In written PDE, clauses are neatly linked into sentences with clearly definable boundaries. In spoken language, however, clauses are not always grammatically complete, interspersed as they are with hedges, hesitations, repetitions and comments of all sorts, not to mention continuations or interruptions by other speakers. This makes it hard at times to see a clear distinction between the different types of clausal relations, or to establish where a new sentence begins or where it ends. The

162

extract in (3) is by no means atypical of natural spontaneous conversation. The passage is coherent and links between clauses are grammatically marked, yet the whole complex of linked clauses does not correspond to our writing-based intuition about a sentence as a unit of text production.

(3) Speaker 1: now his, although it looks [Speaker 2: similar] the same as our house when you open the door here [Speaker 2: mm] his front door, the same, you've got er the stairs going up there [Speaker 2: mm] but, when you go into the passage his door, he's got the door into the front room, same as ours, on the left, but when you get into the bottom of the passage, there's a brick wall in front of ya, and it comes round and his door to the back dining room is on this side here [Speaker2: oh yeah, mm] so he doesn't get a straight through draught like me [Speaker 2: no you not do] by having that wall at the bottom [Speaker 2: that's right of course] the draught always follows where there a, you know, two doors [Speaker 2: mm, mm] two windows open (BNC)

The anacoluthic character of clause-combining in spontaneous conversation can be observed also in historical written texts. This is particularly so in texts from the OE period, when a written standard was still developing, and also in the oral poetry of the ME period, which by its nature was closer to the spoken mode.

For historical texts, difficulties are compounded by the fact that the punctuation used in the early manuscripts is different from what we are used to (cf. Mitchell, 1985: §1879ff.). Editors often have to decide where one sentence or clause begins and another ends because the 'full stops' that are used (dots placed somewhat higher up the line) are meant to indicate pauses and can stand for a comma, a (semi)colon, or a full stop and capitals are not always used to mark the beginning of a clause. To avoid misrepresentation, editors since the 1980s stick much more closely to the original manuscripts, emending the text only in footnotes. Recognizing that clause-combining is sometimes a messier business than the written standard makes it appear is a good starting point to any discussion of the historical developments in this area of grammar.

Additionally, it is helpful to draw a number of distinctions that run through the domain of subordination. The following discussion is organized along two cross-cutting dimensions. First, subordinate clauses can be classified in terms of the kind of position they fill in the main clause. Following tradition, this gives us noun clauses, occupying the position of a noun phrase, adverbial clauses, which function as adverbials, and relative clauses, which function as adnominal modifiers. The correspondences between clausal and phrasal constituents are illustrated in Table 8.1.

Such correspondences are, from a synchronic point of view, often problematic (Huddleston and Pullum, 2002: 1221). For instance, complement clauses are clauses that 'complete' the meaning of a lexical element. When they

Table 8.1. *Correspondences between clausal and phrasal constituents.*

CONSTITUENT TYPE	*Phrasal*	*Clausal*
Nominal	The cat loves *milk.*	The cat loves *being stroked.*
Adverbial	His voice seemed deeper *now.*	His voice seemed deeper *now that he spoke to his own kind.*
Adnominal	The anonymous person *with the superstar's bag.*	The anonymous person *who carries the superstar's bag.*

complement a transitive verb (as in *the cat loves being stroked*) they are analysable as noun clauses, but when they complement an intransitive verb or an adjective (as in *I'm glad to see you*) they do not easily fit any of the categories in Table 8.1.

Even so, the distinctions drawn in Table 8.1 can be insightful from a historical perspective (De Smet, 2010). As we see in the discussion that follows, subordinate clauses may develop from NPs (see Section 8.3.1). Similarly, subordinating conjunctions may develop from structures headed by a preposition, indicating that at least in origin the subordinate clauses they introduce were PPs (Section 8.3.2). So, on historical grounds, some correspondences between clausal and phrasal constituents are only to be expected. At the same time, it is also common for those correspondences to weaken or change over time. For instance, noun clauses may become less 'nouny', gradually losing the features that recalled their nominal origins (the history of the English gerund is a clear example, see Section 8.2.2). Or adverbial clauses often extend into the domain of noun clauses (as is clearly illustrated by the history of the English infinitive, see Section 8.2.1).

Second, subordinate clauses differ in terms of their finiteness. A subordinate clause is the more finite, the more of the trappings of an independent clause it has. These may, among other things, include having an explicit subject, having an inflected verb, having a verb in a main clause mood, or more generally allowing the marking of tense, modality, voice and aspect. In English, a two-way distinction is traditionally made between finite clauses, as in (4), and non-finite clauses, as in (5). The two groups of clauses differ in the presence or absence of verbal inflections.

(4) [*Finite clauses*]
    a Our sources always reported *that they believed Bormann had come here.* (BNC)
    b What power, then, must prayer have *if it be well intentioned?* (BNC)

(5) [*Non-finite clauses*]
    a If the system has broken down it could take days *for it to be sorted out.* (BNC)
    b He phrased it as a question, but she didn't bother *dignifying it with an answer* (BNC)

It is good to be aware, however, of the continuous character of the finite/non-finite distinction. For example, (4a) is in fact slightly more finite than (4b) in having the default mood of main clauses. Similarly, (5a) is slightly more finite than (5b) in having its own explicit subject. Over time, subordinate constructions can shift along the finiteness continuum.

In what follows, we start with non-finite clauses (Section 8.2) and then move on to finite clauses (Section 8.3), each time focusing on the main constructions that can function as noun clauses or adverbial clauses. Relative clauses, which function as modifiers to the NP, are not discussed in this chapter. They have been dealt with in Section 5.5.3).

8.2   Non-Finite Clauses

The English non-finite clauses come in four major types, sometimes with additional subtypes. The four basic types are illustrated in (6).

(6) a *[Bare infinitive]*
        Why did you let it *slip out of your reach*? (BNC)
     b [*To-infinitive*]
        To survive is *to dig into the pit of your own resources* over and over again. (BNC)
     c *[Present participle]*
        I hope that no one has seen you *hanging about round here*. (BNC)
     d *[Gerund]*
        George II was, very typically, in Hanover and there was a disposition to postpone *doing anything decisive* till he got back. (BNC)

From what is known of their histories, the respective developments of the four non-finite clause types have one important commonality. All four developed from phrasal categories, headed by originally deverbal nouns or adjectives that over time picked up verbal behaviour. This type of development is cross-linguistically very common (Disterheft, 1981). For English, the most recent and therefore best documented of these developments is that of the gerund, whose originally phrasal source still exists, in the form of the 'nominal gerund', as in (7a). The present participle, too, still has a phrasal counterpart, the 'adjectival present participle', as in (7b).

(7) a *[Nominal gerund]*
        [I]t was *the mindless pacing of a caged animal*. (BNC)
     b [*Adjectival present participle*]
        She did her best to stimulate a constant flow of love letters, and found the collecting of admirers a *very satisfying* pastime. (BNC)

Similar developments from a phrasal construction into a clausal one can be reconstructed for the two types of infinitive, but with a twist. Both infinitives developed from deverbal nouns, but in the case of the *to*-infinitive, those nouns combined with an allative marker, meaning 'to, in the direction of' (in fact, the *to* of the *to*-infinitive derives from the preposition *to*; Haspelmath, 1989). In other words, the source of the *to*-infinitive would have been a construction more or less analogous to the PDE prepositional phrase with deverbal noun in (8). It follows that the first clause-like use of *to*-infinitives was as adverbials expressing purpose. Noun clause uses developed from the adverbial uses only in a following stage.

(8) It was a strangely anomic creature who strode up to the door of the house of the Frankensteins and rapped *for admittance*. (BNC)

The histories of the English non-finite clauses, then, involve both internal and external changes. Internally, there were the various changes that converted phrasal constituents into clauses, with such clausal properties as clause-like argument structure, clausal negation and (some) marking of tense, aspect and voice. Externally, non-finite clauses came to occupy a broadening range of positions in the higher clause. They typically started out from the positions associated with their phrasal source construction, but then tended to expand to new positions. The main focus in the following discussion is on *to*-infinitives (Section 8.2.1), gerunds (Section 8.2.2) and participles (Section 8.2.3). Bare infinitives are only dealt with in passing because they underwent less change.

8.2.1   *To*-infinitives

From the OE evidence, the prehistory of the *to*-infinitive can be easily surmised. Its *to*-marker can be linked to the homonymous preposition, and the infinitive verb preserved what looks like a fossilized dative case-ending (*-e*) appropriate to a noun in a prepositional phrase. It has even been argued that in OE the *to*-infinitive still was a prepositional phrase. However, Los (2005: 170), following a review of the evidence, concludes otherwise. Among other things, she shows that *to*-infinitives obligatorily followed the finite main verb, as in (9a), whereas prepositional phrases could also precede it, as in (9b).

(9) a *ða eaðmodan ... weorðen geniedde **hiera unðeawas** **to**   **herianne***
       the humble   be   forced   their faults   to   praise
       (*CP*.41.302.13)
       'The humble ... would be forced to praise their faults.'
    b *Gif hwa*   **to hwæðrum þissa**   *genied sie*   on woh
       if anyone to either   of-these forced be   unjustly (*LawAf.*1(1–1))
       'If anyone is forced to either of these unjustly ...'

She also shows that *to* was inseparable from the infinitive verb and that when two infinitive verbs were conjoined, as in (10), *to* was obligatorily repeated – both indications that *to* had cliticised to the infinitive verb. The preposition *to*, in contrast, was again not subject to those restrictions.

(10) *He hæfde þa gleawnesse* **Godes bebodu**   *to*   *healdanne* **&**   *to*   *læranne*
     He had   the wisdom   God's commandments to   obey   and   to   teach
     (*Bede*.3.14.206.10)
     'He had the wisdom to obey and to teach God's commandments.'

Curiously, *to* decliticized again from the infinitive verb in ME, giving rise to conjoined infinitives with a single *to*, as in (11a), as well as to the infamous split infinitive, illustrated in (11b).

(11) a *Bidde we nu þe holigost þat he ... gife us hige and mihte **to forleten and bireusen***
     and beten ure sinnes.
     'Let us now ask the Holy Spirit that he give us the disposition and power to abandon
     and repent of and defeat our sins.' (*OEHom*.Ch.XX)
    b *I kepe nouȝt **to hastiliche afferme** wheþer it be in þat place oþer no.*
     'I do not wish to hastily affirm whether it is in that place or not.'
     (***Polychron*.VI,63.435**)

The decliticization of *to* has attracted some attention in the grammaticalization literature, because it goes against the expected tendency for grammaticalizing elements to undergo progressive formal coalescence and reduction (Norde, 2009: 190–99). Different explanations have been put forward. Fischer (1997) links both the decliticization of *to* and the loss of reinforcing *for* (see the discussion that follows below) to renewed analogical attraction between infinitival *to* and the preposition *to*. Los (2005: 211), following Pullum's (1982) more theory-driven analysis of PDE infinitival *to*, proposes that *to* decliticized when it was reanalysed as the non-finite counterpart of a modal verb.

Several other changes took place in the *to*-infinitive's internal syntax. There was the appearance of formally marked passives. OE *to*-infinitives occasionally conveyed passive meaning, even though this was not marked by a passive auxiliary. A typical context was the construction in (12), which is sometimes called the 'modal passive'. Its subject was the patient of the infinitive verb, and the construction as a whole conveyed root or deontic modality. In PDE, the modal passive survives in a few lexicalized expressions, such as *This house is to let* and *You are to blame*.

(12) a *hit*   *nis*   *no*   *to*   *forseone*
     it   is-not   not   to   despise (*Bo*.24.56.2)
     'It is not to be despised.'
    b *Eac*   *is*   *ðeos*   *bisen*   *to*   *geðencenne ...*
     Also   is   this   example   to   think-of ... (**Bo.23.52.2**)
     'This example can also be thought of ...'

Formally passive infinitives began to appear in the beginning of ME, as in (13a). Their rise has been linked to word-order change and is discussed in some more detail in Chapter 9. As to the modal passive construction, it too was increasingly infiltrated by formally marked passives, as in (13b).

(13) a *he till hiss Fader wass/Offredd forr uss o rode, / All als he wære an lamb **to ben** / **Offredd***
      'He was offered to his Father for us on the cross, just as if he was a lamb to be offered.' (*Orm*.12644–47)
    b *The whiche hevene … nys nat … **to be wondryd upon***
      '… which heaven is not to be marvelled at.' (Chaucer,*Boece*,III.8)

Also in ME, the *to*-infinitive first began to appear with its own explicit subject, in various constructions. An example is given in (14), where (on semantic grounds) *stoones* must be the subject of *be turned* rather than the indirect object of *axid*. This development, too, has been linked to word-order change and is therefore further discussed in Chapter 9.

(14) *Suche men semen to turne þe breed of pore men into stoones, and in þis þei ben more cruelar þan þe deuel þat axid **stoones to be turned into bred**.*
    'Such men seem to turn the bread of the poor into stones, and in that respect, they are crueller than the devil who asked that stones should be turned into bread.'
    (Wycliffe,*Lant.of Liȝt*)

Finally, the infinitive marker *to* was sometimes reinforced, especially in contexts where the *to*-infinitive was to express its original purposive meaning. Perhaps under Scandinavian influence (Kytö and Danchev, 2001), one reinforcement strategy was by adding *for*, as in (15). Except in some traditional dialects, reinforcing *for* again disappeared soon after ME. More recently, *in order* and *so as* were recruited to do a similar job, as illustrated in (15b–c).

(15) a *And þe scherref aboute **Gamelyn for to take**.*
    'The sheriff [went] in all directions in order to capture Gamelyn.'
    (Chaucer,*Gamelyn*,550)
    b I shall next Week come down *in order to take my Seat at the Board.*
    (1711, OED)
    c The devil and his disciples are notable method-mongers, *so as to deceive, if it were possible, the very elect.* (1647, OED)

The introduction of reinforcement strategies may have to do with what happened to the external syntax of the *to*-infinitive. Given their reconstructed prehistory, as well as the evidence from Gothic (Los, 2005: 28–31), it is plausible that *to*-infinitives started out as adverbial clauses marking purpose. Already in OE, however, *to*-infinitives had expanded to a broader range of contexts, including uses as noun clauses, though they typically preserved some sense of purpose. For example, they could be used as theme-argument to intention verbs, as in (16) (Los, 2005: 169).

(16) *Esau   ðin   broðor   þe   ðencð   to   ofsleane*
     Esau   your   brother   you   intends to   kill *(Gen.27.42))*
     'Your brother Esau intends to kill you.'

By PDE, *to*-infinitives can be used in a range of syntactic positions. Sometimes, the original purposive meaning is no longer very prominent, as in (17a) or (17e), possibly explaining why infinitival *to* may occasionally take a reinforcing element when purposive meaning needs highlighting.

(17) a [*Subject*]
        To deny it is therefore impossible. (BNC)
     b [*Subject complement*]
        Their plan was *to feed on the forest as they went* (BNC)
     c [*Noun complement*]
        The idea *to promote an urban walkway/cycleway on the disused railway line from Easter Road to Seafield* goes back to the Leith Local Plan reports of the 1970s. (BNC)
     d [*Verb complement*]
        They wanted *to pass on this property to their children* (BNC)
     e [*Adjective complement*]
        he began to wonder if Smallfry was right *to fear she would poison him at the slightest opportunity*. (BNC)

Some of the constructions in (17) have had complicated histories and deserve a closer look. *To*-infinitives used as verb complements have been on the increase since OE. To an important extent, this went at the expense of *that*-clauses (Manabe, 1989; Los, 2005). Thus, after verbs expressing an order, purpose or intention, the *þæt*-clause was the rule in OE, where the *to*-infinitive would now be much more common. Los (2005: 179–85) demonstrates that this development was already underway in OE. She shows this by comparing two versions of the same text, *Gregory's Dialogues*, one from the late ninth century, and a reworked version about a century older. A good number of *þæt*-clauses in the former have been substituted by *to*-infinitives in the latter, as illustrated in (18).

(18) a *Dauid,   þe   gewunade,   **þæt he hæfde witedomes   gast   in   him***
        David   who   was-accustomed that he had   of-prophecy spirit in   him
        (*GD.*1(C)4.40.24)
     b *Dauid,   þe   gewunode   **to   hæbbenne witedomes   gast   on him***
        David   who   was-accustomed to   have   of-prophecy spirit in   him
        (*GD.*1(H)4.40.22)
        'David, who was accustomed that he had / to have the spirit of prophecy in him.'

Next to *to*-infinitives and *that*-clauses, the domain of verb complementation also saw some variation between *to*-infinitives and bare infinitives. More so than *to*-infinitives, bare infinitives appear to have been used in contexts involving high levels of conceptual integration between the main clause event and the subordinate event.[1] For example, the bare infinitive was favoured in cases where main verb and subordinate verb had a shared time domain and there was direct logical entailment (Fischer, 1995). In (19a), the bare infinitive *stigan* denotes a state of affairs that is understood to be co-temporal with and directly dependent on the main verb *nydan*. In (19b), by contrast, the *to*-infinitive *to beten* denotes a state of affairs in its own time domain, posterior to that of the main clause.

(19) a *Ða   sona   he nydde **his leorningcnihtas on scyp stigan***
    Then at-once he forced his disciples   on ship ascend (*Mk*(WSCp)6.45)
    'Then straightaway he forced his disciples to go on board'
  b *Godde we scullen bihaten, **ure sunnen to beten***
    to-God we must   promise our sins   to atone-for (*Laȝ.Brut*(Clg)9180)
    'We must promise God to atone for our sins.'

Although bare infinitives lost ground since ME, this was not exclusively due to the rise of the *to*-infinitive. In some contexts they were replaced by present participles, as in (20).

(20) *than he will **come renne** vpon vs* (*Merlin*,XII)
    'then he will come running upon us'

In PDE, the bare infinitive has a rather restricted range of occurrence. Apart from its use with the modals (see Chapter 6), it is only common after verbs of perception and some verbs of causation, as in (21).

(21) a Then we saw *the sky burst into red* (BNC)
  b They made *her feel very sophisticated* (BNC)

To-infinitives functioning as adjective complements fall into a number of interrelated types. Quirk *et al.* (1985: 1226) distinguish no less than seven constructions, but for present purposes we can start from the two-way classification illustrated in (22a–b). In the so-called *eager-to-please* construction in (22a), the main clause subject functions also as agent-argument of the infinitive. In the *easy-to-please* construction, the main clause subject corresponds to the patient-argument of the infinitive. The *easy-to-please* construction is therefore somewhat reminiscent of the modal passive, discussed above (cf. (12)), expressing a passive-like meaning without passive marking.

---

[1] The relation between *to*-infinitives and bare infinitives in English strongly recalls the Binding Hierarchy proposed by Givón (1980). The Binding Hierarchy stipulates that closer syntactic integration between the main verb and the verb in the complement clause reflects greater conceptual integration between the two events denoted by main and complement clause.

(22) a [*Eager-to-please construction*]
Andropulos was a bit reluctant *to go* (BNC)
b [*Easy-to-please construction*]
He was lying in wait in the hallway, where he was impossible *to overlook* (BNC)

Note that many of the adjectives in the *easy-to-please* construction also appear with extraposed *to*-infinitives, as in (23), where the infinitive verb again functions as a regular active, in form as well as in meaning.

(23) [*Subject extraposition*]
it is impossible *to overlook the signs of squalor and decay amidst the glamor.*
(2008, COCA)

Both the *eager-to-please* construction and the *easy-to-please* construction were already available in OE, as shown in (24) and (25), respectively. And so was subject extraposition, though the dummy subject (*it*) was still optional (Mitchell, 1985: 18–19; see Chapter 7 and examples (4) and (5) there).

(24) *ic   eom   gearo   to   gecyrrenne to   munuclicere drohtnunge*
I   am   ready   to   turn   to   monastic   way-of-life
(*ÆCHom.*I,35 484.251)
'I am ready to turn to a monastic way of life.'

(25) *ðis   me   is   hefi   to   donne*
this   to-me   is   heavy   to   do   (*Mart.*5(Kotzor)Se.16,A.14)
'This is hard for me to do.'

The *eager-to-please* construction has been essentially stable throughout the history of the language. It is interesting to note, however, that some adjectives in the construction developed into modal markers. A straightforward example is *bound*, originally meaning 'under a binding obligation' but now typically used to mark epistemic necessity. The development is illustrated by the examples in (26).

(26) a *I requyre yow, that ye make the houses as ye **be bound to** repaire and kepe.*
'I ask you that you would mend the houses that you are bound to repair and maintain.' (a1475, *Reg.Godst.Nunnery,*471)
b Remember to keep all the topsoil you remove; you*'re bound to* find a use for it later! (BNC)

On these grounds, expressions like *be bound to* could be regarded as semi-modals – hence auxiliaries (see Chapter 6) – rather than main clause predicates. Other examples include *be sure to* or *be certain to*, as in (27).

(27) a If . . . they shoot at our searchlight they *are pretty sure to* miss us. (1909, COHA)
b whatever it is one has planned to do *is certain to* be altered in the process (BNC)

The *easy-to-please* construction has undergone a number of changes. From around 1400, two slightly more complex variants of the construction are found. One has a stranded preposition in the subordinate clause, as in (28a).[2] The other has a passive infinitive (28b).

(28) a *þei fond hit good and esy* **to dele wiþ** *also*
    'They found it good and easy to deal with as well.' (*Cursor*(Trin-C)16557)
    b *the excercise and vce* [= 'use'] *of suche ... visible signes* [...] *is good and profitable* **to be had at certein whilis** [= 'times'] (Pecock,*Represser,*Ch.XX)

The development in (28b) is reminiscent of that in the modal passive (cf. (12) and (13b) earlier in this chapter), and some degree of mutual influence seems likely. Curiously, however, passive marking eventually became obligatory in the modal passive, but not so in the *easy-to-please* construction, where formal passives never became systematic and sometimes even disappeared again, as shown by the now-ungrammatical example in (29a). Fischer (1991: 175ff) suggests that formally passive infinitives tend to occur with *easy*-type adjectives when the relation between adjective and infinitive rather than between adjective and subject is stressed (cf. 29a). In such cases, an adverb rather than an adjective is also often found, as in (29b).

(29) a when once an act of dishonesty and shame has been deliberately committed, the will having been turned to evil, is difficult *to be reclaimed* (1839, COHA)
    b Jack Rapley is not easily *to be knocked off his feet* (1819, Fischer *ibid.*)

From this, one might speculate that passive forms failed to fully establish themselves in this context because the meaning the construction conveys is not always purely passive. As (30) illustrates, the subject of many *easy-to-please* constructions combines both patient-like and agent-like qualities. While the subject undergoes the action, its intrinsic qualities also contribute to how that action unfolds. The construction could therefore be analysed as marking middle voice.[3]

(30) more experienced opponents ... can sometimes be tricky *to play against.* (BNC)

8.2.2   Gerunds

Gerunds are noun clauses par excellence. They can be found occupying all the positions an ordinary NP can occupy – see the examples in (31) – and hardly any others. Arguably, the only important exception is its use as extraposed subject, as in (32).

---

[2] Such cases of preposition stranding already occurred in OE with a third type of adjective, the *pretty*-class, e.g. *ða syndon swyþe fægere ... on to seonne* (*Or.*1 3.23.7) 'Those are very beautiful to look at.' Adjectives of this *pretty*-class further differed from those in the *easy*-class in that *pretty*-adjectives never occur with an empty or dummy subject (cf. Fischer *et al.*, 2000: 266).
[3] A comparable case is that of 'passive' *get*, which is discussed in Chapter 6.

(31) a *[Subject]*
     Finding the right person for a job can be hard work (BNC)
   b *[Subject complement]*
     Their principal duty is *making sure the two little princesses are safe and well* (BNC)
   c *[Verb complement]*
     Charles bitterly regretted *having allowed the cameras in* (BNC)
   d *[Complement of a preposition]*
     The difficulty lies in *finding an acceptable implied limitation* (BNC)

(32) *[Extraposed subject]*
     I knew it was pointless *expecting him to change his mind.* (BNC)

The gerund looks very similar to the present participle and it has been argued for PDE that the two are in fact just one clause type.[4] Their historical origins are clearly distinct, however. Originally, the present participle had a different ending in -*end*, and even following their formal collapse there has always been one syntactic feature clearly distinguishing the two: only the gerund can have its subject in the possessive form, as in (33).

(33) each day away from Cumbria increased the chance of *his missing the conclusion of the investigation.* (BNC)

The origins of the gerund lie in OE deverbal nouns in -*ing*/-*ung*, as in (34). Such nouns behaved exactly as nouns would. They could combine with adjectives and determiners, as in (34a), where the adjective *gelomum* modifies the deverbal noun *scotungum*. Any participants to the actions these nouns denoted would be expressed by a genitive, such as *deofles* in (34b), which functions as the agent of *tyhttinge*.

(34) a *þa wunda þe þa wælhreowan hæþenan mid* **gelomum scotungum** *on his*
       the wounds that the barbarous   heathens with frequent   shootings   on his
       lice macodon
       body made (*ÆLS*(Edmund)181)
       'the wounds that the barbarous heathens had made on his body with numerous shots'
   b *Ða wearð an þæra twelfa cristes þegena se wæs Iudas gehaten*
       Then became one of-the twelve of-Christ disciples who was Judas called
       þurh **deofles tyhttinge** *beswicen.*
       through devil's persuading deluded (*ÆCHom.*I,1 188.266))
       'Then one of Christ's twelve disciples, the one who was called Judas, was deluded through the devil's persuasive powers'

---

[4] This view has been put forward most explicitly by Huddleston and Pullum (2002: 1220-22). A counterargument is developed in De Smet (2010, 2014).

There have been many attempts to explain how and why nominal gerunds came to adopt verbal behaviour and ended up heading full-fledged non-finite clauses. The most comprehensive overview is provided by Jack (1988), who considers ten possible sources or causes. Eventually, he accepts four as plausible. First, *-ing*-derivation saw an increase in productivity during OE and early ME. This was a preliminary to the emergence of the verbal gerund. Second, French had a gerund – known as the *gérondif* – with clausal qualities. English may have copied the French construction using its forms in *-ing*. Third, the ME genitive sometimes coalesced with the common case, particularly in the plural (see also Chapter 5, especially Section 5.3.2). This might just explain how *-ing*-forms suddenly found themselves accompanied by common case verb arguments.[5] Fourth, verbal gerunds unlike infinitives could follow prepositions, which may account for their subsequent success in ME and ModE. After all, English could well do with a clause type that would pattern with prepositions.

Subsequent work has refined Jack's conclusions, but mostly in the details. Kranich (2006) doubts the role of French. De Smet (2008: 294–96), by contrast, believes French influence is plausible but points not only to the French *gérondif*, but also to French infinitives, which like the gerund could follow prepositions.[6] Additionally, Fanego (2004) and De Smet (2009) nuance the idea that gerunds filled a syntactic gap. It is true that the English infinitive could not combine with prepositions, but this gap in the system could also have been filled by the nominal gerund, as shown in (35). Indeed, the nominal gerund saw a spectacular increase in frequency, exactly in prepositional contexts. This happened just prior to the rise of the verbal gerund. One might therefore speculate that English first filled the gap in its system of noun clauses by exploiting nominal gerunds and then gradually switched to a better alternative in the form of the verbal gerund – the advantage of the latter being its greater syntactic flexibility.

(35) *For þis principle of love moten men suppose, whanne þer ben two þingis put in a mannis chois, and he mut nede leve þe toon for **takinge of þe toþer**.*
(Wyclif, *Bible*,LX,p.182)
'Because men must bear in mind this principle of love, when a man is to choose between two things, and he must abandon the one in return for taking the other.'

As verbal gerunds came to be used more and more, they also acquired more clausal features. Common-case direct objects and adverbs appeared first. Later negation appeared, as well as other clausal constituents such as indirect objects

---

[5] For example, *after is fader buriinge* (Gloucester,*Chron*.7859) is ambiguous between 'after his father's burying' and 'after burying his father'. That is because *fader*, originally an inflectionless genitive singular, could be taken to be a common-case form, entailing verbal status for the form *buriinge*.

[6] Some examples of relevant infinitive constructions, from the *Anglo-Norman Dictionary*, are *Il le trespasserent sanz pardun demander* (c1235, AND) 'they wronged him without asking for pardon' or *Le tierz si est a la feste Seint Johan, pur garder la cite de arsoun pur la graunt secheresce* (1419, AND) 'the third (general assembly) is at the feast of Saint John, for guarding the city against fire on account of the great draught'.

and subject complements. Finally, the gerund began to allow passive and perfect auxiliaries (Tajima, 1985). The examples in (36) illustrate some of the steps in this gradual adoption of clausal syntax.

(36) a [*Gerund with direct object*]
    And thus he slough hem bothe in doinge this orible synne.
    (14[th]c.,*Kn.of LaTour-Landry,*LXII,82)
    'And in this way he killed them both (while they were) in (the act of) committing this terrible sin.'
   b [*Gerund with negation*]
    Al our pes ... is raþer to be sette in meke suffryng þan in not feling contrarieties. (c1430, OED)
    'All our peace of heart is rather in being put in meek suffering than in not feeling any opposition.'
   c [*Gerund with perfect auxiliary*]
    ... *whose pillow she kissed a thousand times for having borne the print of that beloved head.* (1580–1, Tajima, 1999: 269)

In the meantime, nominal gerunds continued to be used, and there also arose various types of mixed nominal-verbal gerunds. For example, in (37) *putting* is preceded by a determiner *the*, like a noun, but takes an object *the prisoners* like a verb. This mixing of nominal and verbal properties has a PDE remnant in the verbal gerunds with possessive subjects illustrated in (33). Another remnant is the occasional gerund with the noun quantifier *no*, as in (38).

(37) Assisting to the sayd Commissioners for *the putting the prisoners ... to suche tortours as they shall think expedient.* (1551, OED)

(38) He spoke softly, but there was *no denying the impatience in his voice.* (BNC)

On the whole, however, mixing between the two clause types declined. The type in (37) disappeared again, possessive subjects in the verbal gerund are being increasingly replaced by common-case subjects, and the type in (38) remains marginal. The result is that the formal distinction between nominal and verbal gerunds has grown sharper.

This formal polarization came with a growing functional differentiation. For example, Fonteyn *et al.* (2015) find that during ModE verbal gerunds became less likely targets for anaphoric reference. That is, examples like (39), where the demonstrative *that* refers back to the verbal gerund *describing the measures of his duty*, became less common. In contrast, nominal gerunds became more likely targets.

(39) So that we cannot discourse of the man's right, without *describing the measures of his duty*; *that* therefore follows next. (1762, Fonteyn *et al.*, 2015: 42)

Being a potential target for anaphoric reference is a typical discourse feature of nominal referents. Therefore, this finding indicates that verbal gerunds, once established, continued to become more clause-like, not so much in their form but in how they are employed in discourse. Nominal gerunds developed in the opposite direction, reverting back to the discourse uses of ordinary NPs. Fonteyn (2016) further shows that nominal gerunds closely match the referential subtypes found in ordinary NPs, showing functional distinctions such as generic/ specific/non-specific and indefinite/definite, whereas verbal gerunds came to be increasingly dissociated from the system of nominal reference.

Although the gerund was originally most common following prepositions, its rise also had a significant impact on the English system of verb complementation, as gerunds came to be used as complements to transitive verbs as well. This development involved a slow process of lexical diffusion that continued throughout ModE and into PDE, as described in detail by De Smet (2013a). The first verbs to select for gerundial complements were typically verbs that collocated with deverbal nouns. For instance, (40a) is an early instance of *love* with a gerund, but the gerund is still part of a series of deverbal nouns (and is therefore probably itself still a noun). From these beginnings, gerundial complement clauses developed and spread to other verbs, initially favouring some clusters of semantically related main verbs, including emotive verbs, such as *love* or *hate*, or negative implicative verbs, such as *forbear, omit* or *avoid* in (40b). As gerundial complement clauses became more productive, they eventually spread beyond these clusters. In PDE they appear with most transitive verbs that are semantically compatible with clausal complementation, such as *imagine, remember, try* or *consider*, as in (40c), with two important groups of exceptions. First, because gerunds themselves convey no temporal or modal information about the state of affairs they denote, they did not spread to main verbs that convey no such information either (e.g. *think, know, say*). Second, gerunds tend to be absent still with many verbs that already took *to*-infinitival complements before the rise of gerund complements (e.g. *want, desire, wish*). With such verbs, the rise of the gerund was often blocked or at least delayed by the availability of the pre-existing pattern.

(40) a *Þe luueden **tening** & stale, hordom & drunken*
'[You] that loved doing harm and theft and whoring and drunkenness'
(early ME, *PoemaMorale*,253)

b If ... I could have avoided *meddling with him*, I should not desirously have begun with a Gentleman ... of so ... turbulent a Disposition. (1635, OED)

c He considered *asking for the feather back* but knew the request would sound foolish. (BNC)

8.2.3   *Participles*

Like *to*-infinitives and gerunds, participles can take up a range of different positions in the clause. Participial subordinate clauses were historical sources for the perfect, passive and progressive constructions illustrated in (41a–c) respectively. In these constructions, an original clause-combining structure has become a mono-clausal one, with the participle now providing the main verb (for details, see Chapter 6). Participles also figure as noun-clause-like complements to perception verbs, as in (42) – the form has its roots in OE (cf. Mitchell, 1985: 895) but the construction's underlying syntax has probably changed subtly since.[7]

(41) a Nails wasn't quite sure what *had hit* him. (BNC)
   b Michael Sweeney *was hit* in the shoulder. (BNC)
   c I *'m hitting* my head repeatedly against something that isn't there and I suppose that that could be a definition of insanity. (BNC)

(42) a He could see her *deciding whether to agree or disagree*, he could see her weigh the advantages and the possible disadvantages. (BNC)
   b to see her *shamed like that* was terrible. (BNC)

In this section, we focus on adverbial past and present participles, as illustrated in (43). As the examples show, such adverbial participle clauses can come with or without a linking element to mark their relation to the main clause, and they can come with or without an explicit subject. When their subject is unexpressed, it typically corresponds to an element in the main clause, mostly the main clause subject. Adverbial participle clauses without subject are sometimes referred to as 'free relatives', the ones with explicit subject as 'absolutes'. Absolutes are said to have been borrowed from Latin, which is probably partly true, as discussed in Chapter 4 (see especially, Section 4.3.1).

(43) a *When stopped by the car park attendant*, the disturbed man shoved the attendant aside, causing him to fall and break his wrist. (BNC)
   b June Roberts went and touched the old silk fabric, *tears filling her eyes* (BNC)

In both the free relative and absolute constructions, participles alternate with other predicate types, particularly adjectives and prepositional phrases. For instance, the head of the free relative is an adjective in (44a), while the absolute in (44b) has as its head a prepositional phrase.

(44) a *Though logical*, these arguments are inaccurate (BNC)
   b *The lassitude still on her*, she came slowly to her feet (BNC)

Even though they are mainly a feature of the written language, free relatives and absolutes are remarkably common in PDE when compared to similar constructions in Dutch and German. This is particularly true of the constructions with present participles and may reflect a more general fondness of English for backgrounding and stativizing grammatical devices as well as the influence of the gerund (Van de Pol and Petré, 2015; cf. Section 6.4.1 in this volume).

Historical developments within free relatives and absolutes have received relatively little scholarly attention. Clearly, however, their use has not been

---

[7] For PDE, Declerck (1981) proposes that (present) participles with perception verbs allow three different syntactic analyses, one of which is analogous to the formally similar 'accusativus-cum-infinitivo' construction with a bare infinitive. The latter analysis presupposes a syntactic change at some stage in the history of the construction (cf. De Smet, 2014: 236).

stable. Focusing on free relatives with a present participle, Killie and Swan (2009) show that the semantic relation between main clause and free relative was more coordinate-like in ME than in PDE. In ME, the free relative just elaborated on the main clause or specified an accompanying circumstance, as in (45a). In eModE, free relatives increasingly came to mark more specific adverbial relations such as manner, time or cause, as in (45b). As the examples show, the semantic change was accompanied by a formal change. From occurring almost exclusively in clause-final position, free relatives began to occupy clause-initial position as well. Killie and Swan take these changes to reflect a tighter syntactic integration between main clause and subordinate clause.

(45) a *Jahel . . . took a neyl of the tabernacle,* **takynge there-with an hamer**
    'Iahel took a nail from the tent and took a hammer with it.'
    (ME, Wyclif,*Bible*,Cap.IV)

   b *Having no alternative,* Fiver accompanied Hazel and Bigwig to the burrow where Hazel had spent the previous night. (BNC)

The history of absolutes shows no such shift. Van de Pol (2016) shows that OE absolutes already covered the full range of adverbial relations and, if anything, came to be used increasingly with the more coordinate-like meanings of elaboration and accompanying circumstance. This suggests that with time free relatives and absolutes grew more alike.

Another area of change is the linking elements free relatives and absolutes combine with. Free relatives tend to allow adverbial subordinators, such as *when, while, if* and the like, as in (43a) and (44a) above, but just when and how those combinations arose is not clear. Absolutes, by contrast, typically take *with* as a linking element, as in (46), and they have done so increasingly over time (van de Pol and Cuyckens, 2013). The source of this use probably lies in prepositional phrases like (47), where the relation between a nominal head and its postmodifying dependent can be reinterpreted as one between a subject and a predicate (see also Section 4.4.1).[8]

(46) I stand up and brush my coat down just in case it got dirty *with me sitting on the ground.* (BNC)

(47) *Heo . . . feng to þonki þus godd* **wið honden up aheuene**.
    'She thus fell to thanking God, with her hands lifted up.' (early ME, *St.Juliana*,60)

Linking elements other than *with* occasionally occurred, too, as in (48).

(48) Wherupon the duke sent him a lettre of defiaunce, and called Paulmer, who *after denial made of his declaracion* was let goe (1550–2,Edward VI,Diary)

---

[8] As argued by van de Pol (2016), an additional factor may have been the fact that the OE absolute construction typically had its subject in the dative. As dative inflections disappeared, *with* may have appeared with absolutes as it did elsewhere to mark relations previously marked by the dative.

Perhaps these point to interference from gerund clauses. Although marginally attested in OE, the bulk of examples occurred in eModE, when the gerund was on the rise (Visser, 1963: 1158, 1271–78). Recall that gerunds also combined with prepositions, could also have subjects, and just like an important subset of absolute constructions they would have a form in *-ing* (Section 8.3.2). The line between gerunds and present participles is particularly thin in non-finite clauses introduced by *what with*, whose convoluted history is discussed by Trousdale (2012).

8.3 Finite Clauses

Finite noun clauses in PDE are mainly *that*-clauses, as in (49a), with *that* serving as a more or less meaningless and often omissible element marking subordination. In contrast, finite adverbial clauses, as in (49b), almost invariably come with dedicated conjunctions, such as *if*, *while*, *as soon as*, *in case* and so on, which are obligatory and specify the semantic relation between subordinate and main clause.

(49) a She was beginning to regret *that Sam had insisted on keeping her wine glass filled during the meal.* (BNC)
     b she didn't approach by Guilford Street *in case the porter came out of his lodge and recognized her.* (BNC)

The following discussion is organized along this distinction, focusing first on *that*-clauses (Section 8.3.1) and then on finite adverbial clauses (Section 8.3.2).

8.3.1 *That*-clauses

PDE *that*-clauses can occupy a range of positions, as shown in (50), functioning as straightforward noun clauses most of the time, though (50c) and (50e) are significant exceptions. Their distribution is similar to that of *to*-infinitives (compare Section 8.2.1).

(50) a [*Subject*]
       That he came at all was surprising; *that he came without a chainsaw* was amazing. (Google)
     b [*Subject complement*]
       The problem is *that they clog up.* (BNC)
     c [*Noun complement*]
       And then there were hats for every occasion, sunglasses, sportswear and even the questionable piece of advice *that a firm corset would prevent seasickness.* (BNC)
     d [*Verb complement*]
       I didn't realize *that he was boss.* (BNC)
     e [*Adjective complement*]
       Only when we are sure that all possible test factors have been controlled can we feel confident *that we understand the causal process at work.* (BNC)

That-clauses, typically with a subjunctive verb, were a very common feature of OE, too. But, while their distribution was more or less similar to that of PDE *that*-clauses, there were some differences, largely purporting to OE *þæt*-clauses being a little less 'noun-clause-like' than the PDE *that*-clause. First, the construction type in (50a) did not yet occur in OE – its appearance is discussed below. Second, OE *þæt* was also frequently used to introduce adverbial purpose clauses, as in (51), making it sometimes hard to decide whether a given *þæt*-clause was an adverbial clause or a noun clause. *Þæt* was also frequently part of complex conjunctive phrases introducing adverbial clauses (see Section 8.3.2).

(51) *he wæs mid wacum cildclaðum   bewæfed,* **þæt** *he us forgeafe þa*
he was with poor   swaddling-cloths covered   that he us bestow the
undeadlican tunecan *þe we forluron on þæs   frumsceapenan mannes*
immortal   coat   that we lost   on of-the first-created   man's
forgægednesse
transgression (*ÆCHom*.I,2 193.88)
'He was wrapped in poor pieces of cloth so that he might return to us the immortal coat that we had lost upon the transgression of the first man.'

When it comes to the origin of *that*-clauses, it is hard to ignore the homonymy between the OE conjunction *þæt* and the demonstrative pronoun – or, for that matter, the relative pronoun (see Section 5.5.3). It is reasonable to assume that the conjunction somehow developed from the demonstrative pronoun (Traugott, 1992: 237), but how exactly that happened is unclear. The most common account states that the conjunction must have been reanalysed from an anticipatory demonstrative in a paratactic structure ([*we heard that*]$_{S1}$ [*the king was dead*]$_{S2}$ > [*we heard* [*that the king was dead*]]$_S$) (Heine and Kuteva, 2007: 241). The best evidence to support this account is that OE *þæt* could indeed function as an anticipatory demonstrative pronoun, as seen in (52).

(52) *Wæs* **þæt** *eac gedefen,* **þætte** **þæt** *swefn gefylled   wære, þætte . . .*
was   that also proper   that   that dream fulfilled   were that . . .
(*Bede*.4.24.336.28)
'It was also proper that that dream was fulfilled that. . .'

Even so, the reanalysis-based account is not entirely convincing. In (52), the pronoun *þæt* is not actually in a position that would allow reanalysis as a conjunction, and in fact such contexts are unattested. Moreover, the account leaves various issues unresolved. One puzzle is the role of the OE subordinating particle *þe*, which was often used to mark subordinate clauses and is sometimes found accompanying *þæt*, mostly contracted to *þætte*, as in (53). Did the combination *þæt þe* only arise after *þæt* had developed into a conjunction, or had it been an ancestor to the conjunction *þæt*? Even though Mitchell (1985: 433) inclines towards the former, the latter is not completely implausible. For what it is worth, while Gothic did not use its demonstrative pronoun *þata* as a conjunction, it did use *þatei* – a contraction of *þata* and the subordinating particle *ei* (van der Horst, 2008: 281–82).

(53) *Ic wene, cwæð Orosius, þæt nan wis mon ne sie, buton he genoh geare wite*
     I believe said Orosius that no wise man not is but he enough clearly knows
     þætte God þone æresetan monn ryhtne godne gesceop
     that God the first man just [and] good created (*Or.*2,1.35.28)
     'I believe, Orosius said, that there isn't a wise man whodoes not clearly know that God created the first man just and good.'

Another puzzle is the role of adverbial *þæt*-clauses and the various other uses of *þæt* where it did not introduce a noun clause. If the conjunction developed directly from the demonstrative pronoun, its first use would have been as a marker of noun clauses, so adverbial and other uses would have been derived. That is what Mitchell (1985: 432–33) suggests, and it is consistent with how Gothic *þatei* was used. However, the opposite direction of change – from adverbial clause to noun clause – seems much better-attested.[9] In all, there is much about the prehistory of *þæt* and, consequently, about its distribution in OE that is still poorly understood.

Less speculative is what happened to *that*-clauses during and after OE. The decline of the subjunctive had consequences for *that*-clauses, too. Sometimes the modals substituted for the old subjunctive forms, or subjunctives were replaced by indicatives (see Chapter 6). But in other cases, the *that*-clause lost ground to the *to*-infinitive (see Section 8.2.1).

In one respect, the distribution of *that*-clauses expanded. *That*-clauses functioning as a subject in preverbal position, as in (50a), first appeared in late ME. The reasons for their non-occurrence in OE and early ME are not clear but may have to do with the fact that subject clauses in initial position are difficult to process. Even today, they are largely restricted to writing, while the preferred option, especially in the spoken language, is to use the dummy subject *it* with the subordinate clause in extraposed position, as in (54) (Biber *et al.*, 1999: 676).

(54) *It* was significant *that it was the Consul General who spoke first*. (BNC)

This option also existed in OE, mainly in impersonal and passive constructions, as in (55a). The alternative was a construction without *it* and the *þæt*-clause in final position, as in (55b). There is some scholarly debate as to whether the *þæt*-clauses in such examples were subjects or not (see Denison, 1993: 61–102, for arguments for and against).

---

[9] Examples of adverbial clauses developing into noun clauses are discussed, for instance, in López-Couso and Méndez-Naya (2015). The English *to*-infinitive, discussed in Section 8.2.1 is another example, as is the case of *in case* briefly discussed in Section 8.3.2.

(55) a *Eac hit awriten is, ðæt sunne aþystrað ær   worulde ende*
　　　also it written is that sun   darkens before world's end (*WHom*.3.41)
　　　'It is also written that the sun will be eclipsed before the world's end.'
　　b *Næs   nanum men forgifen þæt he moste habban* ... *his agen fulluht*
　　　'not-was no   man granted that he might have   his own baptism
　　　buton Iohanne anum
　　　but John   alone (*ÆCHom*.II,3 25.206)
　　　'It was granted to no one to perform his own baptism except to John'

The most remarkable change in the *that*-clause is the increased rate of omission of the conjunction *that*. Finite noun clauses without *that* have always existed but had been uncommon until eModE. A rare OE example is given in (56).

(56) *and cwæð he wolde wiðsacan his Criste*
　　　and said he wanted forsake his Christ (*ÆLS* (Basil) 371)
　　　'... and said (that) he wanted to forsake Christ.'

It is perhaps no coincidence that the subordinate clause in (56) represents reported speech (as do similar examples in Mitchell, 1985: 30–31). As Otsu (2002) points out, the origins of *that*-omission could well be due to influence from direct speech or thought representation, where *that* has always been virtually absent, as in (57). Confusion between indirect and direct reported speech was probably further promoted by the loss of word-order differences between main and subordinate clauses (Fischer, 2007: 304).

(57) *Eft he cuæð be ðæm ilcan: Ðonne ic wæs mid Iudeum ic wæs suelc hie*
　　　'Again he said in the same [manner]: when I was with [the] Jews I was like them'
　　　(*CP*.16.101. 5)

From eModE onwards, the incidence of *that*-omission increased dramatically. The rise of *that*-omission appears to have proceeded faster with main clauses that had a first person subject or an epistemic main verb, such as *I think* or *I believe*. Thompson and Mulac (1991) link this to a change in the status of the main clause itself. They argue that *that*-omission occurs so frequently with specific main clauses because those main clauses were grammaticalizing into modal particles marking speakers' epistemic stance. As a result, the dependent noun clauses became *de facto* main clauses and no longer needed subordinate clause marking. Thompson and Mulac corroborate their argument with the positional flexibility of *I think* and similar main clause chunks, as illustrated in (58). Once main clauses like *I think* lost their main clause status, they argue, there no longer was any reason for them to occur only in sentence-initial position.

(58) Many would regard him, *I think*, as an eligible bachelor. (BNC)

Another indication that some main clauses began to be treated as modal particles is the increasing incidence of so-called negative raising. In negative raising, a negator is formally part of the main clause, but semantically has scope over the subordinate clause. In (59), for instance, *I don't think we should* does not mean 'it is not my opinion that we should' but conveys the stronger meaning 'it is my opinion that we should not'.

(59) 'Dominic – why don't you take Lee to the pub again, then come and see me later?'
     'Too risky, Thea. You're the branch secretary. Everyone knows you here.' 'I meant
     really late. Midnight.' 'I *don't think* we should. Not in this place.' (BNC)

In earlier stages, negative raising was uncommon (Denison, 1998). If a subordinate clause contained a negative proposition, it also contained the negative marker, as in (60).

(60) *I think* there is *not* a more necessary and useful thing to be thought on.
     (1665, Thomas Cock, *Hygieine*)

Negative raising is reminiscent of the behaviour of negation with some of the modals, which are similarly 'transparent' to sentential negation. For example, in (61) *not* does not negate the modal force of *must* ('there is no obligation for letter post items to exceed 610mm in length') but negates the modalized proposition ('there is an obligation for letter post items not to exceed 610mm in length').

(61) Letter post items *must not* exceed 610mm in length (BNC)

As such, negative raising supports the idea that some main clauses have been developing into modal particles.

All this makes Thompson and Mulac's (1991) account of *that*-omission quite attractive. Nevertheless, there is a complication. Thompson and Mulac imply that positionally mobile parenthetical chunks, as in (58), arose as a result of *that*-omission, but that is implausible, because the parentheticals appeared well before *that*-omission became common (Brinton, 1996: 212) – witness the ME example in (59). Brinton (1996) and Fischer (2007: 305) therefore suggest alternative sources for the parenthetical uses.

(62) *Of twenty yeer of age he was, I gesse.* (Chaucer,*Gen.Pr..*82))
     'He was twenty years old, I guess.'

It seems then that the increase in *that*-omission, the rise of negative raising and the rise of positionally mobile parentheticals were developments that started out more or less independently but subsequently converged.

8.3.2   *Adverbial Clauses*

Finite adverbial clauses can be marked by a variety of subordinating conjunctions and it is with respect to these that the main changes in this area of the grammar occurred.[10] The most striking development is probably the expansion of the inventory of subordinators over time, described by Kortmann (1997). There is in PDE a core of high-frequency monomorphemic subordinators – *as, when, if, where, because, while, before, since, after, until* and so on (cf. Kortmann, 1997: 131) – which, from a historical point of view, is both old and relatively stable. The subordinators that make up this core already functioned as subordinators in OE (*as, if, while, since*) or else came to do so no later than ME (*when, where, because, before, after, until*). Remarkably, they also tend to be the subordinators that are first acquired by children. Outside this core, however, fluctuations in the subordinator inventory are more pronounced. Throughout the history of English, the trend has been for the inventory of subordinators to grow. PDE has almost twice as many subordinators as OE, though eModE had even more (Kortmann, 1997: 294). At the same time, many new additions – especially, it appears, the ones that entered the grammar in eModE – again disappeared, witness the subordinators in (63), all of which are now obsolete.

(63) a The Lyons ... brake all their bones in pieces *or euer* [= 'well before'] they came at the bottome of the den. (1611, OED)
   b Such of them as ... had a desire to stay in Spain ... were suffered to do so ... *conditioned, that* [= 'provided that'] *they would be Christened.* (1622–62, OED)
   c The Parts of Musick are in all but four, *howsoever* [= 'even though'] *some skilful Musicians have composed songs of twenty* [...] *parts.* (1674, OED)

English also saw changes in the formal make-up of its subordinators. Apart from its monomorphemic subordinators, OE made frequent use of complex subordinators built on the basis of a case-marked demonstrative, often introduced by a preposition and followed by *þæt* or the subordinating particle *þe*, as in (64a), or an adverb followed by *þe*, as in (64b). In some cases, these complex subordinators alternated with a reduced form, probably reflecting ongoing grammaticalization (e.g. *ær þæm þe* 'before' alternated with *ær*). This construction was more or less lost in the course of ME.

(64) a *Mid þæm þe þa ærendracan to Rome comon, þa com eac mid him...*
       with that that the messengers to Rome came, then came also with them
       (*Or.*3,5.58.8)
       'When the messengers came to Rome, there came also with them...'

---

[10] An interesting type of finite adverbial clause exists without subordinating conjunction, namely conditional clauses marked by VS word order, as in OE *Gewite seo sawul ut: ne mæig se muð clypian* (*ÆCHom* I 10 262.126) ('if the soul departs (lit. goes the soul out), the mouth cannot call out'). The construction existed in OE (see Mitchell, 1985: §§3678-83), although it was not highly frequent and tended to involve mainly past subjunctive forms of the verb *be*. It seems to have become more frequent in ME and eModE (but only with auxiliaries in the past tense) (Denison, 1998: 300). After this, it gradually declined and it is now rare, rather formal, and limited to the auxiliaries *had, were* and *should*, as in *Had he seen the timer in a shop window at half the price, he would have ignored it* (BNC).

b *God   wolde   geswutelian   þurh   þæt syllice   tacn þæt   his   sawl*
God   wanted   show   through that wonderful sign that   his   soul
leofode þeah þe   se   lichama   wære   ofslagen
lived   though   the   body   were   killed (*ÆLS*(Denis)306)
'Through that wonderful sign God wanted to show that his soul lived even if his body was destroyed.'

Another typically OE strategy was the use of correlative adverbs, where main and subordinate clause would each be introduced by one of a pair of identical or related adverbs, as in (65). In such cases, which clause was the main clause and which was the subordinate one would often be clear only from word-order differences. In principle, the main clause was VSO (due to the application of verb-second following the introductory adverb) and the subordinate clause SOV, as in (65a) (cf. Chapter 9). But this was no hard-and-fast rule, as shown by (65b), which has VS-order twice.[11] This correlative pattern, too, largely disappeared in the course of ME.

(65) a *Þa   ða   Ioseph þis smeade: þa   com   him to godes engel.*
Then then Joseph this considered then came him to God's angel
(*ÆCHom*.I,13,284.89)
'When Joseph was considering this, God's angel came to him.'
   b *Nu hæbbe we awriten þære Asian suþdæl, nu wille we fon to hire norðdæle*
Now have we written of-the of-Asia south-part, now will we take to her north-part
(*Or*.1,1.11.25)
'Now that we have described the southern part of Asia, we will continue with the northern part.'

In contrast, from ME onwards, adverbial subordinators began to be increasingly formed on the basis of verbs, such as *save* in (66a), and nouns introduced by a preposition, such as *by cause* in (66b) (Kortmann, 1997: 305). Other examples include *considering, excepting, provided, suppose* or *for fear, in case, on condition*.

(66) a *Te deum was oure song, and nothyng elles, / Save that to crist I seyde an orison, / Thankynge hym of his revelacion.* (Chaucer,*Sum,T.*1866–8)
'*Te Deum* was our song and nothing else, except that I said a prayer to Christ, thanking him for his revelation.'
   b *For though that absolon be wood or wrooth, By cause that he fer was from hire sight,* This nye nicholas stood in his light. (Chaucer,*Mil.T.*3394–6))
'For however insane or angry this Absolon might be, because he was far from her sight, the nearby Nicholas stood in his light (i.e. outshone him).'

---

[11] It is of course also possible that we are dealing with two asyndetically linked main clauses in this example, the distinction between main and subordinate clauses not always being so clear in OE.

Having developed from a lexical head with a dependent *that*-clause, these new subordinators typically continued to combine with *that*, causing an increase in the use of *that* as a marker of subordination. For a while, *that* even spread to subordinators it had not combined with before, such as *if* in (67).

(67) *He myghte wel, **if that he bar hym lowe**, Lyue in atthenes* everemoore unknowe.
     (Chaucer,*Kn.T.*1405–6)
     'He could well live in Athens virtually unknown, provided he behaved humbly.'

Perhaps this extension of *that* was partly in response to the loss of distinctive word order in subordinate clauses. Nevertheless, in ModE and PDE *that* is again increasingly omitted, echoing the behaviour of *that* in noun clauses (see Section 8.3.1), but probably also reflecting the progressive grammaticalization of the new subordinators.

Apart from the changing composition of the subordinator inventory, specific subordinators saw change too. As subordinators grammaticalize, they often undergo formal reduction and coalescence (e.g. OE *eal(l)swa* > ME *as* or ME *by cause (that)* > ModE *because*). At the same time, the semantic relation they establish between main and subordinate clause may change, sometimes along more or less predictable pathways. A well-known example is the conjunction *while* (Traugott and König, 1991: 199–201). Originally, *while* marked simultaneity, as in (68a). This often came with the implication that there was something remarkable about two situations occurring simultaneously, as in (68b) (it is unusual for an intruder to get in just as the gatekeepers are talking about him). Because of this association with unexpectedness, *while* developed into a concessive subordinator, meaning 'although, whereas', as in (68c).

(68) a *& ðat lastede þa xix wintre **wile Stephne was king**. (ChronE*(Irvine)1137.32))
        'and that lasted then nineteen winters during-the-time-when Stephen was king.'
     b *'By my othe,' said a nother, 'it myghte well be mawgys, that is soo dysguysed for to dysceyve vs' / 'It is not soo,' sayd thother / 'mawgys is not a live' / And **while that they devysed thus togyder**, mawgys cam nere to the wycket of the gate, and founde the meanes that he gate in anone* (Caxton,*Sons-of-Aymon*,XXI,462)
        "I swear,' said the one, 'it might well be Mawgys, who is disguised in this way to deceive us.' 'It is not so,' said the other, 'Mawgys is not alive.' And while they were conversing like this, Mawgys approached the opening in the gate and found the way to get in at once.'
     c *While Adorno confines this category to 'serious' music*, Paddison points out that there seems no reason why it could not include a good deal of avant-garde jazz . . . (BNC).

Another kind of change that sometimes affects adverbial subordinators is that they come to introduce complement clauses, including noun clauses (López-Couso and Méndez-Naya, 2015). A recent example is *in case* – originally an adverbial subordinator introducing conditional clauses, but now also marginally used as a 'complementizer' introducing complement clauses with some verbal and adjectival predicates. In (69), *in case* does not introduce the condition under which the subject would have been worried, but the possible state of affairs the subject was worried about.

(69) Oh good. We were worried *in case you couldn't get the band together.* (BNC)

8.4   Concluding Remarks

Subordination would seem to be a quintessentially syntactic phenomenon. It is a prime example of recursion in human language – the capacity of structural units to contain units of the same kind, in a principally endless self-embedding structural complex. One clause contains another, which contains another, and so on. Particularly in formal linguistics, this capacity for recursion has been thought of as the hallmark of syntax. At the same time, there is no denying that subordination also links the formal to the functional, particularly so when it is seen from a historical perspective. Almost any formal change that happened in the history of subordination in English had some functional motivations or repercussions. The preceding discussion provides plenty of examples. The expansion of *to*-infinitives to new syntactic contexts also changed their meanings (Section 8.2.1). The verbalization of the gerund may in part have been a response to a functional gap in the grammar of English (Section 8.2.2). Growing positional flexibility in participial absolute constructions was accompanied by semantic changes (Section 8.2.3). The increasing omissibility of the complementizer *that* may be linked to functional changes in certain main clauses (Section 8.3.1). And so on. The close link between the formal and the functional in the domain of subordination can finally be illustrated by a phenomenon whose history has not yet been well-documented in English. Sometimes clauses with the formal markings of subordination are used without a proper main clause – which is what Evans (2007) refers to as 'insubordination'.

(70) O *that I were a Gloue vpon that hand* (Shakespeare, *Romeo & Juliet*, II.2)

It is typical for such insubordinate clauses to come with specialized functions – the insubordinate *that*-clause in (70) expresses a wish. It is still an unresolved issue, however, exactly how insubordinate clauses originate and develop, and how formal and functional change interact in this.

9   Word Order

9.1   Introduction

Some of the most dramatic syntactic changes in the history of English are the changes in English word order. To appreciate their impact, it may be useful to take an OE sentence, and compare it with its PDE counterpart:

(1)   *ða*   *se*   *Wisdom*   *ða*   *ðis*   *leoð*   *swiðe*   *lustbærlice*   *&*
     when   the   wisdom   then   this   song   very   pleasantly   and
     gesceadwislice   *asungen*   *hæfde,*   *ða*   *hæfde*   *ic*   *ða*   *giet*
     wisely   sung   had   then   had   I   then   still
     hwylchwugu   *gemynd*   *on*   *minum*   *mode*   *ðære*   *unrotnesse*
     what-little   memory   in   my   mind   of-the   sadness
     þe   *ic*   *<ær>*   *hæfde*
     that   I   before   had (*Bo.*36.103.23)
     'When Wisdom had sung this song so pleasantly and wisely, I remembered little of the sadness that I used to feel'

In (1), the subordinate clause *ða se Wisdom ... asungen hæfde* has the entire verbal group in final position, where it follows the direct object *ðis leoð*. In the main clause, the finite verb *hæfde* occupies the second position of the clause, immediately following the word *ða* and preceding the subject. Also note that the direct object of the subordinate clause is separated from the infinitive by the adverbial *swiðe lustbærlice & gesceadwislice*. In grammatical terminology, we would say that the subordinate clause has verb-final order, while the main clause has inversion, or verb-second (to be precise, the finite verb of the verbal group comes after the first constituent, whatever its function may be). A comparison with the PDE translation shows that verb-final order and verb-second have basically disappeared from the language (though, as we shall see, there are some exceptions in the case of verb-second). Furthermore, the direct object and the verb can no longer be separated but must be adjacent. Given these clear differences, it is natural to wonder when, how and why these changes took place.

These and similar questions will be addressed in the following subsections, not only for the changes observable in (1) but also for other word-order changes in the history of English. For our discussion, we make grateful use of the numerous existing studies of word-order change in English. We cannot approach any degree of completeness in the following short overview, but we hope to make clear that close study of word-order changes in English has brought to light many surprising facts and puzzles, some of which have been at least partly solved and others of which still await the serious exploration that they deserve. What we also hope to show is that, in the study of the diachronic syntax of English, cross-linguistic comparisons can often yield valuable insights and ideas. Most significantly, the OE word order in (1) is paralleled quite exactly in modern Dutch or German translations of the same sentence. This means that, with due caution and qualification, we can draw on an enormous amount of work carried out on comparable phenomena attested in living and therefore more fully documented languages (cf. Van Kemenadem, 1987).

The following overview addresses the changing order of subject and verb (Section 9.2), the changing order of object and verb (Section 9.3), direct object and indirect object (Section 9.4), the placement of verb particles (Section 9.5), and the placement of adverbs (Section 9.6). Finally, we discuss some of the more surprising consequences of word-order change on other areas of the grammar (Section 9.7).

9.2 The Order of Subject and Verb

We saw in (1) that, in OE main clauses, the finite verb would typically occupy the second position of the clause. The first constituent could be the subject, or it could be another clausal constituent, in which case the subject usually ends up in the position immediately following the finite verb. Another example of V-S order, with verb and subject in second and third position respectively, is given in (2). The alternative order S-V, with subject and verb in first and second position, is illustrated in (3). Either way, the finite verb occupied the second constituent slot in the clause, which is why this word-order rule is usually referred to as the verb-second rule (or simply verb-second or V2).

(2) *On   twam   þingum   **hæfde**   **God**   þæs   mannes   saule   **gegodod***
   in   two   things   had   God   the   man's   soul   endowed
   (*ÆCHom*.I,1 184.161)
   'With two things God had endowed man's soul'

(3) ***Ic**   **eom**   þin   hælend*
   I   am   your   healer (*AELS*(Eugenia)408)
   'I am your saviour'

Note that (2) also has a non-finite verb, *gegodod*, which appears in clause-final position. This way, the finite and non-finite verbs in this sentence form what is sometimes called a brace construction.

A widely accepted analysis of such OE verb-second sentences, originally developed for modern Dutch and German, is to say that the initial element (*on twam þingum* in (2) and *ic* in (3)) is in a special topic-slot at the left boundary of the clause, and that it somehow attracts the finite verb into a position to its immediate right, while any non-finite verb remains where it was (see Van Kemenade, 1987). This analysis is attractive because it reveals the similarity between declarative main clauses as in (1)–(3) and *wh*-interrogatives such as (4). In OE, *wh*-interrogatives could therefore be regarded as special cases of verb-second main clauses.

(4) *Hwæt*   **witst**   **þu** [. . .]   *us?*
   what   blame   you   us (*Bo.*7.19.11)
   'Why do you reproach us?'

Subordinate clauses generally did not have verb-second in OE, as illustrated in (1) and also (5)–(6).

(5) *ða   lioð   þe   ic   wrecca   geo   lustbærlice   **song***
   the   songs   that   I   exile   formerly   happily   sang (*Bo.*1.8.2)
   'The songs that I, an exile, used to sing so happily'

(6) *sona   swa   ic   þe   ærest   on   þisse unrotnesse   **geseah***
   soon   as   I   you   first   in   this   sadness   saw (*Bo.*5.11.2)
   'As soon as I first saw you in this state of unhappiness'

Instead of second position, the finite verbs here occupied clause-final position. Because this is also the position occupied by the non-finite verb in the main clause, as in (2), it has been suggested that OE, like modern Dutch and German, basically had verb-final order. The one exception to this general pattern, then, is that in main clauses the finite verb moved to second position.

All this may seem quite neat and tidy, but in fact things were more complicated (Pintzuk, 1991; Bech, 2012). For one thing, while verb-second applies quite strictly in modern Dutch and German, it is easy to find OE main clauses that do not have verb-second, as (7)–(9) show.

(7) *nu   **ealle**   **ðas**   **þing**   **sind**   mid   anum   naman   genemnode*
   now   all   these   things   are   with   one   name   named
   gesceaft.
   creature (*ÆCHom.*I,20 335.19)
   'Now, all these things are called with one name: creature'

(8) *Ðillice word   **maria heold**   aræfniende   on   hyre   heortan*
   such   words   Maria   kept   ponderingly   in   her   heart (*ÆCHom.*I,2 197.214)
   'Such words Maria kept and pondered in her heart'

(9) *Forðon   **we sceolan**   mid   ealle   mod   &   mægene   to   Gode*
   therefore   we   must   with   all   mind   and   power   to   God
   gecyrran
   turn (*HomU.*19(BlHom.8)26)
   'Therefore we must turn to God with all our mind and power'

Here, the initial elements *nu*, *ðyllice word* and *forðon* appear to be in the first clausal position, but instead of attracting the finite verb into second position they are followed by the subject. Such exceptions to verb-second were common when the initial element was a disjunct or sentence adverbial, as in (7), but it also occurred with initial elements that were fully integrated clause constituents, as in (8), and it was particularly frequent when the subject of the clause was a pronoun, as in (9). Note that while the finite verb in these examples is not in its usual second position, it is not in clause-final position either (in which case it would be adjacent to the non-finite forms in (7) and (9)). This suggests that we are dealing with a variant on the verb-second rule rather than with no movement at all.[1] That this variant rule was especially common with pronominal subjects makes sense in light of the well-established fact that, in many languages, personal pronouns participate in special word-order patterns. A very simple example can be seen in the French pair in (10), where the object NP *la victime* in (10a) is in postverbal position while for its pronominal counterpart *la* in (10b), preverbal position is obligatory.

(10) a *Le suspect **connaissait la victime***.
  'The suspect knew the victim'
  b *Le suspect **la connaissait**.*
  'The suspect knew her (lit. her knew)'

The precise behaviour of such personal pronouns, which are usually referred to as clitics, can differ from language to language, and their analysis is sometimes far from clear, but the realization that they exist can offer, if not an explanation, then at least partial relief from puzzlement concerning the special position of OE subject pronouns in sentences like (9).[2]

However, there are yet further complications to the OE verb-second rule. While verb-second in general appears to have been optional and was rare (or operated differently) with pronominal subjects, there were a number of contexts where it virtually always applied even when the subject was a pronoun. This is so when the element in first position was a *wh*-word (cf. (4)) or a negative element, as in (11) – and remarkably, it is in these contexts that verb-second survived into PDE, as illustrated in (12) (Los, 2012: 23).

---

[1] Occasionally, the main-clause finite verb would not move at all and remain in clause-final position, particularly in coordinated main clauses (Los, 2015: 167).

[2] Interestingly, the special behaviour of these elements can also be used as a test for personal pronoun-hood. This has been done for the OE element *man* 'people/one', which has its origins in the ordinary noun *man(n)* 'man', but often seems to function as a kind of indefinite pronoun, comparable to Dutch *men*, German *man* and French *on*. OE *man* only occurs in subject position and it appears to resist verb-second, as in *Ac þas tide man sceal mid mycelre forhæfednesse healdan* 'but this time one must with great temperance hold' (*WHom*.14,28). This behaviour suggests that *man* can be classified as a personal pronoun.

(11) *Ne*   *secge*   **we**   *nan*   *þincg*   *niwes*   *on*   *þissere*   *gesetnysse*
NEG say   we   no   thing   of-new   in   this   narrative
forþan ðe hit stod gefyrn awriten on ledenbocum
because it stood before written in latin-books . . . (*ÆLS*(Pref)12)
'We do not say anything new in this narrative because it has already been written
down in Latin books. . .'

(12) a Why *has it* taken you so long? (BNC)
  b Never *would I* have voted against dear Thomas. Never. (BNC)

Verb-second also applied strictly in clauses starting with the adverb *þa* 'then',
as in the main clause in (1) and in the example in (13). Other anaphoric adverbs
such as *þonne* 'then', had a similar effect, albeit somewhat less pronounced.

(13) *þa*   **eodon**   **hie**   *ut*
   then went   they   out (*ChronA*(Plummer)894.83)
   'Then they went out'

Why the adverb *þa*, which was a very frequent word in OE, should have had this
effect is something of a puzzle. It may be possible to find a link between the
special syntax induced by the initial adverb *þa* and its discourse function, which
has been shown to be that of a marker of a new narrative episode (a suggestion
first put forward by Enkvist, 1986). Following this line of thought, Los and
Dreschler (2012) argue that main clauses initiated by *þa* and *þonne* were a special
clause-type dedicated to marking foregrounded events in narrative discourse.

In ME prose, verb-second was still frequent, especially following an initial
adverbial, as in (14). Personal pronouns seem to have retained their resistance
to inversion in most texts; (15) is an example of this.

(14) *and vpon the table **stood a merueillous spere straungely wrought***
   'and upon the table stood a wonderful spear, intricately crafted'
   (Malory, *MorteDarthur*,II.xv)

(15) *bi þis ȝe **mahen** seon ant witen. þat . . .*
   'by this you may see and know that . . .' (*SWard*.263.23)

In the poetry of this period, inversion was, if anything, less usual than in prose,
going against the assumption sometimes made that poetic texts will always be
in the rear-guard rather than the vanguard of linguistic change. In some
northern texts of the thirteenth century, the situation was different, in that
verb-second applied in declarative clauses quite consistently, whatever the
function of the initial element or the nature of the subject. An example from
the early thirteenth-century text *The Rule of St. Benet* is given in (16).

(16) *Oþir*   *labur*   **sal**   **þai**   *do*
   other labour shall they   do (*Ben.Rule*(Lnsd)33.20)
   'They must do other labour'

In these dialects, pronominal subjects appear to have lost clitic status and were eligible for inversion like any other subject. Significantly, as Kroch and Taylor (1997) show, the relevant texts are from the area in which there was heavy influence from Scandinavian, which had consistent verb-second and no clitic pronouns.

In eModE, a decline in the use of verb-second can be observed, and by lModE only those patterns of inversion continued to be regularly used that are still possible in PDE. This concerns clauses with an initial negative or restrictive element and various clause types with initial *there* or a locative phrase and an intransitive verb signifying (non)existence, (dis)appearance or some related notion, as in the following eModE examples.

(17) never *will I* go aboard another fleet (1709, Manley, *The New Atalantis*,10.2)

(18) Seldom *have you* seen anie Poet possessed with avarice
(1594, Nash, *The Unfortunate Traveller*,44.25)

(19) In this place *begins that fruitful and plentiful Country* which was call'd the Vale of Esham (1726 Defoe, *Tour of Great Britain*,441.6)

In general terms, instances of these patterns can be regarded as survivals of an earlier verb-second stage of the language. However, as shown by Nevalainen (1997), the relation is not one of direct continuity: before the eighteenth century, inversion in some contexts was not obligatory, even though it would have been in OE and would be again in PDE. This is illustrated in (20).

(20) *Not long **he had** ben there, whan toward hym arryued a marener*
'Not long had he been there, when a sailor came to him'
(Caxton,*Blanch&Egl.*32.24)

As for the causes of the decline of verb-second, there are several factors that appear to have played a role, though their exact contribution and interaction remains to be established to everybody's satisfaction. Some formal accounts link the decline of verb-second to the decline of verb agreement (Los, 2012; but see Fischer *et al.*, 2000: 135–36). Another factor that has often been cited is language contact. This could have taken the form of influence from French (which lost inversion in most contexts in the Middle Ages), Scandinavian influence (where verb-second was not restricted to full NP subjects), and dialect contact (between Scandinavian-influenced varieties and southern varieties, Kroch and Taylor, 1997). Particularly if some groups of speakers failed to recognize the special 'cliticized' status of preverbal pronouns, such structures would have been reinterpreted as displaying subject-verb order, which would have opened the door to other preverbal subjects, in violation of the original OE verb-second rule.

9.3   The Order of Object and Verb

Ever since Greenberg's (1966) seminal study, linguists have been interested in classifying languages as either OV (object-verb) or VO (verb-object), in the hope of confirming, disconfirming or extending claims about the correlation between basic word-order types and other facts of language. For example, OV languages appear to also typically have verb-auxiliary order, adjective-noun order, noun-preposition order, and possessive-noun order. For VO languages, the orders tend to be exactly reversed (Dryer, 1996). However, these tendencies do not translate easily to the history of one specific language. Research along these lines has shown that OE had some more OV properties, and modern English some more VO properties, but it could not establish a clear explanation of those differences or make further testable predictions. In what follows, we shall of course be using the labels OV and VO, but these must be understood as referring primarily to the ordering of object and verb, and not to any overarching language types. A further restriction that we should make at the outset is that we shall only be considering direct objects here (the position of the indirect object in relation to the direct object and the verb will be dealt with in Section 9.4).

In the preceding discussion, we suggested that in OE verbs were usually in clause-final position, but that a finite verb was typically moved to second position in main clauses. We also saw that there were several complications to this. When the position of the direct object relative to the verb is considered, further complications come to light. Some main clauses had OV order when the object was a personal pronoun, as in example (21).

(21) *Ic*   ***hit***   ***gemunde***   *gio*
     I   it   remembered   formerly (*Bo*.5.13.2)
     'I used to remember it'

Conversely, sometimes OV order might be expected, because a clause is subordinate, but the attested order is nevertheless VO. This was a common pattern with full NP objects, as in (22). It occurred only very occasionally with a pronominal object, as in (23).

(22) *þæt*   *he*   ***forgeafe***   ***godne***   ***willan***   *þam*   *seocan*   *hæðenan*
     that   he   granted   good   will   to-the   sick   heathen
     (*ÆCHom*.II,2.12.28)
     '. . . that he would grant good will to the sick heathen'

(23) *He*   *nolde*   ***genyman***   ***us***   *neadunge*   *of*   *deofles*   *anwealde*
     he   not-wanted   take   us   with-force   of   devil's   power
     (*ÆCHom*.I,1.188.272)
     'He would not forcibly take us from the devil's power'

As in the case of verb-second, it is clear that OV order was not exceptionless in OE. Examples of what was to become the regular order in later English – VO – already existed. It has been argued that VO sentences arose in OE through an operation of extraposition, which can move an object from preverbal to clause-final position (Van Kemenade, 1987). Some support for this can be found in the language of the OE poem *Beowulf*, in which such VO orders tend to have a metrical break between verb and object. Alternatively, VO sentences may simply show that OE allowed VO order in addition to OV order, perhaps with some kind of competition existing between the two variants (Pintzuk, 1991).

After the OE period, the use of OV order continued as a productive option for all kinds of objects, especially pronominal ones, until around 1400. A thirteenth-century example and a fourteenth-century example are given in (24) and (25).

(24) ... *þæt   ich   nule   **þe   forsaken***
       that   I   will-not   you   forsake (*St.Jul.*102/119)
    'that I will not forsake you'

(25) *I may **my persone and myn hous** so kepen and deffenden that...*
    'I can keep and defend myself and my house in such a way that ...'
    (Chaucer,*T.ofMel.*1524)

However, the frequency of OV clauses steadily declined, with Northern texts leading the development. In prose texts written after 1400, OV order also came to be structurally restricted. Specifically, they occurred more or less exclusively in clauses with an auxiliary and a negated or quantified object as in (26)–(27) and in clauses without an overt NP subject, such as relative clauses as in (28).[3] The pattern is remarkably reminiscent of Modern Icelandic, which suggests that there are underlying structural motivations for the restrictions (see Van der Wurff, 1999).

(26) *and sche seyd nay, be here feyth sche wuld **no more days** ʒeve ʒw þer-jn*
    'and she said, no, by her faith she would give you no more time in this matter'
    (*Past.Let.*I.221)

(27) *he haþ on vs mercy, for he may **al þynge do***
    'He has mercy on us, for he can do everything' (*Barlam*,2740)

(28) *alle þat **þis writinge** reden or heere*
    '... all that will read or hear this writing' (Thorpe, *Sermon*,2250)

After the middle of the sixteenth century, OV order disappeared completely from prose texts, except as relics of an earlier era, in the form of quotations, proverbs and fixed expressions like (29). In poetry, OV order survived

---

[3] Pintzuk (2002) and Kroch and Taylor (2000) show that the first two contexts already have a somewhat higher frequency of OV in OE and early ME.

productively much longer and without the restrictions illustrated in (26)–(28), as shown in (30) (which happens to have a remnant of verb-second as well, drawing on operator *do*).

(29) He that *mischief hatches, mischief catches.*

(30) In Xanadu did Kubla Khan / *A stately pleasure-dome decree*
(1797/1816, Coleridge, *Kubla Khan*)

There is no shortage of attempts to explain the shift from OV to VO order. No account is fully satisfactory, however. For one thing, they all leave unexplained the survival of OV order in poetic texts and the curious restrictions on OV order in eModE prose. That said, existing accounts probably touch on at least some of the factors involved. As in the case of verb-second, language contact has been held responsible for the decline of OV order. The situation of bilingualism or perhaps even koineization due to contact with Scandinavian may have promoted the use of VO order (see Weerman, 1993; Kroch and Taylor, 2000; and Chapter 4).

A different approach, pursued by Colman (1988), Ogura (2001) and others, has focussed on the processing costs of embedded clauses in an OV language. If word order is OV, a relative clause to the object can come before the verb and as a result postpone resolution of clausal syntax. Some such 'centre-embedded' constructions are notoriously hard to process, as illustrated by the constructed example with OV order in (31a). One solution is of course to move the object and its relative clauses out of the brace construction, giving VO order, as in (31b). Because OV languages will already have ways to avoid centre-embedding, it is doubtful that processing difficulties necessitated the OV-to-VO shift in English, but it is certainly true that contexts with heavy objects, including objects with relative clauses, favoured the change.

(31) a the dog the cat that the mouse that the cheese ate caught chased.
    b the dog chased the cat that caught the mouse that ate the cheese.

Another recurrent theme in accounts of the OV-to-VO shift is the loss of case distinctions and verbal inflections, as discussed in Chapter 2. When the syntactic function of an NP could no longer be read off of its case endings or inferred from agreement on the verb, word order came to be the sole formal marker of subjects and direct objects. More rigid word-order rules may therefore have compensated for the loss of functional differentiation on the basis of case and agreement. There are many variations on this theme, depending on the particular theory that the writer adopts (e.g. Roberts, 1997). It is good to bear in mind that next to formal markers there are usually contextual, pragmatic and semantic cues to decoding clause structure as well. Where contextual information cannot disambiguate, however, the use of any word order is in principle sufficient to distinguish the subject from the object, as long as word order is consistent. This is proven by modern Afrikaans, which, if anything, has less case or agreement marking than PDE yet retains the Germanic OV system. That the loss of case and verb agreement should result in more consistent word-order patterns is therefore plausible enough (and is reflected in Afrikaans and Dutch as well), but in themselves those morphological changes do not explain the OV-to-VO shift in English.

9.4   The Order of Direct Objects and Indirect Objects

In PDE, the position of the indirect object is relatively fixed. If it is expressed in the form of a full bare NP, the indirect object must immediately follow the verb and precede the direct object (i.e. IO-DO, as in (32a)). No reordering of these elements is allowed – witness the ungrammaticality of (32b).

(32) a We have decided to give *all the competitors a small prize.*
b *We have decided to give *a small prize all the competitors.*

As in the previous two sections, the history of indirect object constructions showed a somewhat wider range of word-order options in OE, which then gradually narrowed down to the more restricted range of PDE.

In OE the order IO-DO was about as frequent as the reverse order. Examples of both orders are given in (33) and (34).

(33) &   *noldon*   **Iuliuse   nænne   weorþscipe**   *don*
and   not-wanted to-Iulius no   worship   do (*Or.*5,10.124.9)
'And did not want to worship Iulius'

(34) *ðonne*   *he*   *nyle*   **ða   bisne**   *oðrum*   *eowian*   *ða*   *he*
when   he   not-wants the example to-others show   that he
mid ryhte eowian sceal
with right show   must (*CP.*59.449.29)
'When he does not want to set the example to others that he properly ought to set'

If one of the objects was pronominal – usually the indirect object – it nearly always preceded the nominal object, illustrating again the tendency for pronouns to favour positions early in the clause. When there were two pronominal objects, the predominant order was DO-IO, as in (35).

(35) *þu*   **hit him**   *of*   *þinum handum sealdest*
you it to-him from your   hands   gave (*LS.*34(Seven-Sleepers)607)
'you gave it to him with your own hands'

As these three examples show, the indirect object was often preverbal, in accordance with the OV-character of OE.

In ME, the order DO-IO continued as the most frequent order when both objects were pronominal, and so did the order IO-DO when only the indirect object was pronominal, as in (36).

(36) *leafdi   do   me   are*
     Lady   do   me   mercy (*AW*.26.3)
     'Lady, have mercy on me'

However, in contexts where both objects were full NPs, the order DO-IO, as in (37), went into decline and had disappeared by the mid-fourteenth century.

(37) *deð   hearm   moni   ancre*
     does   harm   many   anchoress (*AW*.62.21)
     '... does harm to many an anchoress'

After ME, the order DO-IO also began to disappear from contexts where both objects were pronominal, even though it had been predominant in OE and ME. Nevertheless, the old order still exists (see Biber *et al.*, 1999: 929). The examples in (38a–b) illustrate the coexistence of two orders in PDE.

(38) a My great-uncle gave *it me*. (BNC)
     b poor old Mrs Suggett told *me it*. (BNC)

Overall, then, English has become more strictly IO-DO. On the one hand, this increased rigidity may be a response to the loss of distinctive case marking. On the other, that it was the IO-DO order that came to predominate may reflect the situation that was and is most common in discourse. Typically, the indirect object is animate, given and pronominal, whereas the direct object is often inanimate, is potentially new and is more likely to be a full NP. In this typical situation, the natural order is indeed IO-DO. The ordering in more exceptional situations, with both objects being full NPs, or both objects being pronominal, then may have simply converged on the most frequent pattern. Again, however, this line of explanation needs to be taken with some caution. First, variation between IO-DO and DO-IO orders continued long after inflectional distinctions between dative and accusative had worn away. Second, the ditransitive construction decreased in frequency under competition with the prepositional dative, as in (39) (McFadden, 2002; see also Chapter 7). Because the prepositional dative construction nearly always has the order DO-*to*-IO, the DO-IO order is likely to have been the pattern that suffered most under its rise. This, too, could have contributed to the better survival of IO-DO order.

(39) He handed *it to me* as if it was no more than offering me an apple in a market-place. (BNC)

9.5   The Position of Particles

Particles are found in present-day phrasal verbs like *to turn up*, *to hold out* and *to take down*. These combinations go back to OE structures of the type shown in (40) and (41).

(40) *Hi   ða   upastigon*
     they then up-went (*ÆCHom.*II,18 172.95)
     'Then they went up'

(41) *þa   sticode   him   mon   þa   eagan   ut*
     then stuck   him   people   the   eyes   out (*Or.*4.5.90.13)
     'Then they gouged out his eyes'

The forms *upastigan* and *utstician* and scores of others consist of a verb (*astigan*, *stician*) accompanied by an adverb-like element (*up*, *ut*), which can be adjacent to the verb, as in (40), but can also occur in a non-adjacent position, as in (41); these elements are sometimes called separable prefixes, but we shall use the term particles for them, to bring out the continuity with present-day phrasal verbs. They are not to be confused with the OE verbal prefixes, even if the two classes of elements are sometimes hard to distinguish (see Chapter 6). Presumably, particles functioned as or had developed from secondary predicates (Van Kemenade and Los, 2003).

Unsurprisingly, the position of particles was more flexible in OE than in PDE. Theoretically, particles might occur before or after the verb they accompany and they might or might not be separated from the verb by intervening material, as in the four hypothetical orders in Table 9.1.

At first sight, all four orders in Table 9.1 actually occurred in OE. Closer investigation, however, shows that certain positions were disfavoured. Especially the order Part-X-V seems to have been problematic. Sentences with the particle in clause-initial position, as in PDE (42a), were quite rare in OE. The few examples that have been found, such as (42b), are all from poetry.

(42) a *Off* you *go* and not another word. (BNC)
     b *Up   aræmde   Abraham   þa*
       up   rose   Abraham   then (*Ex.*411)
       'Then Abraham got up'

Table 9.1. *Theoretically possible word-order options for verb particles.*

Part	X	V		
X	Part	V		
		V	Part	X
		V	X	Part

Nearly all remaining instances of Part-X-V were of the type in (43), where the intervening element was a prepositional phrase (here *of þam byrene*), suggesting that the particle was the head of a complex prepositional phrase, rather than forming a unit directly with the verb.

(43) he *bæd   hire, þæt heo **ut** of þam byrene **gan** sceolde*
    he asked her   that she out of the stable go   should (*GD*.1(C)9.69.1)
    'He asked her to go out of the stable'

In other words, it appears that particles did not freely appear before the verb except immediately adjacent to it. As for positions following the verb, V-Part-X, as in (44) occurred freely, but it has been noted that the order V-X-Part, as in (41), was uncommon in subordinate clauses, especially when the verb in question was non-finite.

(44) *for ðan þe se   stream   **berð   aweg**   placidum*
    because   the stream   carries away Placidus (*ÆCHom*.II,11 95.97)
    '. . . because the stream carries Placidus away'

These distributional facts fit in well with the more general word-order principles of OE discussed in Sections 9.2 and 9.3.[4] Recall that OE verbs were basically clause-final. If we assume that verbs and particles formed a unit and therefore would have been preferentially adjacent, the predicted order would be X-Part-V. This order is indeed widely attested. Extraposition of preverbal constituents could lead to V-Part-X, which is also attested. Verb-second in main clauses would lead to the order V-X-Part (with the verb moved out of the final position but leaving the particle behind). This order, too, is attested, but is uncommon in subordinate clauses, where verb-second was indeed far less likely to operate. Finally, the order Part-X-V, for which there is little evidence, is not expected to occur, as it disrupts the unity between verb and particle and is not motivated by any movement operation supported by OE clausal syntax.

The interaction between particle placement and general word-order principles in OE had one consequence that still bears on PDE word order. Recall that OE direct objects would often move to postverbal position if they were full NPs, but this tendency did not extend to pronominal objects (see Section 9.3). Therefore, if the order V-Part-X resulted from extraposition of preverbal constituents, X could be a full NP object, but was unlikely to be a pronominal object. In contrast, verb-second in main clauses would place the verb before the direct object and this operation was less sensitive to whether the object was a pronoun or a full NP (again, see Section 9.3). Therefore, if the order

---

[4] Actually, the analysis of OE word order that we present in Sections 9.2 and 9.3 was partly developed on the basis of particle positions, in work such as Koopman (1985) and Van Kemenade (1987).

V-X-Part arose as a result of verb-second, X might be either a full NP object or a pronominal object. This predicts an asymmetry between V-Part-X and V-X-Part that is strikingly confirmed by the OE data. Full NP direct objects occurred as X both in V-Part-X, as in (45a), and in V-X-Part, as in (45b). But pronominal direct objects occurred as X only in V-X-Part, as in (45c) – they are unattested in V-Part-X.

(45) a *Þa* ***ahof*** *Paulus* ***up*** *his heafod*
      Then raised Paul up his head (*LS*.32(PeterandPaul)303)
      'Then Paul raised his head'
  b *þa geleaffullan ælc* ***hylt*** *his æftergengan* ***up***
      the faithful each holds his after-comer up (*ÆCHom*.II,45 339.126)
      'each of the faithful sustains the ones that come after him'
  c *On* *þa* ***ahof*** *Drihten* *hie* ***up***
      And then raised God them up (*LS*.20(AssumptMor)353)
      'And then God raised them up'

What we are looking at here is of course the precursor of the well-known PDE pattern shown in (46), where an NP object, but not a pronominal object, can follow a particle.

(46) a I thanked him and *tore up* the prescription (BNC)
  b ... and *tore* the prescription *up*
  c ... and *tore* it *up*
  d *... and *tore up* it

From a strictly synchronic perspective, it is hard to say exactly what motivates the PDE pattern in (46) (at least judging by the host of divergent and mutually incompatible analyses it has been given, e.g. in Elenbaas 2007 or Cappelle 2005). But from a historical point of view it makes perfect sense, even though the system of word-order rules that gave rise to it in OE is now long defunct.

The order X-Part-V, which as we saw above was common in OE, did not survive into PDE. It began to disappear rapidly after 1100, so that even in ME the great majority of cases had the particle following the verb, in both main and subordinate clauses. Two examples are given in (47)–(48).

(47) *þat he ealle his castles sculde* ***iiuen up***
      that he all his castles should give up (*ChronE*(Plummer)1140.42)
      '... that he should give up all his castles'

(48) 7 *swa me schal, amid te burh,* ***setten*** *hit on heh* ***up***
      and so people shall, amidst the city, set it on high up (*St Kath*.(1)68)
      'and so people shall set it up very high in the middle of the city'

The loss of X-Part-V has been linked to the OV-to-VO shift in English (e.g. in Elenbaas, 2007). Once the verb was no longer taken to be the final element in the predicate, it would come to precede any other clausal constituents apart from the subject. This explanation is not entirely straightforward, however, as other constituents did continue to precede the verb fairly regularly for several centuries even when particles nearly always followed it. Sentence (47) is a case in point, with an object (*ealle his castles*) that is preverbal but a particle (*up*) already in postverbal position. In view of this discrepancy, it may be necessary to regard the change in particle position as being at least partly independent from the change in object position, rather than regard them as being manifestations of one single underlying change.

Since early ME there have been some further changes affecting particles, but as yet little is known about their timing or causes. Thus the pattern with an adverbial in between the verb and the particle, as in (48), died out, leaving objects as the only elements that can separate verb and particle. The pattern *up they went*, with topicalization of the particle (cf. (42)), became more common, also outside poetic texts. Finally, particle verbs in general became much more frequent in ModE and PDE. This appears to a large extent to be due to an increase in combinations having a particle with metaphorical meaning (as in *to let somebody down, to take up a hobby*; see Chapters 6 and 7).

9.6   The Position of Adverbs

Relatively little attention has been given to the position of adverbial phrases relative to other constituents. This is in spite of the fact that they are very frequent – Crystal (1980) reports that nearly two-thirds of all sentences in a corpus of spoken PDE contain an adverbial. One reason for this neglect may be the difficulty of establishing a positional framework for adverbials, which typically show high mobility. That said, the overall historical picture is one of greater freedom in OE slowly giving way to a relatively more constrained system in PDE. However, exactly how and why this happened is a question that for the larger part still awaits an answer.

One particular issue for which somewhat fuller data are available concerns the question whether an adverb can intervene between the object and the verb. In OE, when objects were often preverbal, a clause could have an adverb or even a longer adverbial phrase separating the object from the verb, as shown by the adverb *ærest* and the adverbial phrase *on þisse unrotnesse* in (49) (repeated from (6)).

(49) *sona swa ic þe **ærest on þisse unrotnesse** geseah*
     soon as I   you first in this sadness   saw (*Bo*.5.11.2)
     'As soon as I first saw you in this state of unhappiness'

In ME, preverbal objects slowly become less common, but they could still be separated from the verb by an adverbial, as in (50), where *secrely* intervenes between the object *thy conseil* and the verb *to kepe*.

(50) *If so be that thou ne mayst nat thyn owene conseil hyde, how darstou preyen*
     any oother wight thy conseil **secrely** *to kepe?*
     'If it is the case that you cannot hide your own plans, how dare you ask
     anyone else to keep your plans a secret?' (Chaucer,*T.ofMel.*2338)

However, the intervening element in this type of ME sentence was usually
fairly short, a restriction that is perhaps understandable for a language in which
OV order was becoming more and more marked.

ME clauses with VO order also allowed an adverb to intervene between the
object and the verb. An example is given in (51).

(51) ... *he scapyd of hard & left* **þer** *hir scrippe*
     'He escaped with difficulty and left her bag there' (*MKempe*(A)118.15)

Use of this option declined in ModE, but examples such as (52) show that it
still occurred as late as the nineteenth century.

(52) Accordingly, we had *always* wine and dessert (1851–3 Gaskell, *Cranford*,iii.25)

Significantly, many of these late examples feature the verb *have*, which was
also exceptional in still resisting the use of *do* in questions and interrogatives.
Example (52) may therefore be less like (51) than like the very common
pattern in (53), in which an adverb immediately follows auxiliary *have*.

(53) A medium had *once* told him that a spirit named 'Ellen' was present
     (1873 Amberley Papers,II.534(19 Jan.))

The reason why adverbs ceased intervening between verb and object has
been sought in structural changes in the make-up of the clause. For instance,
in a rather technical account, Roberts (1993) links it to the disappearance
of inflectional marking on verbs, in particular the loss of the -*en* plural
inflection.

A special case of an adverb intervening between verb and object is found in
negative clauses without *do* or another auxiliary. In such clauses, the object NP
can be separated from the verb by the word *not*, as in (54).

(54) a & *ʒit he ʒeuiþ* **not** *þis grace.*
     'And yet he does not give this grace' (*Cl.ofUnknowing*,34.69)
     b ... but saw *not* Betty (1667 Pepys *Diary*,VIII.514.2(1 Nov.))

This pattern is found from the thirteenth century, when *not* started to be used as
the regular marker of negation, until the eighteenth century, when the use of *do*
had become the rule in sentences of this type (see Chapters 6 and 7). During
this entire period, there was a clear split between full NPs and pronouns, with
full NPs always following *not*, as in (54), while pronouns almost invariably
preceded *not*, as in (55).

(55) a *þerfore I do it **nouȝt***
    'Therefore, I don't do it' (*Cl.ofUnknowing*, 125/20)
   b I have it *not* by me, or I would copy you the exact passage.
     (1848 Gaskell, *Mary Barton*,v.62)

Note that (55b), a rather late example of this pattern, again features the lexical verb *have*, which is well-known for having long resisted the use of *do* (and for behaving like an auxiliary also in other ways, see (52)).

9.7   Consequences of Word-Order Change

It is difficult to overestimate the impact word-order change has had on English. Apart from the changes themselves being quite dramatic, they also had consequences on various other aspects of the grammar. In the preceding chapters, word-order change has been discussed several times because of its involvement in a variety of structural changes, such as the rise of operator *do* (Chapter 6), the loss of impersonal verbs (Chapter 7), or the increasing omissibility of the complementizer *that* in finite noun clauses (Chapter 8). Here we consider some additional changes that can plausibly be linked to word-order shifts and that further illustrate some of the more surprising consequences word-order change has had on the grammar of English. The following discussion focuses on just two areas of change, the syntax of infinitival constructions (Section 9.7.1) and the function of the subject (Section 9.7.2). The former involves changes resulting from the OV-to-VO shift, the latter involves changes that followed from the loss of verb-second. There is of course more interesting work on the consequences of word-order change that is not discussed here, including work on the relation between changing word order and the rise of the English progressive (Los, 2012; Petré, 2015) or the expansion and changing functions of *it*-clefts (Los and Komen, 2012).

9.7.1   Infinitival Constructions

The change from predominant OV order to predominant VO order that English underwent especially during the ME period has been associated with the development of several new constructions, including the rise of some new infinitival patterns.

A first infinitival construction that arose in late ME probably in part as a result of the change from OV to VO order, is the '*for* NP-*to*-VP' construction, as in (56). In this construction, the infinitival clause has an overt subject introduced by *for*.

(56) There was nothing Claudia would have liked more than *for Dana to put distance between herself and Roman* (BNC)

The history of the construction is a complicated and somewhat controversial affair (Fischer, 1988; De Smet, 2009). It did not occur in OE but in late ME a predecessor developed with the subject taking the form of a bare NP (i.e. 'NP-to-VP', as in (57)). The *for*-NP-*to*-VP variant developed just before 1500. An early example is (58).

(57) *No thyng ... is so muchel agayns nature as **a man to encressen his owene profit to the harm of another man***
'Nothing is so much against nature as for a man to increase his own profit at the expense of another man' (Chaucer,*T.ofMel*.2776)

(58) *... god that ... in the crosse suffred deth and passyon **for alle soules to be redemed out of the peynes of helle** ...*
'God who suffered death and pain on the cross for all souls to be redeemed from the pains of hell' (Caxton,*S.ofAymon*,24)

The origins of the NP-*to*-VP construction may have to be sought in the OE pattern in (59).

(59) *Hit* *þuncþ* **monige** **monnum** *wunderlice* **to** **herenne** ... **hu** **deofel**
it   seems   to-many   men   miraculous   to   hear   how   devil
æfre **þa** **durstinesse** **hæfde**
ever   the   audacity   had (*HomU*.1(Irv 5)82)
'It seems amazing to many people to hear how the devil ever had the audacity'

In this sentence type, the dative NP *monige monnum* is not the subject of the infinitival clause, but a participant profiled by the main-clause predicate (*þuncþ*) *wunderlic*. In (59), this dative NP precedes the adjective, while the infinitival clause follows it. In analogy to the increasingly strict VO order, however, such dative NPs came to be regularly placed after the predicative element. The results were sentences such as (60).

(60) *if it be a foul thyng **a man to waste his catel on wommen***
'if it is a foul thing for a man to waste his property on women'
(Chaucer,*Pars.T*.850)

Because this construction now had a sequence [NP to VP], it was liable to reanalysis, with the NP being interpreted as the subject of the infinitive, rather than as a complement to the predicate *be a foul thing* – a reinterpretation that would have been further helped by the loss of distinctive dative case endings, and perhaps the roughly simultaneous emergence of AcI constructions (as discussed below).

The *for*-NP-*to*-VP construction familiar from PDE is likely to have been partly modelled on the older NP-*to*-VP construction. The two occurred in overlapping contexts and with similar meanings. Its history is complicated, however, by yet another construction in which *for* is an element reinforcing the *to*-infinitive (see Chapter 8). Typically, this reinforcing *for* would appear immediately adjacent to the infinitive marker *to*, as in (61a), but sometimes *for* and *to* could be separated by a preverbal object, as in (61b).

(61) a ... *after Reynawde was departed from Ardeyne, from hys bretherne, from his wife / and fro hys chyldrene, **for to goe beyonde the sea** ...*
 'After Reynawde had departed from Ardeyne, from his brothers, from his wife and from his children, in order to travel beyond the sea...'
 (Caxton, *S.ofAymon*,13)

 b *That god that created the firmamente, and made alle thynges of noughte, **for the people to susteyne**.*
 'that God who created the firmament and made all things from nothing so as to sustain the people' (Caxton,*S.ofAymon*,24)

Owing to the OV-to-VO shift, contexts like (61b) were becoming increasingly anomalous. One solution would have been to move the object to postverbal position, but another was to passivize the infinitive and turn the object into a subject, producing a PDE-like *for*-NP-*to*-VP construction as a result. This explains why most of the earliest attestations of *for*-NP-*to*-VP are passive, including (58).

 Indeed, the same logic may go some way towards explaining the more general rise of passive infinitives at the end of the ME period (Fischer, 1992a, 1997). Increasingly, the grammar pressured NPs before infinitives into taking the role of subjects and often one way of accomplishing this was by passivizing the infinitive. This is particularly clear in the so-called 'accusativus-cum-infinitivo' or AcI – sometimes also referred to as Exceptional Case Marking or ECM. A modern example is (62a). This type of sentence, in which the matrix verb takes a clausal complement which itself has an overt NP subject, does not occur in OE. Unambiguous examples are found from 1400 onwards, mainly in formal texts. An early example is (62b).

(62) a Few people now believe *this to be possible.* (BNC)
 b *she dare not aventure **her money to be brought vp to London** for feere of robbyng*
 'she dare not venture her money to be brought up to London for fear of robbing'
 (*Past.Let.*I,262)

Careful assessment of a great deal of textual evidence by several scholars has led to a consensus that the construction was promoted by influence from Latin (see Chapter 4); but its development was probably in part also dependent on word-order change. Consider the OE structure in (63):

(63) *Moyses forbead **swyn to etenne***
 'Moses forbade the eating of pigs (lit. pigs to eat).' (*ÆLS*(Maccabees)85)

In (63), the accusative form *swyn* cannot be the object of *forbead*, which assigns dative case, so it must be the object of *etenne*. As far as OE is concerned, this was unproblematic, since OV order was common. But when that was no longer so, *swyn* would be increasingly seen as the subject of the infinitive, necessitating a passive form (as in (62b)). Word-order change, then, promoted both passive infinitives and ACI constructions.[5]

9.7.2 The Subject Slot

The loss of verb-second and the increasingly rigid SV order meant that English lost much of its freedom to move non-subject constituents into clause-initial position. This had important consequences and is especially likely to have affected the functional demands placed on the subject. The clause-initial position is strongly associated with given information. Therefore, the more the subject came to be fixed in initial position, the greater the pressure on the subject to accommodate whatever information was contextually given.

Los and Dreschler (2012) argue that this may explain the 'permissiveness' of English subjects, as compared to subjects in Dutch or German. That is, PDE allows a remarkably wide array of thematic roles in its subject slot, coding information as subject that Dutch or German would preferentially code differently. Some contrastive examples are given in (64)–(66), with PDE coding the given information in its clause-initial subject slot, whereas Dutch codes it as an adverbial, relying on subject-verb inversion to move it into clause-initial position.

(64) a *The woodstove* leaked smoke halfway up the pipe, thin clouds drifting near the ceiling. (2012, COCA)

  b *Uit de tankwagen* *lekt* *nog* *steeds* *veel* *zoutzuur.*
  from the lorry   leaks still ever   much hydrochloric acid
  (Google)
  'The lorry is still leaking a lot of hydrochloric acid'

(65) a Don't be afraid of altitude or power, *it* buys you a very useful commodity – time. (BNC)

  b *Dan kun je een optie nemen op de woning.* *Daarmee* *koop* *je* *jezelf*
                           therewith buy you yourself
  wat *respijt.*
  some respite (Google)
  'Then you can take an option on the house. That buys you a little more time'

---

[5] This interpretation derives further strength from developments in the history of Dutch and German: in both languages, which retained OV order, we can see some toying with ACI constructions in strongly Latin-influenced Renaissance texts, but the construction did not spread and died out again.

(66) a The Chicheley-Smythes have bought an absolutely super villa in Sardinia and say we could rent it if we'd like to. .... *It* sleeps ten with a permanent staff of three. (BNC)

b *Het huis heeft drie verdiepingen met 5 slaapkamers en* **er** *kunnen*
                                     and   there can

acht   *mensen*   *slapen*   *in*   *volledig*   *comfort.*
eight   people   sleep   in   full   comfort (Google)
'The house has three floors with five bedrooms and it can sleep eight people in complete comfort'

Much diachronic research is still to be done in this respect, but one well-documented development that might be linked to the increased functional demands on the subject slot is the loss of the indefinite pronoun *man* (Los, 2005: ch.10). *Man* was a pronoun restricted to subject positions that evoked a non-specified referent as agent of an action. This type of referent has very low salience in the discourse, meaning it has not been mentioned before and is unlikely to be picked up later. When sentences with *man* are translated into PDE, the verb is often passivized so that the referent of *man* can simply be left untranslated, as illustrated by (67). This way, *man* effectively signalled that the agent of an action had no further relevance to the unfolding discourse. Often, *man* was used postverbally, while some other element occupied the clause-initial position to establish a link to the foregoing discourse. In (67), this is done by the deictic adverbial *ða*, integrating the event described in (67) into a bigger temporal sequence of events.

(67) *ða*   *gebrohte* **man** *him to, tomiddes þam folce,* *ænne dumne mann*
     then brought one him to among the people a   dumb man
     (*ÆHom*.18,25)
     'Then was brought to him, among the people, a man who could not speak.'

With the increased pressure on subjects to establish links to the previous discourse, *man* became a less-than-ideal filler of the subject slot. It is therefore likely that the loss of Verb-second was a major blow to indefinite *man*. That the cognates of *man* in Dutch and German did not disappear supports this argument.

Another development that could be linked to the changing role of the English subject is the emergence of prepositional passives. Prepositional passives are structures as in (68), with a stranded preposition whose (notional) complement functions as clause subject. The structure is not found in Dutch or German, and as such fits the general picture of English subjects being more permissive, as indeed suggested by Los (2012: 27).

(68) Out of the corner of her eye, she caught the fact that they *were being stared at* with unveiled interest by most members of the group, the most curious of all, of course, being Mandy. (BNC)

The history of preposition stranding is complicated. In OE, prepositions could be stranded when the complement was a pronoun or the word *þær* 'there', as in examples (69).[6] This particular stranding operation disappeared soon after the end of the OE period. Other cases of stranding were in relative clauses without a relative pronoun and infinitival clauses, as in (70). Prepositional passives did not occur.

(69) a | *þa* | *wendon* | *hi* | *me* | *heora* | *bæc* | *to* | | |
| then | turned | they | me | their | back | to (*Bo.*2.8.9) | | |

'Then they turned their backs on me'

  b | *Be* | *þæm* | *þu* | *meaht* | *ongietan* | *ðæt* | *þu* | *þær* | *nane* | *myrhðe* | *on* |
| by | that | you | can | perceive | that | you | there | no | happiness | on |

  næfdest
  not-had (*Bo.*7.15.11)

'From that you could understand that you did not take joy in it'

(70) a | *þæt* | *gewrit* | *þe* | *hit* | *on* | *awriten* | *wæs* | |
| the | document | that | it | on | written | was (*Or.*6,13.141.21) | |

'The document that it was written in'

  b | *Drihten,* | *þu* | *þe* | *gecure* | *þæt* | *fæt* | *on* | *to* | *eardienne* |
| Lord | you | for-yourself | chose | that | vessel | on | to | live |

  (*LS.*20(AssumptMor)330)

'Lord, you chose yourself to live in that vessel'

This rather limited array of stranding options was greatly extended in the ME period. Already in early ME, preposition stranding began to occur in passive constructions, giving rise to prepositional passives, as shown in (71).

(71) *þis maiden ... feled also bi her þi / þat sche **was yleyen bi***
'This girl felt by her thigh that she had been lain with'
(*Arth.&M.*849, Denison, 1993: 125–6)

Prepositional passives slowly spread to more and more verbs and constructions. They began to be attested in passive infinitive constructions, as in (72), and they extended to collocations consisting of a verb, a nominal, and a preposition, as in (73). Later, they also began to appear with prepositional phrasal verbs, as in (74).

---

[6] Both of these cases also allow an option in which the complement immediately precedes the preposition, as in *and hi ne dorston him fore gebiddan* (*ÆHom* 20. 225) 'and they did not dare to pray for him', or *and com æfter fyrste to ðam treowe. sohte wæstm ðæron and nænne ne gemette* (*ÆCHom.*II,30 237.72) 'And after a while he went to the tree and looked for fruit on it, but found none'. Therefore, Van Kemenade (1987) suggests that the OE stranding constructions in (68) always involved a complement being fronted through the position immediately to the left of the preposition. It follows that any element that could not occur right before its preposition, such as a full NP, also could not move away from its preposition and leave it stranded.

(72) *how worthy it es to **ben wondrid uppon***
'How worthy it is to be marvelled at' (Chaucer,*Bo*.4.pr.1.22)

(73) *and þes oþer wordis of þis bischop ouȝte to **be taken hede to***
'And these other words of this bishop ought to be taken heed of'
(Wyclif,*Clergy*,XXVI,iii)

(74) I understand there there was a servant of yours, and a kynsman of myne, **was**
myschevously *made away with* (c1613 (1502) *Plumpton Let*.130,164.11)

The growth of preposition stranding was not restricted to prepositional
passives, however. Preposition stranding also underwent a widening of possibilities in relative and interrogative clauses. OE only allowed stranding in
relative clauses introduced by the complementizer *þe*, as in (69a); this pattern
was continued when *þe* was replaced by *that* (see Chapter 5). In early ME it
also came to be used in relative clauses introduced by the new relative pronoun
which, as in (75), and from there it appears to have spread to interrogative
clauses with *which* and also *whom*, as in (76).

(75) *And getenisse men ben in ebron / Quilc men mai get wundren **on***
'And there are gigantic men in Hebron, whom people may still marvel at'
(*Gen.&Ex*.3715–16))

(76) *Nuste   nan kempe   whæm he sculde slæn **on***
not-knew   no warrior   who he should strike on (*Laȝ.Brut*(Cal)13719–20)
'No warrior knew whom he should strike'

The full extent of preposition stranding in late ME and beyond suggests that
the need for more permissive subjects was not the only factor motivating its
expansion – in (75)–(76) the subject is not involved in the stranding operation.
Another factor that may have played a role is the increasingly fixed order of
verbal idioms. Once verbs no longer appeared in clause-final position, idiomatic combinations of verb-preposition, verb-noun-preposition, or verb-particle-
preposition came to consistently occur in the same order, which would have
facilitated reinterpretation of the preposition as somehow being part of the
verb. That is, [V] [P NP]$_{PP}$ came to be treated roughly as [V P]$_V$ [NP]. On the
latter analysis, movement operations would target the NP rather than [P NP].
This predicts that new stranding operations would have initially affected only
verbs in which an object interpretation of the complement NP is semantically
plausible, as in (77).

(77) þer   wes sorhe   to seon hire leoflich lich faren so reowliche   **wið**
there was sorrow to see   her   lovely   body dealt so cruelly   with
(*St.Jul.*(Roy)22.195, Denison 1993: 125)
'It was a sad sight to see her lovely body dealt with so cruelly'

In this respect, too, then, word-order change is likely to have influenced the development of preposition stranding, testifying to the pervasive effect word-order change has had on the history of English syntax.

9.8   Concluding Remarks

Word order sits at the cross-roads between syntax and information structure. On the one hand, syntax provides the basic templates that speakers can draw on to manage the information flow in and between clauses. On the other hand, the repertoire of syntactic structures available to speakers is attuned to the demands of information management. Unsurprisingly, then, it is by taking into account information structure that most recent progress in understanding word order and word-order change has been made. The preceding discussion illustrates this – from the special status of pronouns and other light elements in various constructions to the repercussions of word-order change on the pragmatic demands placed on subjects. Even so, much work remains to be done, both at the level of detailed description of word-order phenomena at various stages of English, and when it comes to teasing apart the driving forces of word-order changes, as well as their subsequent effects. In this respect, there is much promise in the relatively recent trend to combine quantitative and qualitative analyses of balanced samples of text material, as provided by the various historical corpora of English.

References

Aarts, B. and McMahon, A. (eds.) 2006. *The Handbook of English Linguistics*. Oxford: Blackwell.

Adamson, S. 2000. 'A lovely little example: Word order options and category shift in the premodifying string', in Fischer *et al.* (eds.), 39–66.

Algeo, J. 2006. *British or American English? A Handbook of Word and Grammar Patterns*. Cambridge: Cambridge University Press.

Allen, C.L. 1980. '*Whether* in Old English'. *Linguistic Inquiry* 11: 789–93.

1992. 'Old English and the syntactician: Some remarks and a syntactician's guide to editions of the works of Ælfric', in F. Colman (ed.), *Evidence for Old English: Material and Theoretical Bases for Reconstruction*. Edinburgh: John Donald, 1–19.

1995. *Case Marking and Reanalysis: Grammatical Relations from Old to Early Modern English*. Oxford: Oxford University Press.

1997. 'Middle English case loss and the "creolization" hypothesis'. *English Language and Linguistics* 1: 63–89.

2001. 'The development of a new passive in English', in M. Butt and T. Holloway King (eds.), *Time over Matter: Diachronic Perspectives on Morphosyntax*. Stanford: CSLI, 43–72.

2002. 'Case and Middle English genitive noun phrases', in D.W. Lightfoot (ed.), *Syntactic Effects of Morphological Change*. Oxford: Oxford University Press, 57–80.

2006. 'Case syncretism and word order change', in Van Kemenade and Los (eds.), 201–23.

2008. *Genitives in Early English. Typology and Evidence*. Oxford: Oxford University Press.

2012. 'Why a determiner? The possessive+determiner+adjective construction in Old English', in Meurman-Solin *et al.* (eds.), 245–70.

Altenberg, B. 1982. *The Genitive v. the Of-Construction: A Study of Syntactic Variation in Seventeenth-Century English*. Lund: CWK Gleerup.

Anderwald, L. 2005. 'Negative concord in British English dialects', in Y. Iyeiri (ed.), *Aspects of English Negation*. Amsterdam: Benjamins, 113–37.

Anttila, R. 2003. 'Analogy: The warp and woof of cognition', in Joseph and Janda (eds.), 425–40.

Arnaud, R. 1983. 'On the progress of the progressive in the private correspondence of famous British people 1800–1880', in S. Jacobson (ed.), *Papers from the Second Scandinavian Symposium on Syntactic Variation*. Stockholm: Almqvist & Wiksell, 83–91.

1998. 'The development of the progressive in 19th century English: A quantitative survey'. *Language Variation and Change* 10: 123–52.

Atkinson, D. 1999. *Scientific Discourse in Sociohistorical Context: The Philosophical Transactions of the Royal Society of London 1675–1975*. London: Erlbaum.

Bache, C. 2000. *Essentials of Mastering English: A Concise Grammar*. Berlin: Mouton de Gruyter.

Baldi, P. 1990. 'Indo-European languages', in B. Comrie (ed.), *The Major Languages of Western Europe*. London: Routledge, 21–57.

Ball, C. 1991. *The Historical Development of the It-Cleft*. PhD dissertation: University of Pennsylvania.

Bandle, O., Braunmüller, K., Jahr, E.H. *et al.* (eds.) 2005. *The Nordic Languages: An International Handbook of the History of the North Germanic Languages*. Vol. 2. Berlin: Mouton de Gruyter.

Baron, N.S. 2008. *Always on: Language in an Online and Mobile World*. Oxford: Oxford University Press.

Barðdal, J., Smirnova, E., Sommerer, L. and Gildea, S. (eds.) 2015. *Diachronic Construction Grammar*. Amsterdam: Benjamins.

Beal, J.C., Corrigan, K.P. and Moisl, H.L. (eds.) 2007. *Creating and Digitizing Language Corpora*, vol. 2: *Diachronic Databases*. Houndsmills: Palgrave Macmillan.

Bech, K. 2012. 'Word order, information structure, and discourse relations: A study of Old and Middle English verb-final clauses', in Meurman-Solin *et al.* (eds.), 66–86.

Bennett, P., Durrell, M., Scheible, S. and Whitt, R.J. (eds.) 2013. *New Methods in Historical Corpora*. Tübingen: Narr.

Bergs, A. 2005. *Social Networks and Historical Sociolinguistics: Studies in Morphosyntactic Variation in the Paston Letters 1421–1503*. Berlin: Mouton de Gruyter.

Bermúdez-Otero, R., Denison, D., Hogg, R.M. and McCully, C.B. (eds.) 2000. *Generative Theory and Corpus Linguistics: A Dialogue from 10 ICEHL*. Berlin: Mouton.

Biber, D. 1988. *Variation across Speech and Writing*. Cambridge: Cambridge University Press.

Biber, D. and Clark, V. 2002. 'Historical shifts in modification patterns with complex noun phrase structures: How long can you go without a verb?', in T. Fanego, M.J. López-Couso, and J. Pérez-Guerra (eds.), *English Historical Syntax and Morphology: Selected Papers from 11 ICEHL*. Amsterdam: Benjamins, 43–66.

Biber, D. and Finegan, E. 1989. 'Drift and the evolution of English style: A history of three genres'. *Language* 65: 487–517.

Biber, D. and Gray, B. 2011. 'Grammatical change in the noun phrase: The influence of written language use'. *English Language and Linguistics* 15: 223–50.

Biber, D., Johansson, S., Leech, G., Conrad, S. and Finegan, E. 1999. *Longman Grammar of Spoken and Written English*. Harlow: Longman.

Blake, N. (ed.) 1992. *The Cambridge History of the English Language,* vol. 2: *1066–1676*. Cambridge: Cambridge University Press.

Bolinger, D. 1952. 'Linear modification'. *Language* 67: 1117–44.

1967. 'Apparent constituents in surface structure'. *Word* 23: 47–56.

Brazil, D. 1995. *A Grammar of Speech*. Oxford: Oxford University Press.

Breban, T. 2010. *English Adjectives of Comparison: Lexical and Grammaticalized Uses*. Berlin: Mouton de Gruyter.

2012. 'Functional shifts and the development of English determiners', in Meurman-Solin *et al.* (eds.), 271–300.

Brems, L. and Davidse, K. 2010. 'The grammaticalization of nominal type noun constructions with *kind/sort of*: Chronology and paths of change'. *English Studies* 91: 180–202.

Bresnan, J.W. and Ford, M. 2010. 'Predicting syntax: Processing dative constructions in American and Australian varieties of English'. *Language* 86: 168–213.

Brinton, L.J. 1988. *The Development of English Aspectual Systems: Aspectualizers and Post-Verbal Particles*. Cambridge: Cambridge University Press.

1996. *Pragmatic Markers in English: Grammaticalization and Discourse Functions*. Berlin: Mouton de Gruyter.

Brinton, L.J. and Akimoto, M. (eds.) 1999. *Collocational and Idiomatic Aspects of Composite Predicates in the History of English*. Amsterdam: Benjamins.

Brinton, L.J. and Traugott, E.C. 2005. *Lexicalization and Language Change*. Cambridge: Cambridge University Press.

Britain, D. 2002. 'Space and spatial diffusion', in Chambers *et al.* (eds.), 603–37.

Bybee, J.L., Perkins, R. and Pagliuca, W. 1994. *The Evolution of Grammar: Tense, Aspect, and Modality in the Languages of the World*. Chicago, IL: University of Chicago Press.

Bybee, J.L. and Torres Cacoullos, R. 2009. 'The role of prefabs in grammaticization: How the particular and the general interact in language change', in R.L. Corrigan, E.A. Moravcsik, H. Ouali and K. Wheatley (eds.), *Formulaic Language*, vol. 1: *Distribution and Historical Change*. Amsterdam: Benjamins, 187–217.

Cappelle, B. 2005. *Particle Patterns in English. A Comprehensive Coverage*. PhD dissertation: KU Leuven.

Chambers, J.K., Trudgill, P. and Schilling-Estes, N. (eds.) 2002. *The Handbook of Language Variation and Change*. Oxford: Blackwell.

Chomsky, N. 1981. *Lectures on Government and Binding*. Dordrecht: Foris.

Christiansen, M.H. and Kirby, S. (eds.) 2003. *Language Evolution*. Oxford: Oxford University Press.

Claridge, C. 2000. *Multi-Word Verbs in Early Modern English: A Corpus-Based Study*. Amsterdam: Rodopi.

Claridge, C. and Walker, T. 2001. 'Causal clauses in written and speech-related genres in Early Modern English'. *ICAME Journal* 25: 31–63.

Cloutier, R. 2005. Review of Carola Trips 2002. *From OV to VO in Early Middle English. English Language and Linguistics* 9: 181–91.

Coates, R. 2002. 'The significances of Celtic place-names in England', in Filppula *et al.* (eds.), 47–85.

Colman, F. 1988. 'Heavy arguments in Old English', in J. Anderson and N. Macleod, (eds.), *Edinburgh Studies in the English Language*. Edinburgh: John Donald, 33–89.

Croft, W. 2000. *Explaining Language Change: An Evolutionary Approach*. London: Longman.

2012. *Verbs. Aspect and Causal Structure*. Oxford: Oxford University Press.

Crystal, D. 1980. 'Neglected grammatical factors in conversational English', in S. Greenbaum, G. Leech and J. Svartvik (eds.), *Studies in English Linguistics for Randolph Quirk*, London: Longman, 153–66.

Dąbrowska, E. 2004. *Language, Mind and Brain: Some Psychological and Neurological Constraints on Theories of Grammar.* Washington D.C.: Georgetown University Press.

Dahl, Ö. 2010. 'The grammar of future time reference in European languages', in Ö. Dahl (ed.), *Tense and Aspect in the Languages of Europe.* Berlin: Mouton de Gruyter, 309–28.

Davidse, K. 1996. 'Functional dimensions of the dative in English', in W. van Belle and W. Langendonck (eds.), *The Dative,* vol. 1: *Descriptive Studies.* Amsterdam: Benjamins, 289–338.

Davidse, K., Breban, T. and Van linden, A. 2008. 'Deictification: The development of secondary deictic meanings by adjectives in the English NP'. *English Language and Linguistics* 12: 475–503.

Deacon, T.W. 1997. *The Symbolic Species.* London: Norton.

Declerck, R. 1981. 'On the role of the progressive aspect in nonfinite perception verb complements'. *Glossa* 15: 83–113.

De Cuypere, L. 2015. 'The Old English *to*-dative construction'. *English Language and Linguistics* 19: 1–25.

De Haan, F. 2010. 'Typology of tense, aspect, and modality systems', in J. Jung Song (ed.), *The Oxford Handbook of Linguistic Typology.* Oxford: Oxford University Press, 443–64.

De Haas, N.K. 2011. *Morphosyntactic Variation in Northern English. The Northern Subject Rule, Its Origins and Early History.* Utrecht: LOT.

Denison, D. 1985a. 'The origins of periphrastic "do": Ellegård and Visser reconsidered', in R. Eaton, O. Fischer, W.F. Koopman and F. van der Leek (eds.), *Papers from the Fourth International Conference on English Historical Linguistics.* Amsterdam: Benjamins, 45–60.

1985b. 'The origins of completive *up* in English'. *Neuphilologische Mitteilungen* 86: 37–61.

1993. *English Historical Syntax.* London: Longman.

1998. 'Syntax', in S. Romaine (ed.), *The Cambridge History of the English Language,* vol. 4: *1176–1997,* Cambridge: Cambridge University Press, 92–329.

2006. 'Category change and gradience in the Determiner system', in Van Kemenade and Los (eds.), 279–304.

Denison, D., Bermúdez-Otero, R., McCully, C. and Moore, E. (eds.), 2012. *Analysing Older English,* Cambridge: Cambridge University Press.

Depraetere, I. and Reed, S. 2006. 'Mood and modality in English', in Aarts and McMahon (eds.), 269–90.

De Smet, H. 2008. *Diffusional Change in the English System of Complementation: Gerunds, Participles and* for. . .to-*Infinitives.* PhD dissertation: KU Leuven.

2009. 'Analyzing reanalysis'. *Lingua* 19: 1728–55.

2010. 'Grammatical interference: Subject marker *for* and phrasal verb particle *out*', in Traugott and Trousdale (eds.), 75–104.

2013a. *Spreading Patterns: Diffusional Change in the English System of Complementation.* Oxford: Oxford University Press.

2013b. 'Does innovation need reanalysis?', in E. Coussé and F. von Mengden (eds.), *Usage-Based Approaches to Language Change.* Amsterdam: Benjamins, 23–48.

2014. 'Constrained confusion: The gerund/participle distinction in Late Modern English', in M. Hundt (ed.), *Late Modern English Syntax.* Cambridge: Cambridge University Press, 224–38.

De Smet, H. and Vancaeyzele, E. 2014. 'Like a rolling stone: The changing use of English premodifying present participles'. *English Language and Linguistics* 19: 131–56.

De Smet, H., Flach, S., Tyrkkö, J. and Diller, H.-J. 2015. *The Corpus of Late Modern English (CLMET), version 3.1: Improved tokenization and linguistic annotation.* KU Leuven, FU Berlin, U Tampere, RU Bochum. Available from https://perswww.kuleuven.be/~u0044428/clmet3_1.htm.

Diewald, G. 2011. 'Grammaticalization and pragmaticalization', in Narrog and Heine (eds.), 438–61.

Disterheft, D. 1981. 'Remarks on the history of the Indo-European infinitive'. *Folia Linguistica Historica* 2: 3–34.

Dixon, R.M.W. 1982. *Where Have All the Adjectives Gone?* Berlin: Mouton de Gruyter.

Dreschler, G. 2015. *Passives and the Loss of Verb Second. A Study of Syntactic and Information-Structural Factors.* Utrecht: LOT.

Drinka, B. 2013. 'Sources of auxiliation in the perfects of Europe'. *Studies in Language* 37: 599–644.

Dryer, M. 1996. 'Word order typology', in J. Jacobs, A. von Stechow, W. Sternefeld and T. Vennemann (eds.) *Syntax: An International Handbook of Contemporary Research*, vol. 2. Berlin: Walter de Gruyter, 1050–65.

Elenbaas, M. 2007. *The Synchronic and Diachronic Syntax of the English Verb-Particle Combination.* Utrecht: LOT.

Ellegård, A. 1953. *The Auxiliary Do. The Establishment and Regulation of Its Use in English.* Stockholm: Almqvist & Wiksell.

Emonds, J.E. and Faarlund, J.T. 2014. *English: The Language of the Vikings.* Olomouc: Palacký University.

Engel, D.M. and Ritz, M.-E. 2000. 'The use of the present perfect in Australian English', *Australian Journal of Linguistics* 20: 119–40.

Enkvist, N.E. 1986. 'More about the textual function of Old English adverbial *þa*', in D. Kastovsky and A. Szwedek, (eds.), *Linguistics across Historical and Geographical Boundaries: In Honour of Jacek Fisiak on the Occasion of his Fiftieth Birthday*, vol. 1. Berlin: Mouton de Gruyter, 301–09.

Evans, N. 2007. 'Insubordination and its uses', in I. Nikolaeva (ed.), *Finiteness: Theoretical and Empirical Foundations.* Oxford: Oxford University Press, 366–431.

Faarlund, J.T. 1990. *Syntactic Change: Towards a Theory of Historical Syntax.* Berlin: Mouton de Gruyter.

Fanego, T. 2004. 'On reanalysis and actualization in syntactic change: The rise and development of English verbal gerunds'. *Diachronica* 21: 5–55.

Filppula, M. 1999. *The Grammar of Irish English: Language in Hibernian Style.* London: Routledge.

  2000. 'Inversion in embedded questions in some regional varieties of English', in Bermúdez-Otero *et al.* (eds.), 439–53.

  2009. 'The rise of *it*-clefting in English: Areal-typological and contact-linguistic considerations'. *English Language and Linguistics* 13: 267–93.

Filppula, M., Klemola, J. and Pitkänen, H. (eds.) 2002. *The Celtic Roots of English.* Joensuu: Faculty of Humanities.

Finkenstaedt, Th., Leisi, E. and Wolff, D. 1970. *A Chronological English Dictionary*. Heidelberg: Winter.

Fischer, O. 1988. 'The rise of the *for NP to V* construction: An explanation', in G. Nixon and J. Honey (eds.), *An Historic Tongue: Studies in English Linguistics in Memory of Barbara Strang*. London: Routledge, 67–88.

1991. 'The rise of the passive infinitive in English', in D. Kastovsky (ed.), *Historical English Syntax*. Berlin: Mouton de Gruyter, 141–88.

1992a. 'Syntactic change and borrowing: The case of the accusative-and-infinitive construction in English', in Gerritsen and Stein (eds.), 17–88.

1992b. 'Syntax', in Blake (ed.), 207–408.

1994a. 'The development of quasi-auxiliaries in English and changes in word order'. *Neophilologus* 78: 137–64.

1994b. 'The fortunes of the Latin-type accusative and infinitive construction in Dutch and English compared', in T. Swan, E. Mørck and O. Jansen-Westvik (eds.), *Language Change and Language Structure: Old Germanic Languages in a Comparative Perspective*. Berlin: Mouton de Gruyter, 91–133.

1995. 'The distinction between *to* and bare infinitival complements in late Middle English'. *Diachronica* 12: 1–30.

1997. 'The grammaticalisation of infinitival *to* in English compared with German and Dutch', in Hickey and Puppel (eds.), vol. 1, 265–80.

1998. 'On negative raising in the history of English', in I. Tieken-Boon-van Ostade, G. Tottie and W. van der Wurff (eds.), *Negation in the History of English*. Berlin: Mouton de Gruyter, 55–100.

2000. 'The position of the adjective in Old English', in Bermúdez-Otero *et al.* (eds.), 153–81.

2001. 'The position of the adjective in Old English from an iconic perspective', in O. Fischer and M. Nänny (eds.), *The Motivated Sign*. Amsterdam: Benjamins, 249–76.

2004. 'Developments in the category adjective from Old to Middle English'. *Studies in Medieval English Language and Literature* 19: 1–36.

2006. 'On the position of adjectives in Middle English'. *English Language and Linguistics* 10: 253–88.

2007. *Morphosyntactic Change: Functional and Formal Perspectives*. Oxford: Oxford University Press.

2012. 'The status of the postposed "*and*-adjective" construction in Old English: Attributive or predicative?', in Denison *et al.* (eds.), 251–84.

2013. 'The role of contact in English syntactic change in the Old and Middle English periods', in Schreier and Hundt (eds.), 18–40.

2015. 'The influence of the grammatical system and analogy in processes of language change: The case of the auxiliation of *have to* once again', in F. Toupin and B. Lowrey (eds.), *Studies in Linguistic Variation and Change: From Old to Middle English*. Newcastle: Cambridge Scholars, 120–50.

Fischer, O., Rosenbach, A. and Stein, D. (eds.) 2000. *Pathways of Change: Grammaticalization in English*. Amsterdam: Benjamins.

Fischer, O., Van Kemenade, A., Koopman, W. and Van der Wurff, W. 2000. *The Syntax of Early English*. Cambridge: Cambridge University Press.

Fischer, O. and Van der Leek, F. 1987. 'A "case" for the Old English impersonal', in W. F. Koopman, F. van der Leek, O. Fischer and R. Eaton, (eds.), *Explanation and Linguistic Change*. Amsterdam: Benjamins, 79–120.

Fisiak, J. and Krygier, M. (eds.) 1998. *Advances in English Historical Linguistics.* Berlin: Mouton de Gruyter.

Fonteyn, L. 2016. 'From nominal to verbal gerunds: A referential typology'. *Functions of Language* 23: 60–83.

Fonteyn, L., De Smet, H. and Heyvaert, L. 2015. 'What it means to verbalize: The changing discourse functions of the English gerund'. *Journal of English Linguistics* 43:1–25.

Fries, C. 1927. 'The expression of the future'. *Language* 3: 87–95.

Fulk, R.D. 2014. '*Beowulf* and language history', in L. Neidorf (ed.), *The Dating of Beowulf: A Reassessment.* Cambridge: Brewer, 19–36.

Gerritsen, M. and Stein, D. 1992. 'Introduction: On "internal" and "external" in syntactic change', in Gerritsen and Stein (eds.), 1–16.

 (eds.) 1992. *External and Internal Factors in Syntactic Change.* Berlin: Mouton de Gruyter.

Ghesquière, L. 2014. *The Directionality of (Inter)subjectification in the English Noun Phrase: Pathways of Change.* Berlin: Mouton de Gruyter.

Givón, T. 1979. *On Understanding Grammar.* New York: Academic Press.

 1980. 'The binding hierarchy and the typology of complements'. *Studies in Language* 4: 333–77.

 2001. *Syntax: An Introduction.* Vol. 1. Amsterdam: Benjamins.

Godden, M.R. 1992. 'Literary language', in Hogg (ed.), 490–535.

Görlach, M. 1999a. *English in Nineteenth-Century England: An Introduction.* Cambridge: Cambridge University Press.

 1999b. 'Regional and social variation', in R. Lass, (ed.) *The Cambridge History of the English Language,* Vol. 3: *1476–1776.* Cambridge: Cambridge University Press, 459–538.

González-Díaz, V. 2008. *English Adjective Comparison: A Historical Perspective* Amsterdam: Benjamins.

 2009. 'Little old problems: Adjectives and subjectivity in the English NP'. *Transactions of the Philological Society* 107: 376–402.

 2010. 'Iconicity and subjectivisation in the English NP: The case of *little*', in J. Conradie, R. Johl, M. Beukes, O. Fischer and C. Ljungberg (eds.), *Signergy.* Amsterdam: Benjamins, 319–45.

Gotti, M., Dossena, M. and Dury, R. (eds.) 2008. *English Historical Linguistics 2006,* vol. 1: *Syntax and Morphology.* Amsterdam: Benjamins.

Greaves, C. and Warren, M. 2010. 'What can a corpus tell us about multi-word units?', in A. O'Keeffe and M. McCarthy (eds.), *The Routledge Handbook of Corpus Linguistics.* London: Routledge, 212–26.

Greenberg, J. 1966. 'Some universals of grammar with particular reference to the order of meaningful elements', in J. Greenberg (ed.), *Universals of Grammar* (2nd ed.). Cambridge, MA: MIT Press, 73–113.

Gronemeyer, C. 1999. 'On deriving complex polysemy: The grammaticalization of *get*'. *English Language and Linguistics* 3: 1–39.

Hadley, D.M. 1997. '"And they proceeded to plough and to support themselves": The Scandinavian settlement of England', *Anglo-Norman Studies* 19: 69–96.

Hadley, D.M. and Richards, J.D. (eds.) 2000. *Cultures in Contact: Scandinavian Settlement in England in the Ninth & Tenth Centuries.* Turnhout: Brepols.

Haeberli, E. 2010. 'Investigating Anglo-Norman influence on late Middle English syntax', in R. Ingham (ed.), *The Anglo-Norman Language and its Contexts*. Woodbridge: York Medieval Press, 143–63.

Haeberli, E. and Ingham, R. 2007. 'The position of negation and adverbs in Early Middle English'. *Lingua* 117: 1–25.

Haegeman, L. 1997. 'Register variation, truncation, and subject omission in English and in French'. *English Language and Linguistics* 1: 233–70.

Harris, A.C. and Campbell, L. 1995. *Historical Syntax in Cross-Linguistic Perspective*. Cambridge: Cambridge University Press.

Haspelmath, M. 1989. 'From purposive to infinitive - A universal path of grammaticization'. *Folia Linguistica Historica* 10: 287–310.

Haumann, D. 2003. 'The postnominal *and* adjective construction in Old English'. *English Language and Linguistics* 7: 57–83.

2010. 'Adnominal adjectives in Old English'. *English Language and Linguistics* 14: 53–81.

Heine, B., Claudi, U. and Hünnemeyer, F. 1991. *Grammaticalization: A Conceptual Framework*. Chicago, IL: University of Chicago Press.

Heine, B. and Kuteva, T. 2002. *World Lexicon of Grammaticalization*. Cambridge: Cambridge University Press.

2007. *The Genesis of Grammar*. Oxford: Oxford University Press.

Hickey, R. (ed.) 2010. *The Handbook of Language Contact*. Chichester: Wiley-Blackwell.

Hickey, R. and Puppel, S. (eds.) 1997. *Language History and Linguistic Modelling*, 2 vols. Berlin: Mouton de Gruyter.

Higham, N. 2002. 'The Anglo-Saxon/British interface: History and ideology', in Filppula *et al.* (eds.), 29–46.

Hilpert, M. 2008. *Germanic Future Constructions: A Usage-Based Approach to Language Change*. Amsterdam: Benjamins.

2013. *Constructional Change in English: Developments in Allomorphy, Word Formation and Syntax*. Cambridge: Cambridge University Press.

Hiltunen, R. 1983. *The Decline of the Prefixes and the Beginnings of the English Phrasal Verb: The Evidence from some Old and Early Middle English Texts*. Turku: Turun Yliopisto.

Hinrichs, L. and Szmrecsanyi, B. 2007. 'Recent changes in the function and frequency of standard English genitive constructions: A multivariate analysis of tagged corpora'. *English Language and Linguistics* 11: 437–74.

Hofstadter, D. 1995. *Fluid Concepts and Creative Analogies: Computer Models of the Fundamental Mechanisms of Thought*. New York: Basic Books.

Hogg, R.M. (ed.) 1992. *The Cambridge History of the English Language*, vol. 1: *The Beginnings to 1066*. Cambridge: Cambridge University Press,

2004. 'The spread of negative contraction in early English', in A. Curzan and K. Emmons (eds.), *Studies in the History of the English Language II: Unfolding Conversations*. Berlin: Mouton de Gruyter, 459–82.

Hollmann, W. and Siewierska, A. 2011. 'The status of frequency, schemas, and identity in Cognitive Sociolinguistics: A case study on definite article reduction'. *Cognitive Linguistics*. 22: 25–54.

Holyoak, K.J. and Thagard, P. 1995. *Mental Leaps: Analogy in Creative Thought*. Cambridge, MA: MIT Press.

Hopper, P.J. and Thompson, S.A. 1980. 'Transitivity in grammar and discourse'. *Language* 56: 251–99.

1984. 'The discourse basis for lexical categories in Universal Grammar'. *Language* 60: 703–52.

Hopper, P.J. and Traugott, E.C. 2003. *Grammaticalization* (2nd ed.). Cambridge: Cambridge University Press.

Huber, M. 2007. 'The Old Bailey proceedings, 1674–1834: Evaluating and annotating a corpus of 18th- and 19th-century spoken English'. *Studies in Variation, Contacts and Change in English* 1 [www.helsinki.fi/varieng/journal/volumes/01/index.html].

Huddleston, R., and Pullum, G. 2002. *The Cambridge Grammar of the English Language*. Cambridge: Cambridge University Press.

Hübler, A. 2007. *The Nonverbal Shift in Early Modern English Conversation*. Amsterdam: Benjamins.

Hurford, J.R. 2003. 'The language mosaic and its evolution', in Christiansen and Kirby (eds.), 38–57.

Iglesias-Rábade, L. 2001. 'Composite predicates in Middle English with the verbs *nimen* and *taken*'. *Studia Neophilologica* 73:143–63.

Ihalainen, O. 1994. 'The dialects of England since 1776', in R. Burchfield (ed.), *The Cambridge History of the English Language*, vol. 5: *English Language in Britain and Overseas: Origins and Development*. Cambridge: Cambridge University Press, 197–274.

Ingham, R. 2000. 'Negation and OV order in Late Middle English'. *Journal of Linguistics* 36: 13–38.

2002. 'Negated subjects and objects in 15th-century nonliterary English'. *Language Variation and Change* 14: 291–322.

Itkonen, E. 2005. *Analogy as Structure and Process*. Amsterdam: Benjamins.

Iyeiri, Y. 2001. *Negative Constructions in Middle English*. Kyushu University Press.

Jack, G.B. 1978. 'Negation in later Middle English prose'. *Archivum Linguisticum* 9 n. s.: 58–72.

1988. 'The origins of the English gerund'. *NOWELE* 12: 15–75.

Janda, R.D. 1980. 'On the decline of declensional systems: The overall loss of Old English nominal case inflections and the Middle English reanalysis of -ES as HIS', in E.C. Traugott, R. Labrum, S. Shepherd and P. Kiparsky (eds.), *Papers from the 4th International Conference on Historical Linguistics*. Amsterdam: Benjamins, 243–52.

Jespersen, O. 1909–1949. *A Modern English Grammar on Historical Principles*. Heidelberg/Copenhagen: Carl Winters/Ejnar Munksgaard.

Joseph, B.D. and Janda, R.D. 2003. (eds.) *The Handbook of Historical Linguistics*. Oxford: Blackwell.

Kahneman, D. 2011. *Thinking, Fast and Slow*. New York: Farrar, Strauss, Giroux.

Kastovsky, D. and Mettinger, A. (eds.) 2003. *Language Contact in the History of English*. Bern: Lang.

Keizer, E. 2007. *The English Noun Phrase: The Nature of Linguistic Categorization*. Cambridge: Cambridge University Press.

Keller, R. 1994. *On Language Change: The Invisible Hand in Language*. (translated from the German by B. Nerlich). London: Routledge.

Kerswill, P. 2002. 'Koineization and accommodation', in Chambers *et al.* (eds.), 669–702.

Kerstens, J., Ruys, E. and Zwarts, J. 1996–2001. *Lexicon of Linguistics online*, www2.let.uu.nl/UiL-OTS/Lexicon/.

Killie, K. 2008. 'From locative to durative to focalized? The English progressive and "PROG imperfective drift"', in Gotti *et al.* (eds.), 69–88.

Killie, K., and Swan, T. 2009. 'The grammaticalization and subjectification of adverbial *-ing*-clauses (converb clauses) in English'. *English Language and Linguistics* 13: 337–63.

Kirby, S. and Christiansen, M.H. 2003. 'From language learning to language evolution', in Christiansen and Kirby (eds.), 272–94.

Kirch, M.S. 1959. 'Scandinavian influence on English syntax'. *Publications of the Modern Language Society* 74: 503–10.

Klemola, J. 2002. 'Periphrastic DO: Dialectal distribution and origins', in Filppula *et al.* (eds.), 199–210.

2013. 'English as a contact language in the British Isles', in Schreier and Hundt (eds.), 75–87.

Kohnen, Th. 2003. 'The influence of "Latinate" constructions in early Modern English: Orality and literacy as complementary forces', in Kastovsky and Mettinger (eds.), 171–94.

Komen, E. 2009. 'CESAC: Coreference Editor for Syntactically Annotated Corpora'. Paper presented at 7th Symposium on the History of English Syntax, 6–7 June 2009, Nijmegen, Netherlands: Radboud University Nijmegen.

Koopman, W. 1985. 'The syntax of verb and particle combinations in Old English', in H. Bennis and F. Beukema (eds.), *Linguistics in the Netherlands 1985*. Dordrecht: Foris, 91–9.

1998. 'Inversion after single and multiple topics in Old English', in Fisiak and Krygier (eds.), 135–50.

Kortmann, B. 1997. *Adverbial Subordination: A Typology and History of Adverbial Subordinators Based on European Languages*. Berlin: Mouton de Gruyter.

Kortmann, B. and Wagner, S. 2010. 'Changes and continuities in dialect grammar', in R. Hickey (ed.), *Eighteenth-Century English: Ideology and Change*. Cambridge: Cambridge University Press, 269–92.

Kranich, S. 2006. 'The origin of English gerundial constructions: A case of French influence?', in A.J. Johnston, F. von Mengden and S. Thim (eds.), *Language and Text: Current Perspectives on English and German Historical Linguistics and Philology*. Heidelberg: Universitätsverlag Winter, 179–95.

2010. *The Progressive in Modern English. A Corpus-Based Study of Grammaticalization and Related Changes*. Amsterdam: Rodopi.

Krickau, C. 1877. *Der Accusativ mit dem Infinitiv in der englischen Sprache, besonders im Zeitalter der Elisabeth*. PhD dissertation: University of Göttingen.

Kroch, A.S. 1989. 'Reflexes of grammar in patterns of language change'. *Language Variation and Change* 1: 199–244.

Kroch, A.S. and Taylor, A. 1997. 'Verb movement in Old and Middle English: Dialect variation and language contact', in Van Kemenade and Vincent (eds.), 297–325.

2000. 'Verb-object order in Early Middle English', in Pintzuk *et al.* (eds.), 132–63.

Krug, M. 2000. *Emerging English Modals: A Corpus-Based Study of Grammaticalization*. Berlin: Mouton de Gruyter.

Kytö, M. 1996. *Manual to the Diachronic Part of the Helsinki Corpus of English Texts: Coding Conventions and Lists of Source Texts* (3rd ed.). Department of English, University of Helsinki.

Kytö, M. and Danchev, A. 2001. 'The Middle English *for to*+infinitive construction', in Kastovsky and Mettinger (eds.), 35–55.

Kytö, M. and Romaine, S. 2006. 'Adjective comparison in nineteenth-century English', in M. Kytö, M. Rydén and E. Smitterberg (eds.), *Nineteenth-Century English: Stability and Change*. Cambridge: Cambridge University Press, 194–213.

Labov, W. 1994. *Principles of Linguistic Change*, vol. 1: *Internal Factors*. Oxford: Blackwell.

   2001. *Principles of Linguistic Change*, vol. 2: *Social Factors*. Oxford: Blackwell.

   2010. *Principles of Linguistic Change*, vol. 3: *Cognitive and Cultural Factors*. Oxford: Blackwell.

Laitinen, M. 2004. 'Indefinite pronominal anaphora in English correspondence between 1500 and 1800', in C. Kay, S. Horobin, and J. Smith (eds.), *New Perspectives on English Historical Linguistics*, vol. 1: *Syntax and Morphology*. Amsterdam: Benjamins, 65–81.

   2008. 'Sociolinguistic patterns in grammaticalisation: *he, they*, and *those* in human indefinite reference'. *Language Variation and Change* 20: 1–31.

   2009. 'Singular *you was/were* variation and English normative grammars in the eighteenth century', in Nurmi *et al.* (eds.), 199–217.

Lange, C. and Schaefer, U. 2008. '*Tis he, 'tis she, 'tis me – I don't know who* . . .. Cleft and identificational constructions in 16ᵗʰ and 18ᵗʰ century plays', in Gotti *et al.* (eds.), 203–22.

Lass, R. 1980. *On Explaining Language Change*. Cambridge: Cambridge University Press.

   (ed.) 1999. *The Cambridge History of the English Language*, vol. 3: *1476–1776*. Cambridge: Cambridge University Press.

   2004. '*Ut custodiant litteras*: Editions, corpora and witnesshood', in M. Dossena and R. Lass (eds.), *Methods and Data in English Historical Dialectology*. Bern: Lang, 21–48.

Leech, G., Hundt, M., Mair, C. and Smith, N. 2009. *Change in Contemporary English: A Grammatical Study*. Cambridge: Cambridge University Press.

Lehmann, C. 1985. 'Grammaticalization: Synchronic variation and diachronic change'. *Lingua e Stile* 20: 303–18.

Lehmann, H.M., auf dem Keller, C. and Ruef, B. 2006. 'Zen Corpus 1.0', in R. Facchinetti and M. Rissanen (eds.) *Corpus-Based Studies of Diachronic English*. Bern: Lang, 135–55.

Leung, A.H. and Van der Wurff, W. 2011. 'Anaphoric reference in Early Modern English: The case of *said* and *same*'. Paper read at the 2ⁿᵈ International Workshop on the Noun Phrase in English, Newcastle University, September 2011.

Light, C. and Wallenberg, J. 2015. 'The expression of impersonals in Middle English'. *English Language and Linguistics* 19: 227–45.

Lightfoot, D.W. 1979. *Principles of Diachronic Syntax*. Cambridge: Cambridge University Press.

   1981. 'The history of noun phrase movement', in C.L. Baker and J. McCarthy (eds.), *The Logical Problem of Language Acquisition*. Cambridge MA: MIT Press, 86–119.

   1991. *How to Set Parameters: Arguments from Language Change*. Cambridge, MA: MIT Press.

1999. *The Development of Language: Acquisition, Change, and Evolution.* Oxford: Blackwell.

López-Couso, M.J. and Méndez-Naya, B. 2015. 'Secondary grammaticalization in clause combining: From adverbial subordination to complementation in English'. *Language Sciences* 47: 188–98.

Los, B. 2005. *The Rise of the to-Infinitive.* Oxford: Oxford University Press.

2012. 'The loss of Verb-second and the switch from bounded to unbounded systems', in Meurman-Solin *et al.* (eds.), 21–46.

2015. *A Historical Syntax of English.* Edinburgh: Edinburgh University Press.

Los, B. and Dreschler, G. 2012. 'The loss of local anchoring: From adverbial local anchors to permissive subjects', in Nevalainen and Traugott (eds.), 859–72.

Los, B. and Komen, E. 2012. 'Clefts as resolution strategies after the loss of a multifunctional first position', in Nevalainen and Traugott (eds.), 884–98.

Lüdeling, A. and Kytö, M. (eds.) 2008–2009. *Corpus Linguistics: An International Handbook*, 2 vols. Berlin: de Gruyter.

Lutz, A. 1998. 'The interplay of external and internal factors in morphological restructuring: The case of *you*', in Fisiak and Krygier (eds.), 189–210.

2009. 'Celtic Influence on Old English and West Germanic'. *English Language and Linguistics* 13: 227–49.

Mair, C. and Leech, G. 2006. 'Current changes in English syntax', in Aarts and McMahon, (eds.), 318–42.

Manabe, K. 1989. *The Syntactic and Stylistic Development of the Infinitive in Middle English.* Fukuoka: Kyushu University Press.

McFadden, T. 2002. 'The rise of the *to*-dative in Middle English', in Lightfoot (ed.), 107–23.

McIntosh, A., Samuels, M.L. and Benskin, M. 1985. *A Linguistic Atlas of Late Mediaeval English.* Aberdeen: Aberdeen University Press.

McMahon, A. 2000. *Change, Chance and Optimality.* Oxford: Oxford University Press.

McWhorter, J.H. 2002. 'What happened to English?', *Diachronica* 19: 217–72

Meurman-Solin, A. 2007. 'Relatives as sentence-level connectives', in U. Lenker and A. Meurman-Solin (eds.), *Connectives in the History of English.* Amsterdam: Benjamins, 255–87.

Meurman-Solin, A., López-Couso, M.-J., and Los, B. (eds.) 2012. *Information Structure and Syntactic Change in the History of English.* Oxford: Oxford University Press.

Miller, D.G. 2001. 'Subject and object in Old English and Latin copular deontics', in J.T. Faarlund (ed.), *Grammatical Relations in Change.* Amsterdam: Benjamins, 223–39.

2012. *External Influences on English: From Its Beginnings to the Renaissance.* Oxford: Oxford University Press.

Miller, J. and Weinert, R. 1998. *Spontaneous Spoken Language: Syntax and Discourse.* Oxford: Oxford University Press.

Milroy, J. 1992. 'Dialectology', in Blake (ed.), 156–206.

Mitchell, B. 1985. *Old English Syntax.* 2 vols. Oxford: Clarendon Press.

Mitkovska, L. and Bužarovska, E. 2012. 'An alternative analysis of the English *get*-past-participle constructions: Is *get* all that passive?'. *Journal of English Linguistics* 40: 196–215.

Moerenhout, M. and Van der Wurff, W. 2000. 'Remnants of the old order: OV in the *Paston Letters*'. *English Studies* 81: 513–30.

2005. 'Object-Verb order in early sixteenth-century English prose: An exploratory study'. *English Language and Linguistics* 9: 83–114.

Moessner, L. 1999. 'The negative relative marker *but*: A case of syntactic borrowing', in Tops *et al.* (eds.), 65–78.

Mondorf, B. 2009. *More Support for More-Support: The Role of Processing Constraints on the Choice between Synthetic and Analytic Comparative Forms*. Amsterdam: Benjamins.

Moralejo-Gárate, T. 2001. 'Composite predicates and idiomatisation in Middle English: A corpus-based approach'. *Studia Anglistica Posnaniensia* 36: 171–87.

Mustanoja, T. 1960. *Middle English Syntax*. Part I. Helsinki: Société Néophilologique.

Nagle, S.J. 1989. *Inferential Change and Syntactic Modality in English*. Frankfurt: Lang.

Nagucka, R. 2003. 'Latin prepositional phrases and their Old English equivalents', in Kastovsky and Mettinger (eds.), 251–65.

Narrog, H. and Heine, B. (eds.) 2011. *The Oxford Handbook of Grammaticalization*. Oxford: Oxford University Press.

Nehls, D. 1974. *Synchron-diachrone Untersuchungen zur Expanded Form im Englischen*. Munich: Hueber.

Nevalainen, T. 1997. 'Recyling inversion: The case of initial adverbs and negators in early Modern English'. *Studia Anglica Posnaniensia* 31: 203–14.

2011. 'Reconstructing syntactic continuity and change in Early Modern English regional dialects: The case of *who*', in Denison *et al.* (eds.), 159–84.

Nevalainen, T. and Raumolin-Brunberg, H. (eds.) 1996. *Sociolinguistics and Language History: Studies Based on The Corpus of Early English Correspondence*. Amsterdam: Rodopi.

2003. *Historical Socio-Linguistics: Language Change in Tudor and Stuart England*. London: Pearson.

Nevalainen, T. and Traugott, E.C. (eds.), 2012. *The Oxford Handbook of the History of English*. Oxford: Oxford University Press.

Newmeyer, F.J. 2003. 'What can the field of linguistics tell us about the origin of language?', in Christiansen and Kirby (eds.), 58–76.

Nickel, G. 1967. 'An example of a syntactic blend in Old English'. *Indogermanische Forschungen* 72: 261–74.

Nicolle, S. 2011. 'Pragmatic aspects of grammaticalization', in Narrog and Heine (eds.), 401–12.

Noël, D. 2007. 'Diachronic construction grammar and grammaticalization theory'. *Functions of Language* 14: 177–202.

Norde, M. 2009. *Degrammaticalization*. Oxford: Oxford University Press.

Nurmi, A., Nevala, M. and Palander-Collin, M. (eds.) 2009. *The Language of Daily Life in England 1400–1800*. Amsterdam: Benjamins.

Ogura, M. 2001. 'Perceptual factors and word order change in English'. *Folia Linguistica Historica* 22: 233–53.

Ohlander, U. 1943. 'Omission of the object in English'. *Studia Neophilologica* 16: 105–27.

Otsu, N. 2002. 'On the presence or absence of the conjunction *þæt* in Old English, with special reference to dependent sentences containing a *gif*-clause'. *English Language and Linguistics* 6: 225–38.

Patten, A.L. 2010. 'Grammaticalization and the *it*-cleft construction', in Traugott and Trousdale (eds.), 221–43.

Paul, H. 1909, 4th ed.[1886]. *Prinzipien der Sprachgeschichte*. Halle: Niemeyer.

Petré, P. 2014. *Constructions and Environments: Copular, Passive, and Related Constructions in Old and Middle English*. Oxford: Oxford University Press.

2015. 'Grammaticalization by changing co-text frequencies. Or why [BE V*ing*] became the "progressive"'. *English Language and Linguistics* 19: 1–24.

Phillipps, K.C. 1970. *Jane Austen's English*. London: Deutsch.

Pintzuk, S. 1991. *Phrase Structures in Competition: Variation and Change in Old English Word Order*. PhD dissertation: University of Pennsylvania.

2002. 'Morphological case and word order in Old English'. *Language Sciences* 24: 381–95.

Pintzuk, S. and Kroch, A.S. 1989. 'The rightward movement of complements and adjuncts in the Old English of Beowulf'. *Language Variation and Change* 1: 115–43.

Pintzuk, S. and Taylor, A. 2006. 'The loss of OV order in the history of English', in Van Kemenade and Los (eds.), 249–78.

Pintzuk, S., Tsoulas, G. and Warner, A. 2000. 'Syntactic change: Theory and method', in Pintzuk et al. (eds.), 1–22.

(eds.) 2000. *Diachronic Syntax: Models and Mechanisms*. Oxford: Oxford University Press.

Plank, F. 1983. 'Coming into being among the Anglo-Saxons', in M. Davenport, E. Hansen and H.F. Nielsen (eds.), *Current Topics in English Historical Linguistics*. Odense: Odense University Press, 239–78.

1984. 'The modals story retold'. *Studies in Language* 8: 305–64.

2007. 'Extent and limits of linguistic diversity as the remit of typology – but through constraints on WHAT is diversity limited?'. *Linguistic Typology* 11: 43–68.

Polo, C. 2002. 'Double objects and morphological triggers for syntactic case', in Lightfoot, (ed.), 124–42.

Poppe, E. 2009. 'Standard Average European and the Celticity of English intensifiers and reflexives: Some considerations and implications'. *English Language and Linguistics* 13: 251–66.

Posner, R. 1986. 'Iconicity in syntax: The natural order of attributes', in P. Bouissac, M. Herzfeld and R. Posner (eds.), *Iconicity: Festschrift for Thomas A. Sebeok*. Tübingen: Stauffenburg, 305–37.

Poussa, P. 1982. 'The evolution of early standard English: The creolization hypothesis', *Studia Anglica Posnaniensia* 14: 69–85.

Pratt, L. and Denison, D. 2000. 'The language of the Southey-Coleridge circle'. *Language Sciences* 22: 401–22.

Prins, A.A. 1952. *French Influence in English Phrasing*. Leiden: Universitaire Pers.

Pullum, G. 1982. 'Syncategorematicity and English infinitival *to*'. *Glossa* 16: 181–215.

Quirk, R., Greenbaum, S., Leech, G. and Svartvik, J. 1985. *A Comprehensive Grammar of the English Language*. London: Longman.

Raumolin-Brunberg, H. 1994. 'The position of adjectival modifiers in Late Middle English noun phrases', in U. Fries, G. Tottie and P. Schneider (eds.), *Creating and Using English Language Corpora*. Amsterdam: Rodopi, 159–68.

2009. 'Lifespan changes in the language of three early modern gentlemen', in Nurmi et al. (eds.), 165–96.

2000. 'WHICH and THE WHICH in Late Middle English: Free variants?', in I. Taavitsainen, T. Nevalainen, P. Pahta, and M. Rissanen (eds.) *Placing Middle English in Context.* Berlin: Mouton de Gruyter, 209–26.

Raumolin-Brunberg, H. and Nevalainen, T. 2007. 'Historical sociolinguistics: The corpus of Early English Correspondence', in Beal *et al.* (eds.), 148–71.

Rissanen, M. 1967. *The Uses of* One *in Old and Early Middle English.* Helsinki: Société Néophilologique.

1999. 'Syntax', in Lass (ed.), 187–331.

Rissanen, M., Ihalainen, O., Nevalainen, T. and Taavitsainen, I. (eds.) 1992. *History of Englishes: New Methods and Interpretations in Historical Linguistics.* Berlin: Mouton de Gruyter.

Rissanen, M., Kytö, M. and Heikkonen, K. (eds.) 1997. *English in Transition: Corpus-Based Studies in Linguistic Variation and Genre Styles.* Berlin: Mouton de Gruyter.

Rissanen, M., Kytö, M. and Palander-Collin, M. (eds.) 1993. *Early English in the Computer Age: Explorations through the Helsinki Corpus.* Berlin: Mouton de Gruyter.

Roberts, I. 1993. *Verbs and Diachronic Syntax: A Comparative History of English and French.* Dordrecht: Kluwer.

1997. 'Directionality and word order change in the history of English', in Van Kemenade and Vincent (eds.), 397–426.

2007. *Diachronic Syntax.* Oxford: Oxford University Press.

Rohdenburg, G. 2009. 'Grammatical divergence between British and American English in the nineteenth and early twentieth centuries', in I. Tieken-Boon van Ostade and W. van der Wurff (eds.), *Current Issues in Late Modern English.* Bern: Lang, 301–30.

Rohdenburg, G. and Schlüter, J. (eds.) 2009. *One Language, Two Grammars? Differences between British and American English.* Cambridge: Cambridge University Press.

Ronan, P. 2002. 'Subordinating *ocus* "and" in Old Irish', in Filppula *et al.* (eds.), 213–36.

Rosenbach, A. 2002. *Genitive Variation in English: Conceptual Factors in Synchronic and Diachronic Studies.* Berlin: Mouton de Gruyter.

2003. 'Aspects of iconicity and economy in the choice between the *s*-genitive and the *of*-genitive in English', in G. Rohdenburg and B. Mondorf (eds.), *Determinants of Grammatical Variation in English.* Berlin: Mouton de Gruyter, 379–411.

2007. 'Emerging variation: Determiner genitives and noun modifiers in English'. *English Language and Linguistics* 11: 143–89.

Rosenbach, A., Stein, D. and Vezzosi, L. 2000. 'On the history of the *s*-genitive', in Bermúdez-Otero *et al.* (eds.), 183–210.

Rubba, J. 1994. 'Grammaticization as semantic change: A case study of preposition development', in W. Pagliuca (ed.), *Perspectives on Grammaticalization.* Amsterdam: Benjamins, 81–101.

Sairio, A. 2009. *Language and Letters of the Bluestocking Network: Sociolinguistic Issues in Eighteenth-Century Epistolary English.* Helsinki: Société Néophilologique.

Samuels, M.L. 1969. 'Some applications of Middle English dialectology', in R. Lass (ed.), *Approaches to English Historical Linguistics. An Anthology.* New York: Holt, Rinehart & Winston, 404–18.

Sankoff, G. 2002. 'Linguistic outcomes of language contact', in Chambers *et al.* (eds.), 638–68.

2005. 'Cross-sectional and longitudinal studies', in U. Ammon, N. Dittmar, K.J. Mattheier and P. Trudgill (eds.), *Sociolinguistics: An International Handbook of the Science of Language and Society*, vol. 2. Berlin: de Gruyter, 1003–13.

Sapir, E. 1921. *Language*. Cambridge: Cambridge University Press.

Sawyer, P.H. 1971. *The Age of the Vikings*. London: Arnold.

Schendl, H. and Wright, L. (eds.) 2011. *Code-Switching in Early English*. Berlin: Mouton de Gruyter.

Schlüter, J. 2005. *Rhythmic Grammar: The Influence of Rhythm on Grammatical Variation and Change in English*. Berlin: Mouton de Gruyter.

Schmid, H.-J. 2015. 'A blueprint of the Entrenchment-and-Conventionalization Model'. *Yearbook of the German Cognitive Linguistics Association* 3: 1–27.

Schreier, D. and Hundt, M. (eds.) 2013. *English as a Contact Language*. Cambridge: Cambridge University Press.

Schrijver, P. 2002. 'The rise and fall of British Latin: Evidence from English and Brittonic', in Filppula *et al.* (eds.), 87–110.

Seidlhofer, B. and Widdowson, H. 2007. 'Idiomatic variation and change in English: The idiom principle and its realizations', in U. Smit, S. Dollinger, J. Huettner, G. Kaltenboeck and U. Lutzky (eds.), *Tracing English through Time: Explorations in Language Variation*. Wien: Braumüller, 359–74.

Sommerer, L. 2015. 'The influence of constructions in grammaticalization: Revisiting category emergence and the development of the definite article in English', in Barðdal et al. (eds.), 107–38.

Stein, D. 1990. *The Semantics of Syntactic Change: Aspects of the Evolution of 'do' in English*. Berlin: Mouton de Gruyter.

Suárez-Gómez, C. 2009. 'On the syntactic differences between Old English dialects: Evidence from the Gospels'. *English Language and Linguistics* 13: 57–75.

Sweetser, E.E. 1990. *From Etymology to Pragmatics: Metaphorical and Cultural Aspects of Semantic Structure*. Cambridge: Cambridge University Press.

Tajima, M. 1985. *The Syntactic Development of the Gerund in Middle English*. Tokyo: Nan'un-do.

1999. 'The compound gerund in Early Modern English', in S. Embleton, J.E. Joseph and H.J. Niederehe (eds.), *The Emergence of the Modern Language Sciences: Studies on the Transition from Historical-Comparative to Structural Linguistics in Honour of E.F.K. Koerner*. Amsterdam: Benjamins, 265–76.

Tanaka, T. 2000. 'On the development of transitive expletive constructions in the history of English'. *Lingua* 110: 473–95.

Taylor, A. 2005. 'Prosodic evidence for incipient VO order in Old English'. *English Language and Linguistics* 9: 139–56.

2008. 'Contact effects of translation: Distinguishing two kinds of influence in Old English'. *Language Variation and Change* 20: 341–65.

Taylor, A. and Pintzuk, S. 2012. 'Rethinking the OV/VO alternation in Old English: The effect of complexity, grammatical weight, and information status', in Nevalainen and Traugott (eds.), 1199–1213.

Thomason, S.G. 2003. 'Contact as a source of language change', in Joseph and Janda (eds.), 687–712.

Thomason, S.G. and Kaufman, T. 1988. *Language Contact, Creolization, and Genetic Linguistics*. Berkeley: University of California Press.

Thompson, S.A. 1988. 'A discourse approach to the cross-linguistic category "adjective"', in J. Hawkins (ed.), *Explaining Language Universals*. Oxford: Blackwell, 168–85.

1995. 'The iconicity of "dative shift" in English: Considerations from information flow in discourse', in M.E. Landsberg (ed.), *Syntactic Iconicity and Linguistic Freezes: The Human Dimension*. Berlin: Mouton de Gruyter, 155–75.

Thompson, S.A. and Mulac, A. 1991. 'A quantitative perspective on the grammaticization of epistemic parentheticals in English', in Traugott and Heine, (eds.), vol. 2, 313–29.

Tieken-Boon van Ostade, I. 1987. *The Auxiliary Do in Eighteenth-Century English: A Sociohistorical Linguistic Approach*. Dordrecht: Foris.

Timofeeva, O. 2010. *Non-Finite Constructions in Old English, with Special Reference to Syntactic Borrowing from Latin*. Helsinki: Société Néophilologique.

Tomasello, M. 2003. 'On the different origins of symbols and grammar', in Christiansen and Kirby (eds.), 94–110.

Tops, G.A., Devriendt, B. and Geukens, S. (eds.) 1999. *Thinking English Grammar: To honour Xavier Dekeyser*. Leuven: Peeters.

Tottie, G. 2002. *An Introduction to American English*. Oxford: Blackwell.

Traugott, E.C. 1989. 'On the rise of epistemic meanings in English. An example of subjectification in semantic change'. *Language* 57: 33–65.

1992. 'Syntax', in Hogg (ed.), 168–289.

2008. 'The grammaticalization of *NP of NP* patterns', in A. Bergs and G. Diewald (eds.), *Constructions and Language Change*. Berlin: Mouton de Gruyter, 23–45.

2011. 'Grammaticalization and mechanisms of change', in Narrog and Heine (eds.), 19–30.

Traugott, E.C. and Dasher, R.B. 2002. *Regularity in Semantic Change*. Cambridge: Cambridge University Press.

Traugott, E.C. and Heine, B. (eds.) 1991. *Approaches to grammaticalization*, 2 vols. Amsterdam: Benjamins,

Traugott, E.C. and König, E. 1991. 'The semantics-pragmatics of grammaticalization revisited', in Traugott and Heine (eds.), vol. 1, 189–218.

Traugott E.C. and Trousdale G. (eds.) 2010. *Gradience, Gradualness and Grammaticalization*. Amsterdam: Benjamins.

Traugott, E.C., and Trousdale, G. 2013. *Constructionalization and Constructional Changes*. Oxford: Oxford University Press.

Trips, C. 2002. *From OV to VO in Early Middle English*. Amsterdam: Benjamins.

Tristram, H.L.C. 2002. 'Attrition of inflections in English and Welsh', in Filppula *et al.* (eds.), 111–49.

Trousdale, G. 2012. 'Theory and data in diachronic Construction Grammar: The case of the *what with* construction', *Studies in Language* 36: 576–602.

2013. 'Multiple inheritance and constructional change', *Studies in Language* 37: 491–514.

Trousdale, G. and Adger, D. (eds.) 2007. 'Special Issue on Theoretical Accounts of Dialect Variation', *English Language and Linguistics* 11.ii.

Van Bergen, L. 2013. 'Early progressive passives'. *Folia Linguistica Historica* 34: 173–208.

Van Coetsem, F. 1988. *Loan Phonology and the Two Transfer Types in Language Contact*. Dordrecht: Foris.

Van de Pol, N. 2016. *The Development of the Absolute Construction in English*. PhD dissertation: KU Leuven.

Van de Pol, N. and Cuyckens, H. 2013. 'Gradualness in change in English augmented absolutes', in A. Giacalone Ramat, C. Mauri and P. Molinelli (eds.), *Synchrony and Diachrony: A Dynamic Interface*. Amsterdam: Benjamins, 341–66.

Van de Pol, N. and Petré, P. 2015. 'Why is there a Present-day English absolute?' *Studies in Language* 39: 198–228.

Van de Velde, F. 2009. *De Nominale Constituent: Structuur en Geschiedenis*. Leuven: Leuven University Press.

2011. 'Left-peripheral expansion of the English NP'. *English Language and Linguistics* 15: 387–415.

Van de Velde, F. and Van der Horst, J. 2013. 'Homoplasy in diachronic grammar'. *Language Sciences* 36: 66–77.

Van der Auwera, J. 1999. 'Periphrastic *do*: Typological prolegomena', in Tops *et al.* (eds.), 457–70.

2009. 'The Jespersen cycles', in E. van Gelderen (ed.), *Cyclical Change*. Amsterdam: Benjamins, 35–71.

Van der Auwera, J. and Genee, I. 2002. 'English *do*: On the convergence of languages and linguists'. *English Language and Linguistics* 6: 283–307.

Van der Horst, J. 2008. *Geschiedenis van de Nederlandse Syntaxis*. Leuven: Universitaire Pers Leuven.

Van der Wurff, W. 1990. *Diffusion and Reanalysis in Syntax*. PhD dissertation: University of Amsterdam.

1999. 'Objects and verbs in modern Icelandic and fifteenth-century English: A word order parallel and its causes'. *Lingua* 109: 237–65.

Van Gelderen, E. 2013. 'Null subjects in Old English'. *Linguistic Inquiry* 44: 271–85.

Van Kemenade, A. 1987. *Syntactic Case and Morphological Case in the History of English*. Dordrecht: Foris.

1997. 'V2 and embedded topicalization in Old and Middle English', in Van Kemenade and Vincent (eds.), 326–52.

Van Kemenade, A. and Los, B. 2003. 'Particles and prefixes in Dutch and English', in G. Booij and J. van Marle (eds.), *Yearbook of Morphology 2003*. Dordrecht: Kluwer, 79–117.

(eds.) 2006. *The Handbook of the History of English*. Oxford: Blackwell.

Van Kemenade, A. and Vincent, N. (eds.) 1997. *Parameters of Morphosyntactic Change*. Cambridge: Cambridge University Press.

Vandelanotte, L. 2002. 'Prenominal adjectives in English: structures and ordering'. *Folia Linguistica* 36: 219–59.

Varga, E. 2005. 'Lexical V-to-I raising in Late Modern English'. *Generative Grammar in Geneva* 4: 261–81.

Vartiainen, T. 2013. 'Subjectivity, indefiniteness and semantic change'. *English Language and Linguistics* 17: 157–79.

Vaughan, J. and Mulder, J. 2014. 'The survival of the subjunctive in Australian English: Ossification, indexicality and stance'. *Australian Journal of Linguistics* 34: 486–505.

Vennemann, T. 2009. 'Celtic Influence in English? Yes and no'. *English Language and Linguistics* 13: 309–34.

Viana, V., Zyngier, S. and Barnbrook, G. (eds.) 2011. *Perspectives on Corpus Linguistics*. Amsterdam: Benjamins.

Visser, F.Th. 1963–73. *An Historical Syntax of the English Language*. 4 vols. Leiden: Brill.

Walkden, G. 2013. 'Null subjects in Old English', *Language Variation and Change* 25: 155–78.

Warner, A.R. 1982. *Complementation in Middle English and the Methodology of Historical Syntax*. London: Croom Helm.

1993. *English Auxiliaries: Structure and History*. Cambridge: Cambridge University Press.

Weerman, F. 1993. 'The diachronic consequences of first and second language acquisition: The change from OV to VO'. *Linguistics* 31: 903–31.

Westin, I. and Geisler, C. 2002. 'A multi-dimensional study of diachronic variation in British newspaper editorials', *ICAME Journal* 26: 133–52.

White, D.L. 2002. 'Explaining the innovations of Middle English: What, where, and why', in Filppula *et al.* (eds.), 153–74.

Wiik, K. 2002. 'On the Origin of the Celts', in Filppula *et al.* (eds.), 285–94.

Wischer, I. 2000. 'Grammaticalization versus lexicalization: *Methinks* there is some confusion', in Fischer *et al.* (eds.), 355–70.

2010. 'On the use of *beon* and *wesan* in Old English', in U. Lenker, J. Huber, and R. Mailhammer (eds.), *English Historical Linguistics 2008*, vol. 1: *The History of English Verbal and Nominal Constructions*. Amsterdam: Benjamins, 217–35.

Wolk, C., Bresnan, J., Rosenbach, A. and Szmrecsanyi, B. 2013. 'Dative and genitive variability in late Modern English: Exploring cross-constructional variation and change'. *Diachronica* 3: 382–419.

Zeitlin, J. 1908. *The Accusative with Infinitive and Some Kindred Constructions in English*. New York: Columbia University Press.

Name Index

231

Subject Index